Liberal Learning and the Art of Self-Governance

Concerns over affordability and accountability have tended to direct focus away from the central aims of liberal learning, such as preparing minds for free inquiry and inculcating the habits of mind, practical skills, and values necessary for effective participation in civil society. The contributors to this volume seek to understand better what it is that can be done on a day-to-day basis within institutions of liberal learning that shape the habits and practices of civil society.

The central argument of this volume is that institutions of liberal learning are critical to a developing and flourishing civil society. It is within these "civil society incubators" that the habits of open discourse are practiced and honed; that a collaborative (often contentious) commitment to truth-seeking serves as the rules that govern our work together; that the rules of personal and widespread social cooperation are established, practiced, and refined. Many have made this argument as it relates to community-based learning, and we explore that theme here as well. But acquiring and practicing the habits of civil society recur within and throughout the college context – in the classrooms, in college governance structures, in professional associations, in collaborative research, in the residence halls, and on the playing field. To put it another way, when they are at their best, institutions of liberal learning are contexts in which students learn how to live in a free society and learn the art of self-governance.

Emily Chamlee-Wright is Provost and Dean of the College at Washington College, U.S.A.

Routledge Frontiers of Political Economy

Liberal Learning and the Art of Self-Governance

Edited by Emily Chamlee-Wright

Routledge
Taylor & Francis Group

LONDON AND NEW YORK

First published 2015
by Routledge

2 Park Square, Milton Park, Abingdon, Oxfordshire OX14 4RN
52 Vanderbilt Avenue, New York, NY 10017

Routledge is an imprint of the Taylor & Francis Group, an informa business

First issued in paperback 2020

British Library Cataloguing in Publication Data
A catalogue record for this book is available from the British Library

Library of Congress Cataloging in Publication Data
A catalog record for this title has been requested.

ISBN: 978-0-415-70832-6 (hbk)
ISBN: 978-0-367-59968-3 (pbk)

Typeset in Times New Roman
by Taylor & Francis Books

Contents

Illustrations

Figures

Tables

Boxes

This volume is dedicated to the faculty at our institutions who create intellectual community, cultivate the habits of self-governance, and perform minor transformational miracles with our students every day.

Contributors

Paul Dragos Aligica is a senior research fellow at the F. A. Hayek Program for Advanced Study in Philosophy, Politics, and Economics at the Mercatus Center at George Mason University. His latest book is *Institutional Diversity and Political Economy: The Ostroms and beyond* (Oxford University Press, 2014).

Emily Chamlee-Wright is Provost and Dean of the College at Washington College. She is the author of *The Cultural and Political Economy of Recovery* (Routledge, 2010), *Culture and Enterprise* with Don Lavoie (Routledge, 2000), *The Cultural Foundations of Economic Development* (Routledge, 1997), and co-editor of *The Political Economy of Hurricane Katrina and Community Development* (Edward Elgar, 2010) with Virgil Storr.

Traci Fordham, formerly Department Chair and Associate Professor of Performance and Communication Arts at St. Lawrence University in Canton, New York, is now Chief of Staff at Portland Community College in Portland, Oregon. With almost three decades of teaching and scholarly experience in Communication, Fordham specializes in critical and transdisciplinary approaches to pedagogy, faculty development, and organization.

Robert F. Garnett is Professor of Economics at Texas Christian University. He writes on the history and philosophy of economics, primarily on questions of pluralism, liberal education, and the moral philosophy of Adam Smith.

Adam Goodheart is the Director of Washington College's C. V. Starr Center for the Study of the American Experience. He is the author of *1861: The Civil War Awakening*, and his essays appear in *National Geographic*, the *New York Times*, and many other publications.

Laura Grube is a Mercatus Dissertation Fellow with the Mercatus Center at George Mason University. She is also Visiting Instructor of Economics at Beloit College in Beloit, Wisconsin. Grube received her B.A. in Economics and Management from Beloit College (about which she writes in this volume) and her M.A. in Economics from George Mason University.

Steven Horwitz is Charles A. Dana Professor and Chair of the Department of Economics at St. Lawrence University in Canton, New York, where he also served as Associate Dean of the First Year Program from 2001 to 2007.

Jonathan B. Imber is Jean Glasscock Professor of Sociology at Wellesley College. He is author of *Abortion and the Private Practice of Medicine* (Yale University Press, 1986) and *Trusting Doctors: The decline of moral authority in American medicine* (Princeton University Press, 2008). He has been editor-in-chief of *Society* since 1998.

Heather Wood Ion is a chief executive and cultural anthropologist specializing in turning around troubled organizations and communities. She currently manages the Athena Charitable Trust and is Founder of the Epidemic of Health. Her books include: *Third-class Ticket*, *Against Terrible Odds*, *Making Doctors*, and *The Shaman's Child*.

David M. Levy is Professor of Economics at George Mason University. He and Sandra Peart are co-directors of the Summer Institute for the Preservation of the History of Economics. He has a Ph.D. from the University of Chicago and is a Distinguished Fellow of the History of Economics Society.

Sandra J. Peart is Dean of the Jepson School of Leadership Studies. She obtained her doctorate from the University of Toronto. She is a past president of the History of Economics Society and President of the International Adam Smith Society. Her research focuses on the transition from classical to neoclassical economics.

John L. Seidel is Lammot DuPont Copeland Associate Professor of Anthropology and Environmental Studies at Washington College. Seidel is also the Director of the Center for Environment and Society at Washington College.

Virgil Henry Storr is Senior Research Fellow and the Director of Graduate Student Programs at the Mercatus Center as well as a Research Associate Professor in the Department of Economics, George Mason University.

Charles Westerberg is Associate Dean of the College, Director of the Liberal Arts in Practice Center, and Brannon-Ballard Professor of Sociology at Beloit College. His current work focuses on developing structures that advance the goals of liberal education.

Carol Wickersham is the Director of Community-Based Learning, and serves as a Visiting Instructor and Coordinator of the Duffy Community Partnerships in the Department of Sociology at Beloit College. She is also a pastor in the Presbyterian Church (U.S.A.).

Introduction

The extraordinary lessons of self-governance all around us

Emily Chamlee-Wright

Preparing for life within civil society has always been a core value of liberal education. Even though they operated in highly illiberal societies, the likes of Socrates, Plato, and Cicero considered non-vocational education essential for free citizens as it was they who would attend to the common good. As the concepts of liberalism advanced with the ideas of John Locke, and later, Scottish Moral Enlightenment thinkers the connection between one's ability to think freely – to acquire the habits of rational thought, throwing off dogma in its various forms – were increasingly considered fundamental to one's moral development and ability to attend to the affairs of civil society.[1] Liberal education's role in supporting a healthy civil society gained a particular and pointed emphasis in the context of American institutions of higher learning. As Tocqueville ([1835] 2011) pointed out, democracy carried with it the very real threat that mob rule, not rational thought and civic virtues, might shape the course of a new nation. Revolution Era leaders in higher education such as William Smith and Thomas Jefferson recognized that liberal education was the principal path to securing a widespread and enduring commitment to civil and religious liberty and the values of tolerance and public civility (Goodheart). In short, the role that liberal education would play in fostering a healthy and robust civil society was critical to the American democratic experiment.

Yet much of the contemporary national discourse on higher education seems to ignore this critical role. Concerns over affordability (Vedder 2004, 2007) and accountability (Arum and Roksa 2011) have directed our focus away from the less tangible and more difficult-to-measure outcomes of liberal learning such as preparing minds for free inquiry and inculcating the habits of mind, practical skills, and values necessary for effective participation in civil society.

Judging by several high-profile publications on civic learning and engagement, however, the academy appears to be deeply interested in reclaiming this territory as a central value. For example, in a recent publication of the Association of American Colleges and Universities (AAC&U) titled *A Crucible Moment: Civic learning and democracy's future*, the National Task Force on Civic Learning and Democratic Engagement (2012: 2) identified this period of American higher education as a turning point calling for "invest[ment] on a massive scale in higher education's capacity to renew this nation's social, intellectual, and civic capital." In *Civic Provocations,* editor Donald Harward (2012) offers a complementary volume examining the implications of *A Crucible Moment*'s call to action. In *Civic Studies*, editors Peter Levine and Karol Edward Soltan (2014) argue that academic research and teaching ought to be in service to citizens, citizenship, and a healthy civil society. And in *Remaking College: Innovation and the liberal arts*, Rebecca Chopp (2014: 17) argues:

> The case we must make for liberal arts education is that the residential educational setting serves as an incubator for intellectual agility and supports the creation of new models of engagement to help both individuals and communities survive and flourish in this century.[2]

According to the contributors to *A Crucible Moment*, investment in civic learning and democratic engagement should take the form of a national movement involving transformative leadership at all levels of higher education and significantly expanded funding from a variety of federal and state agencies. The goals of such a national call to action include fostering a civic ethos across all parts of campus and educational culture, making civic literacy a core expectation for all students, practicing civic inquiry across all fields of study, and advancing civic action through transformative partnerships at home and abroad.

This ambitious and visionary charge will no doubt inspire some faculty, academic leaders, and public figures to take up the call. And yet, the scale of transformation that is being called for may inadvertently (and ironically) undermine the academy's effort to reclaim its role in fostering a robust civil society as a central value. The notion, for example, that success requires complete institutional transformation may intimidate and overwhelm faculty and academic leaders into inaction if the challenge appears unachievable. Similarly, the insistence that success requires significant funding from state and federal agencies may cast the effort as a lost cause, suspending progress if that funding is not forthcoming. More generally, the notion that success in the academy's effort to renew our civic health depends upon funding decisions made in the halls of political power diminishes the sense of agency and efficacy teacher-scholars and academic leaders will require if we are to reclaim attention to civic life as being central to our craft and institutional missions.

In one sense, the present project is very much in keeping with the goals and spirit set forth in *A Crucible Moment* and other treatises aimed at infusing greater attention to the role institutions of higher learning have in fostering a robust civil society. The contributors to this project agree with those who seek to weave civic learning throughout the entire enterprise of liberal education, and reject the impulse to treat it as a sort of window dressing that the student checks off with a single discrete experience. But the present project locates the conversation in a different space. Instead of the ten-thousand-foot view of a national call to action, the current project seeks to understand better what it is that we do on a day-to-day basis within institutions of liberal learning that shape the habits and practices of civil society, with attention to how we can do this work better. The hope is that by identifying places in the classroom and curriculum, in institutional governance structures, in the connections between college and community, and in the norms and practices across the academy as a whole in which this work is already being accomplished, we will see the challenge of reclaiming the essential role institutions of liberal learning have in fostering robust civil society as less daunting. And if in our day-to-day work we come to recognize the civic learning that is taking place, the hope is that we will become more deliberate and effective practitioners of this parti-cular aspect of our craft. Finally, by recognizing the civic learning that is unfolding in our daily work with students and fellow colleagues, the trans-formative success civic engagement visionaries are seeking remains in *our* hands and is freed from the political winds that may or may not favor government investment in such endeavors.

Creating spaces of self-governance

The central argument of this volume is that institutions of liberal learning are critical to a developing and flourishing civil society. It is within these "civil society incubators" that the habits of open discourse are practiced and honed; that a collaborative (often contentious) commitment to truth seeking serves as the rules that govern our work together; that the rules of personal and widespread social cooperation are established, practiced, and refined. Many have made this argument as it relates to community-based learning, and we explore that theme here as well (Couto and Guthrie 1999, Beere *et al.* 2011, Finley 2012). But acquiring and practicing the habits of civil society recur within and throughout the college context: in the classrooms, in college governance structures, in professional associations, in collaborative research, in the resi-dence halls, and on the playing field. To put it another way, when they are at their best, institutions of liberal learning are contexts in which we learn how to live in a free society – contexts in which we learn the art of self-governance.

The present project considers the concept of "self-governance" as a layered set of meanings, with each layer connecting to what it means to become a liberally educated person. At the most "macro" level, the concept of self-governance creates a space in which a people imagine national identity and sovereignty as legitimate. In such a space, it becomes possible, for example, to throw off colonial dominance. Though we now take it for granted that by the latter part of the eighteenth century, England no longer had a legitimate claim of sovereignty over the American colonists, consider how radical the idea was at the time. The notion that we were no longer subject to the authority of a distant king was inspiring to some but considered foolhardy, frightening, and even blasphemous to others. Following the American Revolution, institutions of liberal learning would play a distinctive role in developing citizen-leaders who were intellectually and morally equipped to guide a new nation without the "benefit" of royal mandate, the divine right of kings, or a singular religious doctrine with the force of state power behind it.

My own institution Washington College offers a clear example of how essential liberal learning was considered to building a new nation's confidence that self-governance was indeed possible. Founded in 1782, Washington College was the first to be established in an independent United States. As Adam Goodheart observes:

> With the nation's political independence barely secured on the battlefield, a group of visionary educators on the Eastern Shore of Maryland declared: "We must attend to the rising generation. The souls of our youth must be nursed up to the love of LIBERTY and KNOWLEDGE ... for LIBERTY will not deign to dwell, but where her fair companion KNOWLEDGE flourishes by her side."[3] No new college had been chartered on the continent since Dartmouth in 1769, in the days when Americans were subjects of George III, it was time to found an institution that would educate its students to be not subjects, but rather citizens of the new United States.[4]

Notably, the college's mission "to educate responsible citizens who could lead government, start businesses, and promote peace and knowledge" was decidedly secular, and its founding documents explicitly eschewed any religious affiliation or religious litmus test for students, faculty, or administrators. At this point of American history, there was no question as to the importance liberal learning would play in promoting self-governance through a tolerant and open civil society.

Self-governance can also refer to the ability of local communities to manage their affairs without higher levels of authority stepping in and taking control. The research of Nobel Laureate Elinor Ostrom (1990) and her colleagues at the Workshop in Political Theory and Policy Analysis at Indiana University has been particularly influential in how we understand the workings of self-governance at this "meso" level. Ostrom's research investigates social coordination problems such as those associated with managing common pool resources (CPRs) – resources vulnerable to overexploitation and degradation if left unmanaged. The provision of key public goods, such as effective monitoring of individual behavior, represents another social coordination problem in that the incentive to "free ride" means that such services are likely to be under-produced unless some solution can be found. Ostrom's research finds that communities around the globe have evolved varied and creative solutions to the challenges associated with common pool resource management and public goods provision through self-governance within civil society. For example, informal norms and cultural practices, voluntary associations, and formal cooperative agreements within communities have served as effective mechanisms for managing common pool resources such as water reservoirs, fisheries, and forests and providing effective monitoring and policing of individual behavior.

Colleges and universities face many of these same social coordination problems. Campus facilities, financial resources, the curriculum, institutional reputation are all examples of common pool resources that require appropriate management. And even the smallest colleges provide a remarkable array of public goods from open lectures to public scholarship. And yet, these social coordination problems that are (in theory) impossible to resolve at the local level are routinely resolved in the context of faculty-, student-, and co-governance structures. And as will be argued in some of the contributions to this volume, it is the institutions most explicitly committed to liberal learning that tend to have the most robust formal and informal rules of civic engagement that enable this level of self-governance. Such institutions, in other words, tend to practice what they teach, and in doing so, offer students opportunities to develop the habits of associative life.

And of course we must also consider the most literal and individual meaning of self-governance, as implied in the question, "Am I capable of governing my*self*?" The connection between this meaning of self-governance and liberal learning is quite familiar. The original seven liberal arts emphasized the ability to think as the primary purpose of education, superseding the customary purpose, which was vocational training. In the contemporary context, we understand the liberally educated person to be someone who is capable of self-governance because she or he is able to navigate uncharted intellectual territory and make genuine discoveries, whether they be artistic discoveries through, for example, collaborative choreography, or scientific discoveries in the lab or in the field, or entrepreneurial discoveries that generate greater value from the same resources that have always been available. The claim of liberal learning is that in order to bear the responsibilities and enjoy the fruits of a free society, we must develop intellectual agency in ourselves and in those who entrust their education to us.

Thus on all three levels of meaning, self-governance is fundamentally tied to liberal learning, in each case creating a space in which freedom can be pursued.

So, what is the quality and character of these spaces that liberal learning creates? These spaces can be and often are physical spaces in which faculty, students, and colleagues meet, exchange ideas, consider together a common text, or experience something great or beautiful or puzzling in one another's presence. Similarly, the concepts that rest at the foundation of liberal learning also create a specific kind of space that is less physical but just as critical to the emancipating potential of liberal education (Palmer 2011). The principles and habits of liberal learning create an intellectual and creative space in which discovery can unfold. In this space students and their teachers learn that they are co-creators of the ideas essential to a life of purpose and meaning. In these intellectual and physical spaces students learn that such discovery and meaning creation are collaborative projects, whether their collaborators are the great thinkers of antiquity, a colleague or professor who asks probing questions, or the student who insists that the matter at hand is not yet settled.

It is this intellectual and creative space that connects liberal learning to robust civil society so intimately. Consider, for example, the idea of liberty itself. The concept of negative freedom – freedom from arbitrary coercive power from the state and other hegemonic forces – is the essential and necessary condition that makes this physical and conceptual space we call "free inquiry" possible. Freedoms of speech, assembly, and the press guarantee that one is free in the physical sense to speak and write to others and learn from others in turn, without fear of losing one's self-sovereignty. But assuring this critical necessary condition through formal guarantees triggers the development of norms, values, and informal institutional arrangements that grow this space in which individuals develop intellectual and creative agency and in which communities flourish in the context of voluntary cooperation. Or more accurately, it is in such spaces that individuals and communities *can* flourish if those norms, values, and informal institutional arrangements are appropriately aligned with the requirements of free inquiry and if they are appropriately nurtured and passed on.

Michael Oakeshott's (1950, 1975) work is particularly helpful in identifying the special quality of spaces that institutions of liberal learning create. Oakeshott (1975) argues that the temporal space between one's school lessons and one's career that the traditional college represents, and the rich physical and social context in which the student is given reprieve from the cares of making a living, providing for a family, advancing in one's career is the well-spring of liberal learning. According to Oakeshott (1975: 31), university is a:

> somewhat unexpected invitation to disentangle oneself from the here and now of current happenings and engagements, to detach oneself from the urgencies of the local and the contemporary, to explore and enjoy a release from having to consider things in terms of their contingent features ... [It is] an invitation to be concerned not with the employment of what is familiar but with understanding what is not yet understood.

Places of liberal learning offer us pathways to develop our capacity to "see further and more deeply," to "gather resources for reflection [and develop] the capacity to catch sight of the poetic in the midst of the ordinary, which is the grace of life" (Fuller's "Foreword" to Oakeshott 2001: xi, xiii).

But just when we might think that Oakeshott is advocating a "monastic" educational model of intellectual seclusion, he makes it clear that there is much to be learned in the space where intellectual tradition and lived experience intersect. In his essay "Political Education" Oakeshott (1951: 159–160) explores the question of what it means to be educated for civil society.[5] For Oakeshott, concepts like freedom, equality, and social responsibility are born out of engagement in civic life, born out of attending to the arrangements that bring people together. To become productive members of political (civic) life, the practices of that political culture have to be *lived*:

> What has to be learned is not an abstract idea, or set of tricks, not even a ritual, but a concrete, coherent manner of living in all its intricacy ... Moreover, political education is not merely a matter of coming to

understand a tradition, it is learning how to participate in a conversation: it is at once initiation into an inheritance in which we have a life interest, and the exploration of its intimations.

(Oakeshott 1951: 179)

Environments of liberal learning prepare us for civic life by creating a space in which we are invited to acquire the manners, and practice the intellectual skills and moral disposition, of civil discourse. The implications for civil society are clear in Oakeshott's (1975: 30) characterization of liberal learning as fundamentally "conversational," involving multiple voices, each expressing:

distinct and conditional understanding of the world and a distinct idiom of human self-understanding ... [The] culture itself [can be thought of] as these voices joined, as such voices could only be joined, in a conversation – an endless unrehearsed intellectual adventure in which, in imagination, we enter into a variety of modes of understanding the world and ourselves and are not disconcerted by the differences or dismayed by the inconclusiveness of it all. And perhaps we may recognize liberal learning as, above all else, an education in imagination, an initiation into the art of this conversation in which we learn to recognize the voices; to distinguish their different modes of utterance, to acquire the intellectual and moral habits appropriate to this conversational relationship and thus to make our debut dans la vie humaine [make our entrance into the life of humanity].

Institutions of liberal learning create the physical, intellectual, and social space in which these conversations – conversations that invite us to explore and expand our humanity – define who we are.

Changing the nature of the debate: liberal learning and the workplace as civic space

So what is it that stands in our way? What are the forces that threaten a more deliberate effort to claim civic learning as a core value of a liberal education? In her book *Not for Profit* Martha Nussbaum (2012) argues that the singular drive toward economic productivity has led us to a crisis of global proportions. Profitability as a primary goal of the educational system, she argues, fundamentally threatens our ability to think critically and respond humanely in the world. Andrew Delbanco (2012) agrees, arguing that students' anticipation of and obsessive concern over preparation for commercial life has guided higher education down the wrong path.[6]

And public policy debates seem to be fueling the notion that job preparedness is the sole purpose of higher education. As noted in *A Crucible Moment* (3):

The National Governors Association's report *Degrees for What Jobs? Raising Expectations for Universities and Colleges in a Global Economy* serves as only one example of a policy discourse that focuses higher education directly and solely on jobs. The report openly challenges higher education's historic commitment to provide students with a broad liberal arts education (Sparks and Waits 2011). US higher education, of course, has proudly owned liberal education as a form of college learning that prepares citizens for the responsibilities of freedom. Rejecting the value of what has differentiated US higher education and made it an intellectual powerhouse and an economic driver, the report describes higher education's function and future funding as dependent singly on promoting "economic goals," "workforce preparation," and "competitive advantage."

These warnings are not new. In 1998 the National Commission on Civic Renewal cautioned that we were in danger of becoming a "nation of spectators" and that part of the problem was that preparation for economic productivity was being conflated with civic health (7). According to Oakeshott (1975) business schools, training of journalists and corporate lawyers and the like corrupt liberal education because it legitimizes the notion that higher education ought to be for the express purpose of readying one for a career.

If the central claim of this book is correct, that institutions of liberal learning serve as incubators for civil society by cultivating the art of self-governance, then clearly our central missions must be much more than delivering marketable skills that render students "job ready on day one." And yet, I believe that those of us who are champions of place-based liberal education as a source of a thriving civil society cede too much when we suggest that we are not interested in preparing students for professional life, or when we say, "yes, we will offer students some preparation for their eventual careers, but only reluctantly, and only as something that is secondary to our *real* mission." Preparing students to be productive contributors to civil society includes attention to the fact that workplaces are civic spaces too. As Parker Palmer (2011: 162) observes in *Healing the Heart of Democracy*:

> The workplace where we spend so many hours of our lives is one of the prepolitical spaces where our habits of the heart get formed or deformed. It is a human-scale setting where questions arise about our capacity for mutual respect and trust, open listening and courageous speaking, and individual and collective resolve to work for the common good. The way we answer those questions in the workplace often spills over into the larger society, for better or worse.

Many of the habits of association that make for healthy civil societies (rules of collaborative engagement, norms and values of tolerance, pluralism, and inclusion, and so on) make for healthy business and workplace environments. In turn, workplace norms of professional ethics and boundaries can often serve as a guide for keeping our non-market civic engagement civil.

Most important, despite what personnel recruiters might say, it is the intellectual agency we develop in our students (not the knowledge of the latest statistical software) that represents the most important contribution institutions of liberal learning offer to the workplaces that will eventually employ our students (Battistoni and Longo 2005).

The workplace can be and is often a context in which we are invited to exercise our creativity and engage in discovery – the discovery of the genuinely novel. Such discovery can indeed take the form of entrepreneurial innovation, but it can also take the form of better business practices that improve the quality of life and work for employees. The claim here is not that all workplace environments are incubators of creative discovery. Unfortunately this is far from the case. The point, rather, is that the liberally educated mind – the mind that has learned to engage in a creative discovery process in uncharted terrain – is the mind that is most likely to turn workplaces into incubators of creative discovery either through example or through direct leadership.

It is appropriate and understandable, I would argue, that students will think and worry about their employability, career development, and even income earning potential. Our job as liberal educators is to help them understand and articulate to others that it is the ability to deploy their acquired skills in productive and creative ways in unscripted environments that is the value of what they bring to the table. When asked in their first job interview about specific business-oriented knowledge, we want our graduates to be able to say something like, "Yes, I know that statistical package, but more importantly, let me tell you about how I used that knowledge to help a local housing non-profit reconfigure its model for client services so that it could expand its client base by 30 percent without any increase in staff." When asked about their ability to manage people, we want our graduates to be able to say something like, "Let me tell you about how I led the effort to establish a summer concert series that involved local officials, college administrators, and performing artists from the community and student body." And ideally, such students would be able to reflect on the ways in which courses across the curriculum and co-curricular involvement were the source of novel insight that helped them navigate this uncharted territory.

The point here is that if properly understood, student interest in their career is not a threat to the status of liberal learning. And to put it more strongly, we (those who understand the central role liberal learning plays in fostering healthy civil society) have the rightful claim that it is we who are more fully preparing students for the world of work; not those who focus too narrowly on finding the most efficient way to deliver specific content that will be obsolete by the time the first round of hiring is complete.

This book

This volume is structured in four parts. Part I explores the connections between liberal learning and civic learning in the context of the classroom. Particular emphasis is placed on pedagogies that foster intellectual agency necessary for self-governance. In his essay "Knowledge and Community in the Undergraduate Classroom," Robert Garnett argues that liberal educators have the potential to cultivate the habits of self-governance not only by *what* they teach, but also by *how* they teach. Garnett argues that by shifting away from an "expert-centered" pedagogy and toward a "polycentric" pedagogy, liberal educators turn their classrooms into learning communities in which students actively participate in the creation of new knowledge and experience the generative potential of critical thinking and collaborative discourse.

The classroom discussion is so ubiquitous within institutions that value liberal learning – such an obvious part of the liberal educator's toolkit – that the question "why is discussion important?" may seem rather silly; somewhat like asking why a framing carpenter needs a hammer or why a cook needs fire. But a moment's thought reveals that each of these questions is far from silly. (Think of the physics and the chemistry involved in carpentry and cooking.) In their essay, "On 'Strongly Fortified Minds': Self-restraint and cooperation in the discussion tradition," Sandra Peart and David Levy examine the "discussion tradition" within the mainline of political economy, beginning with Adam Smith and J. S. Mill, through more contemporary figures within that tradition, including Frank Knight, James Buchanan, and Amartya Sen, to identify the specific ways in which discussion as a pedagogical practice develops the habits of critical thought, intellectual openness, and cooperation.

Drawing upon the sociology of knowledge literature, Traci Fordham's essay "Teaching the Art of Speaking Across Ideological Paradigms," examines the theory and practice of developing in our students (and ourselves) the "literacy of citizenship" that makes democracy possible. Fordham argues that the very notion of citizenship requires an ability to engage (civilly) viewpoints and perspectives different from one's own. As such, she offers practical guidance for how liberal educators can deploy the pedagogies of dialogue and deliberation to fulfill our responsibility to help students navigate a world defined by difference.

Part II of the volume examines the intersections between liberal learning and self-governance that are created when we go beyond the traditional classroom to include pedagogies of place, community, and context. In their essay "More than Community-Based Learning: Practicing the liberal arts," Charles Westerberg and Carol Wickersham argue that by putting the liberal arts into *practice* – in the field, and in professional and community environments – students develop the habits of judgment ("What's important in this circumstance?"), confidence ("When should I step forward?"), and humility ("When should I let someone else lead?").

Community- and context-based learning facilitates what Westerberg and Wickersham call the "learning stance," in which students become practiced at the art of finding and learning from unlikely characters and situations. Such a learning stance is precisely what is cultivated in the programs my co-authors Adam Goodheart, John Seidel, and I describe in our essay "Developing the Art of Self-Governance: Teaching the role of place in associative life." In this essay we illustrate the power of place in cultivating the student's ability to read and navigate complex social terrain through place-based history and environmental student programs.

Part III of the volume draws our attention to the fact that most institutions of liberal learning are *social* spaces, and as such afford particular opportunities to practice the art of self-governance. In her essay "The Essential Role of Abrasion in Developing Healthy Institutions of Liberal Learning," Heather Wood Ion explores the theme of social abrasion – how the formal and informal structures of college life create the kind of friction that frustrates, transforms, shapes, and polishes. In their essay "Communities of Liberal Learning and Social Spaces," Laura Grube and Virgil Henry Storr examine the ways in which the residential liberal arts college as a social space fosters habits of association in ways that are profound (e.g., collective student response to social issues involving race or gender dynamics on campus) and mundane (e.g., learning to live compatibly with others in tight dormitory quarters). Further, through case study analysis, Grube and Storr argue that it is within the context of these social spaces that young adults gain experience in building community with others significantly different from themselves.

Part IV of the volume explores the formal and informal governance structures that shape interaction across campuses and across the academy as a whole; structures that either expand or inhibit the development of collaborative relationships, allow for widespread experimentation, and uphold standards of academic freedom. In our essay "Polycentricity and the Principles of Effective Co-Governance: What the Bloomington School can teach us," Paul Dragos Aligica and I consider the principles and practices of co-governance as a form of self-governance that is worthy of our analytical attention. We examine the polycentric (as opposed to top-down hierarchical) nature of decision-making authority within higher education, identifying both opportunities for robust well-functioning processes of institutional governance and common pitfalls administrators and boards encounter when they fail to understand the overlapping spheres of authority that define and limit their ability to control every aspect of college governance.

Arguing that faculty-led curricular and pedagogical change is among the most important forms of faculty self-governance, Steven Horwitz underscores the importance of understanding the social ecology of faculty life in his essay "Meaningful Change Comes from the Shop Floor: Generating, growing and governing in liberal education." Horwitz argues that the most effective and sustainable pedagogical changes come not from top-down mandates about how better to teach, but rather faculty coming together on their own to organize formal or informal arenas to discuss their work. And finally, in his essay "Academic Freedom as a Basis for Self-Governance," Jonathan Imber

examines critical turning points in the history of academic freedom, particularly those surrounding the life and career of Arthur O. Lovejoy, a founding
leader of the American Association of University Professors (AAUP), that
has shaped the culture of the modern academy.

In these essays the reader will hear from scholars who have honed their
craft as teachers, and will encounter programs, campuses, and historical figures that are extraordinary in many respects. But, and here I trust (hope) that
the contributors to this volume will forgive me for saying so, what is being
described here is also ordinary. By this I mean that in some form or another
we see examples of these pedagogical practices and these kinds of programs,
campus life, and faculty culture throughout institutions of liberal learning.
Yes, they do seem extraordinary when they are our own, but what is more
extraordinary is that readers teaching and learning within institutions of liberal learning will see them as familiar. The aim of this volume is to draw our
analytic eye to these familiar aspects of liberal learning so that we become
practiced at recognizing the opportunities for cultivating the art of self-
governance that are all around us. By recognizing these opportunities, we
become more deliberate about and skilled at cultivating the habits of self-
governance within ourselves and within our students. Most importantly, by
doing so, we become more practiced at delivering on the promise of liberal
education.

Notes

1 See Locke's *Essay Concerning Human Understanding* ([1689] 1824) and *Some
   Thoughts Concerning Education* ([1690] 1824).
2 See also Dedrick *et al.*'s (2008) *Deliberation and the Work of Higher Education,*
   Couto and Guthrie's (1999) *Making Democracy Work Better,* Beere *et al.*'s (2011)
   Becoming an Engaged Campus, Finley's (2012) *Making Progress? What we know
   about the achievement of liberal education outcomes,* and Dey and Associates' series
   that includes *Civic Responsibility, Developing a Moral Compass,* and *Engaging
   Diverse Viewpoints* (2009, 2010a, 2010b, respectively).
3 William Smith, *An Account of Washington College, in the State of Maryland* (Philadelphia, 1784) p. 4.
4 See Goodheart, op. cit.
5 By "political education," Oakeshott (1951: 159–160) was referring to what I have
   called here "civic learning." "Politics I take to be the activity of attending to the
   general arrangements of a set of people whom chance or choice have brought
   together. In this sense, families, clubs, and learned societies have their 'politics.' …
   [T]he activity [of attending to these arrangements] is one in which every member of
   the group who is neither a child nor a lunatic has some part and some responsibility. With us it is, at one level or another, a universal activity."
6 See also Checkoway (2012), Schneider (2012).

References

Arum, R. and Roksa, J. (2011) *Academically Adrift: Limited learning on college
   campuses,* Chicago, IL: University of Chicago Press.

Battistoni, R. M. and Longo, M. V. (2005) *Connecting Workforce Development and Civic Engagement: Higher education as public good and private gain*, Washington, DC: Public Policy Institute.

Beere, C., James, A., Votruba, C., and Wells, G. W. (2011) *Becoming an Engaged Campus: A practical guide for institutionalizing public engagement*, Hoboken, NJ: Jossey-Bass.

Checkoway, B. (2012) "Civic engagement, civic learning, and higher education," in D. Harward (ed.) *Civic Provocations*, Washington, DC: Bringing Theory to Practice, pp. 25–30.

Chopp, R. (2014) "Remaking, renewing, reimagining: The liberal arts college takes advantage of change," in R. Chopp, S. Frost, and D. H. Weiss (eds) *Remaking College: Innovation and the liberal arts*, Baltimore, MD: Johns Hopkins University Press, pp. 13–24.

Chopp, R., Frost, S., and Weiss, D. H. (eds) (2014) *Remaking College: Innovation and the liberal arts*, Baltimore, MD: Johns Hopkins University Press.

Couto, R. and Guthrie, C. (1999) *Making Democracy Work Better: Mediating structures, social capital, and the democratic prospect*, Chapel Hill: University of North Carolina Press.

Dedrick, J., Grattan, L., and Dienstfrey, H. (eds) (2008) *Deliberation and the Work of Higher Education*, Dayton, OH: Kettering Foundation Press.

Delbanco, A. (2012) *College: What it was, is, and should be*, Princeton, NJ: Princeton University Press.

Dey, Eric L. and associates. (2009) *Civic Responsibility: What is the campus climate for learning?* Washington, DC: Association of American Colleges and Universities.

Dey, Eric L. and associates. (2010a) *Developing a Moral Compass: What is the campus climate for ethics and academic integrity?* Washington, DC: Association of American Colleges and Universities.

Dey, Eric L. and associates. (2010b) *Engaging Diverse Viewpoints: What is the campus climate for perspective-taking?* Washington, DC: Association of American Colleges and Universities.

Finley, A. (2012) *Making Progress? What we know about the achievement of liberal education outcomes*, Washington, DC: Association of American Colleges and Universities.

Fuller, T. (2001) "Foreword," in M. Oakeshott, *The Voice of Liberal Learning*, Indianapolis: Liberty Fund, pp. xv–xxxv.

Goodheart, A. (n.d.) "The birth of Washington College," *Revolutionary College Project*, http://revcollege.washcoll.edu/firstcollege/birthofwc.html (accessed 24 June 2012).

Harward, D. W. (ed.) (2012) *Civic Provocations*, Washington, DC: Bringing Theory to Practice.

Levine, P. and Soltan, K. E. (2014) *Civic Studies*, Washington, DC: Bringing Theory to Practice.

Locke, J. ([1689] 1824) "Essay Concerning Human Understanding," in *The Works of John Locke in Nine Volumes, Volume II*, 12th edn, London: Rivington.

Locke, J. ([1690] 1824) "Some Thoughts on Education," in *The Works of John Locke in Nine Volumes, Volume II*, 12th edn, London: Rivington.

National Commission on Civic Renewal. (1998) "Nation of spectators: How civic disengagement weakens America and what we can do about it," www.civicengagement.org/agingsociety/links/nationspectators.pdf (accessed 10 July 2014).

National Task Force on Civic Learning and Democratic Engagement. (2012) *A Crucible Moment: College learning and democracy's future*, Washington, DC: Association of American Colleges and Universities.

Nussbaum, M. (2012) *Not for Profit: Why democracy needs the humanities*, Princeton, NJ: Princeton University Press.

Oakeshott, M. (1950) "The idea of a university," in *The Voice of Liberal Learning*, Indianapolis, IN: Liberty Fund, pp. 105–117.

Oakeshott, M. (1951) "Political education," in *The Voice of Liberal Learning*, Indianapolis, IN: Liberty Fund, pp. 159–188.

Oakeshott, M. (1975) "A place of teaching," in *The Voice of Liberal Learning*, Indianapolis, IN: Liberty Fund, pp. 1–34.

Oakeshott, M. (2001) *The Voice of Liberal Learning*, Indianapolis, IN: Liberty Fund.

Ostrom, E. (1990) *Governing the Commons: The evolution of institutions for collective action*, Cambridge: Cambridge University Press.

Palmer, P. (2011) *Healing the Heart of Democracy: The courage to create a politics worthy of the human spirit*, Hoboken, NJ: Jossey-Bass.

Smith, W. (1784) *An Account of Washington College, in the State of Maryland*, Philadelphia. http://revcollege.washcoll.edu/firstcollege/anaccount.html (accessed 24 June 2012).

Schneider, C. G. (2012) "To democracy's detriment: What is the current evidence, and what if we fail to act now?" in D. Harward (ed.) *Civic Provocations*, Washington, DC: Bringing Theory to Practice, pp. 7–12.

Sparks, E., and Waits, M. J. (2011) *Degrees for What Jobs? Raising expectations for universities and colleges in a global economy*, Washington, DC: National Governors Association, Center for Best Practices.

Tocqueville, A. ([1835] 2011) *Democracy in America*, Chicago, IL: University of Chicago Press.

Vedder, R. (2004) *Going Broke by Degree: Why colleges cost too much*, Washington, DC: AEI Press.

Vedder, R. (2007) "Overinvested and Overpriced: American higher education today," Washington, DC: Center for College Affordability and Productivity.

Part I

Cultivating the habits of self-governance in the classroom

1 Knowledge and community in the undergraduate classroom

Robert F. Garnett

College professors occupy a liminal space: academic professionals with little or no formal training as educators who nonetheless wield the authority of disciplinary expertise in their classrooms (DeMartino 2011: 106). In the current U.S. context, undergraduate faculties also face structural uncertainties about the future of postsecondary education (Ginsberg 2011, Schrecker 2010). Long-standing concerns about unsustainable revenue/cost structures in private and public higher education (Bowen 1980, Vedder 2004) are now amplified by the specter of massive open online courses and renewed evidence of limited student learning, particularly in the arts of critical thinking, complex reasoning, and writing (Bok 2008, Arum and Roksa 2011). Widening divisions of labor between teachers and researchers within departments and across disciplines are also evident. As a growing share of students and courses are taught by contingent faculty members and more institutions offer lower teaching loads to more productive scholars, faculty members increasingly feel compelled to become more specialized in either research or teaching (Rowland 2006, Nelson 2010).

In light of these foreboding trends, readers who might otherwise share our enthusiasm for liberal education and civic learning may hear our redoubled advocacy of these ideals as a counsel of perfection. It becomes our challenge to persuade anxious or dispirited colleagues, and indeed ourselves, that the perils facing the twenty-first-century professorate strengthen rather than undercut the case for liberal learning. More than ever we must keep our eyes (and our stakeholders' eyes) on the only ball that makes a higher education worth having, namely: our ability to expand students' capacities for creative, disciplined, fair-minded thought and effective participation in the world beyond the academy.

Emily Chamlee-Wright argues, and I agree, that "institutions of liberal learning are contexts ... in which we learn the art of self-governance" (see her Introduction to this volume). Note the "we" in Chamlee-Wright's claim – referring to students *and* faculty members. The cultivation of students' capacities for self-governance outside the classroom requires students and their professors to act as academic citizens in the self-governing learning communities where higher education principally occurs. To help their students become liberally educated individuals, faculty members must take seriously their duties as liberal educators. As Deirdre McCloskey (2006: 8) argues, "You can't get virtue Y from a starting point consisting only of virtue X. Y has to be in from the start. You have to put the rabbits in the hat if you are going to pull them out." When we as professors define our educational mission narrowly, as expert-centered instruction only, we forget our academic citizenship duties and reduce our students' chances of acquiring the intellectual and civic virtues necessary for free and responsible citizenship.

In this essay I outline a liberal vision of teachers' and students' duties as co-appropriators of a common pool resource: the undergraduate classroom. I argue that educators and students each play dual roles in the classroom knowledge commons: not just as expert and novice but as senior and junior citizens of the academic community. In support of this claim, I contrast the epistemic, educational, and ethical dimensions of teachers' and students' dual roles in two stylized settings: the expert-centered classroom and the liberal classroom. I examine each vision of the classroom enterprise by way of addressing three fundamental questions:

- What counts as knowledge and where does it come from?
- By what processes do students learn, and what roles do educators and students each play in the learning process?
- As academic citizens, what minimal duties must educators and students each perform in the learning process?

The core of my argument draws from the Socratic perspectives of John Dewey (1916), William Perry (1970), Kenneth Strike (1982), Martha Nussbaum (1997), Parker Palmer (1998), and David Ellerman (2005), and from the U.S. tradition of academic freedom (American Association of University Professors (AAUP) 1915, 1940, 1967, 1987, 2007). To highlight the liberal character of these Socratic approaches, I also explore their resonance with the liberal political economy of Friedrich Hayek (1948, 1979), Don Lavoie (1985, 1995a, 1995b), and Elinor Ostrom (1990, 2011).

Liberal education and self-governance

Before comparing the tacit assumptions of liberal and expert-centered approaches to undergraduate education, we must clarify the terms "liberal education" and "self-governance." Each pertains at all levels of academic organization, from the academy at large to individual institutions, departments, and courses, all the way down to the individual teacher and student.

Writing in defense of liberal education at every level of academic life, Nussbaum (1997: 19) claims that liberal education is the proper aim of all baccalaureate institutions.

> Liberal education in our colleges and universities is and should be Socratic, committed to the activation of each student's independent mind

and to the production of a community that can reason together about a problem, not just trade claims and counterclaims.

Education is liberal, Nussbaum argues, when it produces "citizens who are free not because of wealth or birth" but because they "can call their minds their own," because they "have looked into themselves and developed the ability to separate mere habit and convention from what they can defend by argument" and have gained thereby "ownership of their own thought and speech" (ibid.: 293).

The process of intellectual self-ownership – becoming an autonomous thinker – is classically described by Perry's (1970) nine stages of intellectual development, ranging from students who view education as the delivery of Truth from experts to novices, to students who are able to assume responsibility for their own minds and ideas despite the absence of absolute epistemic warrants for their positions. In Perry's words, "The liberally educated [person] ... can take responsibility for [his or her] own stand and negotiate – with respect – with other men" (ibid.: 39–40). Liberal education names the developmental process by which students become intellectual free agents: responsible, self-directed learners.

Hungarian philosopher Laszlo Versényi (1963: 117) neatly summarizes the Socratic view of knowing and learning as acts of intellectual (self-)ownership:

> Real education aims at imparting knowledge rather than opinion ... [K]nowledge cannot be handed over ready-made but has to be appropriated by the knower ... [and] that appropriation is only possible through one's own search.

Taking Versényi's thesis as his starting point, Ellerman (2005: 252) foregrounds the ethical dimension of teaching and other forms of "autonomy-respecting help":

> Helpers can at best use indirect, enabling, and autonomy-respecting methods to bring doers to the threshold. [But] the doers have to do the rest on their own in order to make it their own. The doers will acquire [knowledge] only as the fruits of their own labor.

Autonomy-respecting help is a delicate art, fraught by the paradox of "assisted autonomy": "If the helpers are supplying help that directly influences the doers, then how can the doers really be 'helping themselves'? Autonomy cannot be externally supplied" (ibid.: 4).

Nussbaum and Ellerman each envision the undergraduate classroom as a community of inquiry, affirming John Dewey's view of the college classroom and college itself as "a form of community life" (Dewey 1929: 293). Ellerman's "labor theory of intellectual property," whereby each learner is inalienably responsible for integrating new ideas into his or her web of prior knowledge, underscores the inherent indirectness of the Socratic teacher's role: providing resources and opportunities that bring students to the threshold of discovery and learning without undercutting their capacity for self-reliance. Worrying aloud about the enervating effects of teacher-centered education, Dewey argues that "neglect of the idea of the school as a form of social life" gives rise to educational philosophies and practices wherein "far too much of the stimulus and control proceeds from the teacher" (Dewey 1929: 293).

The classroom knowledge commons is governed not by any single authority but by an evolving constellation of formal and informal rules, specifying the duties of instructors and students as academic citizens. In the United States, the principal repository of these rules is the century-old institution of academic freedom. As a system of self-governance and ongoing dialogue on the rights and duties of instructors and students in shared spaces of inquiry, the academic freedom regime is notably decentralized, "a nested, polycentric system [arranged] from small to very large" (Ostrom 2011: 371) that serves to define, protect, and manage the common pool resources of college faculty members and students (AAUP 1915, 1940, 1967, 1987, 2007, Association of American Colleges and Universitites (AAC&U) 2006).

In her celebrated work on common pool resource (CPR) management, Ostrom foregrounds the complex ecology of CPR governance. In the case of academic freedom, she would alert us to the possibility of dysfunctional imbalances in the academic property rights claimed by teachers or students, e.g., professors who construe academic freedom as a doctrine of professorial private property, or student rights advocates who contend that students should not be forced to learn anything that violates their religious, political, or ethical preferences (Grossman 1998, Garnett 2009a, Nelson 2010). Ostrom would also remind us that "getting the institutions right" is a "difficult, time-consuming, conflict-invoking process" (Ostrom 1990: 14) and that the rules governing the classroom commons are continually evolving in response to pressures within and beyond the academy. Our role as academic citizens is to ensure that prevailing rules and norms of academic freedom enhance rather than diminish the prospects for liberal education.

What's wrong with expert-centered education?

To appreciate the character and value of liberal education, we must understand its departures from the "expert-centered" model. Our discussion will focus on the latter's implicit assumptions regarding knowledge, learning, and academic citizenship. These assumptions are depicted schematically in Figure 1.1, an adaptation of Palmer's "objectivist myth of knowing" (1998: 100).

Knowledge

Any sensible philosophy of undergraduate education recognizes the epistemic hierarchy between teacher and student. What distinguishes the expert-centered

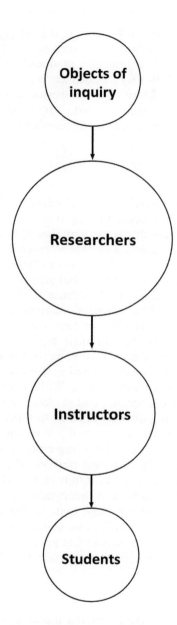

Figure 1.1 Knowledge and learning in the expert-centered classroom

model is the assumption that no knowledge is *produced* in the undergraduate classroom. The knowledge conveyed to students by teachers and textbooks consists of concepts and arguments produced by disciplinary experts upstream (Palmer 1998: 100–101). "Education is a system for delivering those propositions to students; and an educated person is one who can remember and repeat the experts' propositions" (ibid.: 101). Undergraduate students *and teachers* are cast as amateurs in this scheme; neither is regarded as a knowledge producer.

Learning

Teaching in the expert-centered model is fundamentally a process of instruction. Mutual learning may occur among students or between student and teacher but there is no sense that something special has been created if it does or sense of failure if it does not. The expert-centered space is thus devoid of learning *community.* "Teachers and students gather in the same room at the same time not to experience community but simply to keep the teacher from having to say things more than once" (Palmer 1998: 116).

Here we see concretely how teachers' "assumptions about knowing can open up, or shut down, the capacity for connectedness on which good teaching depends" (Palmer 1998: 51). In their earnest efforts to help students understand the nature and value of their subjects, teachers working under the default assumptions of the expert-centered model often fail to elicit or utilize student feedback as their courses unfold. Without effective feedback loops, the knowledge gaps between teacher and student – ever present, since "when you know something, it is extremely difficult to think about it from the perspective of someone who does not know it" (Wieman 2007) – multiply to the point of mutual incomprehension. Reflecting on the pedagogical ramifications of these knowledge gaps, Carl Wieman observes that even "a lesson that is very carefully thought out and is beautifully clear and logical to experts may be interpreted totally differently (and incorrectly) by the student," since students often "think about a topic in ways quite unimagined by the instructor."

Wieman concludes that "it is dangerous, and often profoundly incorrect, to think about student learning based on what appears best to faculty members, as opposed to what has been verified with students" (ibid.).

Academic citizenship

Another side effect of the expert-centered model is the eclipse of academic citizenship in the classroom, as the teacher's role is reduced to "instructor only" and the student's role to "amateur learner only." Neither party bears any obligation to the classroom learning community beyond compliance with institutional codes of conduct. Professors are not expected to cultivate students' autonomy as learners, for example. When students raise questions about the assumptions or implications of a particular argument, the liberal educator would be duty-bound "to give reasons" and to respect the student's right "to question and debate the conclusions reached by experts" (Strike 1982: 49). An expert-centered ethic conveys no such duty. Kinder souls may elect to give reasons; but no ethical line is crossed by the professor who illiberally responds, "Just learn what's in the textbook; then we'll talk."

The liberal classroom

Liberal education proceeds from fundamentally different assumptions about the educational process, envisioning the college classroom as neither teacher-centered nor student-centered but subject-centered (Palmer 1998: 103–104). These assumptions are reflected in Figure 1.2, a modified version of Palmer's "community of truth" (1998: 102).

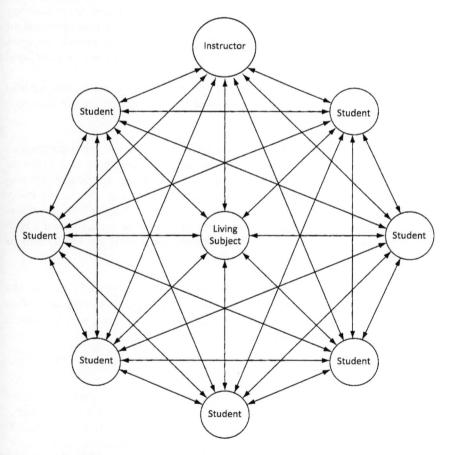

Figure 1.2 Knowledge and learning in the liberal classroom

Knowledge

Liberal educators see the undergraduate classroom as a locus of knowledge production, not merely a site for the redistribution of expert knowledge produced elsewhere. Without effacing the hierarchies of knowledge and authority between instructor and student (highlighted in Figure 1.2 by the relative sizes of the "Instructor" and "Student" circles), all parties in the liberal classroom act as knowers. Students are treated as active educational subjects, as learners whose tacit knowledge and intellectual agency are activated when teachers put them "behind the wheel" (Palmer 1998: 40–47).

In support of the liberal vision, Strike (1982) argues that teachers and students are participants in a common process of inquiry, "a community united by a shared commitment to some intellectual enterprise" (Strike 1982: 51). Strike acknowledges the epistemic inequality of students and teachers *qua* junior and senior participants in the disciplinary learning community. At the same time, student learning entails the appropriation of new ideas by a unique human mind and thus constitutes new knowledge, even if it does not advance the frontiers of human knowledge in any conventional sense.

In their joint emphasis on the knowledge of amateur learners, Palmer and Strike echo Hayek's (1948: 80) celebration of the valuable, albeit inexpert, knowledge possessed by each individual:

> [T]here is beyond question a body of very important but unorganized knowledge which cannot possibly be called scientific in the sense of knowledge of general rules: the knowledge of the particular circumstances of time and place. It is with respect to this that practically every individual has some advantage over all others because he possesses unique information of which beneficial use might be made, but of which use can be made only if the decisions depending on it are left to him or are made with his active cooperation.

Just as the Palmerian student finds her voice when placed "behind the wheel," the Hayekian individual's "man-on-the-spot" knowledge often remains tacit or inarticulate (Lavoie 1995a) until she is "faced with a problem where this [knowledge] will help" (Hayek 1979: 190).

Learning

Palmer's vision of the classroom as a subject-centered "community of truth" foregrounds the communal dimension of the liberal learning process. "To teach," says Palmer, "is to create a space where the community of truth is practiced" (1998: 90), "to draw students into the process, the community, of knowing" (1990: 12). Each classroom is a microcosm of the larger realm of inquiry, a single node within an extended network comprised of:

many communities, far-flung across space and ever-changing through time ... made one by the fact that they gather around a common subject and are guided by shared rules of observation and interpretation that require them to approach the subject in the same way.

(Palmer 1998: 101–102)

Liberal learning emerges from each learner's discovery of new connections to a living subject, connections derived in part from the learner's previously inarticulate knowledge (Hayek 1979, Lavoie 1995a). To facilitate the discovery process, liberal educators must recognize and exploit the fact that within each classroom, "the knowledge of the circumstances of which we must make use is not given to anyone in its totality" (Hayek 1948: 77–78). The core pedagogical problem is not how to deliver prepackaged information to students but how to induce and enable diverse learners to forge new connections to the subject matter and to communicate their discoveries to others (Hayek 1979: 190, Lavoie 1995a). Learning opportunities proliferate when students put their unique insights and confusions on the table so that privately held ideas ("money in their pocket") become intellectual resources ("money in the bank") available to other members of the classroom community (Garnett 2009b).

The liberal learning process is thus inherently polycentric, with new knowledge potentially emancipating each member of the classroom community. In contrast to the expert-centered premise that all relevant knowledge flows from disciplinary researchers, teachers, and textbooks, the liberal approach redefines teaching as a process of epistemic system design. To teach is to set in motion a framework of resources, rules, and incentives, seeking to generate – for each learner and for the class as a whole – not just an "accumulation of data" but "an enhancement of our interpretive powers and our tacit understanding of an unfolding reality" (Lavoie 1985: 58), "a kind of 'intelligence' that is far greater than the sum of its parts" (Lavoie 1995a: 125).

Our default notion of learning itself is transformed in the liberal setting, shifting from the expert-centered idea of learning as absorption or manipulation of experts' propositions to increased capacity for dialogue with a living subject and with fellow investigators (Garnett and Klopfenstein 2003). The more students are drawn into "the process, the community, of knowing," the more their thinking is enlarged and constrained by ideas and feedback from numerous sources and the better they are able to act as free, responsible thinkers.

With regard to classroom strategies, the liberal education model is wholly pluralist. Ostrom's "no panaceas!" mantra for CPR governance (Ostrom 2009) is affirmed in spades by Palmer's motto, "Good teaching cannot be reduced to technique" (Palmer 1990: 11):

Engaging students in the community of truth does not require that we put the chairs in a circle and have a conversation ... Different teachers with different gifts create community in surprisingly diverse ways ... in classes large and small ... through lectures, ... and many other pedagogies, traditional and experimental.

(Palmer 1998: 115)

The intellectual energy and persona of a relentless lecturer, for example, may elicit more engagement and critical thinking from students than would be achieved by means of "active learning" techniques (Palmer 1998: 136–137). Hayek argues a similar point regarding the imposition of textbook "perfect competition" as a normative benchmark for evaluating real-world markets, advising economists to "worry much less about whether competition in a given case is perfect and worry much more whether there is competition at all" (Hayek 1948: 105).

The essential task for the liberal educator is to bring the subject matter to life for students, "to give the subject an independent voice – a capacity to speak its truth quite apart from the teacher's voice in terms that students can hear and understand" (Palmer 1998: 118). Analogous to Hayek's theory of market process in which price fluctuations express not the personal dictates of sellers or buyers but the voice of the market as a whole (Lavoie 1995b: 392), Palmer envisions a learning process in which "the subject has a presence so real, so vivid, so vocal, that it can hold teacher and students accountable for what they say and do," in contrast to student-centered or teacher-centered classrooms "where either the teacher reigns supreme or students can do no wrong" (Palmer 1998: 117).

A second vital task for the liberal educator is to establish rules and norms that inspire trust among members of the classroom community. A classroom favorable to free exchange and critical give-and-take is only possible if the transaction costs of engaging in these risky behaviors are held to a reasonable minimum. Hence Palmer's (1990: 15) attention to the affective side of the classroom commons:

> The most important thing a teacher can do to encourage classroom conflict is to make the classroom a hospitable place. Only under these conditions are students likely to do the hard things ... exposing one's ignorance, challenging another's facts or interpretations, claiming one's truth publicly and making it vulnerable to the scrutiny of others.

Academic citizenship

For liberal educators, the college classroom is a site of academic self-governance, a learning commons occupied jointly by faculty members and students, each of whom bears certain academic duties (American Association of University Professors 1915, 1940, 1967, 1970, 2005). The special role of faculty members in the provision of "autonomy-respecting help" in the classroom was addressed in the AAUP's founding document (AAUP 1915), which stipulates that the university teacher shall not "provide his students with ready-made conclusions" and must "guard against taking unfair advantage of the student's immaturity by indoctrinating him with the teacher's own opinions before the student has ... sufficient knowledge and ripeness of judgment to be entitled to form any definitive opinion of his own."

The AAUP also charges faculty members with the positive duty to "train (students) to think for themselves and to provide them access to those materials which they need if they are to think intelligently." In the illustrative words of the 1915 report:

> The university teacher ... while he is under no obligation to hide his own opinion under a mountain of equivocal verbiage ... should cause his students to become familiar with the best published expressions of the great historic types of doctrine upon the questions at issue ... (including) the divergent opinions of other investigators.

The ethical rationale for these professorial duties is subject to ongoing debate. Some critics contend that the intellectual immaturity of undergraduate students means they "do not possess any academic rights except the right to competent instruction" (Fish 2008: 123, Saito 2003: 25). Socratic educators like Strike (1982), on the other hand, argue that the epistemic gap between teacher and student is precisely the *justification* for students' academic rights. Strike (ibid.: 148) grants that undergraduate students *qua* students possess no First Amendment free-speech rights:

> The rights of students in schools are not simply the civil rights of adults in society. Civil liberties are rooted in a presumption of equality between the parties ... [Postsecondary education] is not a marketplace of ideas where truth emerges from a multitude of tongues. It is a place where the student strives to master a rational enterprise under the guidance of an expert. Treating the expert-novice relationship as though it were governed by civil rights distorts its character.

Yet Strike defends students' academic rights on moral and epistemic grounds. "Students do have rights," Strike argues, because "[t]hey are persons and moral agents, and must, therefore, be treated as objects of value and respect" (ibid.: 148). The moral equality of teacher and student, as persons who each bear moral responsibility "for what they choose and what they do," obliges teachers to respect the autonomy of students, "to give students reasons for what they are asked to believe, within students' capacity to grasp them, and to teach so as to expand the students' capacity to comprehend and assess reasons" (ibid.: 43).

Epistemically, the "significant inequality between the student (as novice) and the teacher (as expert) in terms of their current capacity to understand and assess the ideas and arguments of a field" (Strike 1982: 49), obliges the teacher to treat each student "as a junior member of a community united by a shared commitment to some intellectual enterprise." The teacher's job is "to represent the field to the student honestly and fairly, to evaluate the student's work on relevant criteria" and to "secure for the student the right to participate in the intellectual affairs of the classroom in a way that assists the student in internalizing the standards and procedures of a discipline" (ibid.: 51, 49).

In sum, the Socratic duty of the undergraduate educator is to provide ample resources and opportunities for each student to achieve a liberal education: an education that honors the student's personhood and brings him or her "into a position of intellectual independence" (Strike 1982: 135, also see Garnett and Butler 2009, Garnett 2011).

Cultivating the liberal educator

If we accept the idea that the undergraduate classroom (like the academy at large) is a civil society in its own right, the practical question becomes: How might we encourage the formation and flourishing of liberal classrooms on our campuses? A conventional response would be to declare a shortage of qualified faculty members and arrange expert-led workshops on course design and teaching methods. Fink (2003: 23) recommends this very solution:

> "Design of instruction" … is one skill for which few college-level teachers have extensive training … Most faculty members simply follow the traditional ways of teaching in their particular discipline. They lack the conceptual tools they need to significantly rethink and reconstruct the set of teaching and learning activities they use.

Educational consultants can indeed provide valuable inspiration and classroom-ready techniques; but their expert-centered ethos should give us pause. Granted, most Ph.D. programs do not prepare students for "the full range of roles faculty play," particularly with regard to teaching (Gaff *et al.* 2003: 2–3); so expert-led conferences and workshops provide training that addresses real gaps in the professional development of many faculty members. Yet the professorate's demand for the wisdom of outside experts is notably limited. Most faculty members ignore their monthly teaching excellence newsletter. In addition to lack of time, the specialized language of pedagogical experts is alien to most faculty audiences, especially when it comes across as a discourse of imperious outsiders who do not appreciate the norms and histories of particular programs, institutions, or disciplinary traditions.

A liberal alternative would be to think in terms of expanding the resources, opportunities, and incentives for all Ph.D. faculty members to discover and develop their latent liberal education capabilities. If colleges and universities are academic civil societies, and if the driving force of any thriving civil society is voluntary cooperation (Cornuelle [1965]), it follows that busy colleagues with well-established courses and pedagogies will be more likely to engage in productive reflection on their teaching if induced to so do voluntarily rather than required to do so as a mandatory assessment exercise. When faculty members gather informally over lunch or coffee, or in more structured settings like reading groups or round-robin class visits, they are more likely to come away with fresh ideas and inspiration due to the civic character of the experience: voluntary, "off the record" interactions whose value often exceeds expectations.

The civil society concept pays further dividends when extended to the college classroom, opening up new ways for seasoned educators to discuss problems of perennial concern. For example, when departments treat student perceptions of teaching as the principal measure of teaching effectiveness, faculty members may understandably be troubled by the authority accorded to students as customers whose preferences and demands trump all. Recasting the classroom as an academic civil society provides a firm basis on which to insist that students are never simply consumers (receivers of information, motivation, and grades from faculty "suppliers" of these goods). Even as novice learners, they bear certain responsibilities and enjoy corresponding freedoms as citizens of the academic learning commons.

The liberal vision of undergraduate education can also provide a useful way to address the frustration of faculty members who struggle to conduct meaningful classroom-based courses in competition with students' phones and the Internet. Every college instructor grows accustomed to competition from students' other coursework, family emergencies, illnesses, work schedules, co-curricular activities, and the like. But when a quarter or more of the students in our classrooms are routinely distracted by their devices, it can be hard to sustain one's faith in the possibility of effective education in the digital age. Formal rules about the use of phones, tablets, and laptops in the classroom are necessary but rarely sufficient to resolve these issues. The most effective responses employ formal rules in combination with the instructor's demonstrated commitment to the students and subject matter, and, where possible, the creation of assignments or pedagogies that enlist students as co-investigators based on their expertise as digitally networked learners (Bakera *et al.* 2012, McLaughlin 2013).

In addition, three sets of resources stand ready to support the development of faculty members' nascent interest in liberal alternatives to expert-centered instruction.

The U.S. tradition of academic freedom

Academic freedom – the evolving dialogue on the rights and duties of instructors and students – is a neglected but defining rubric for U.S. higher education (Nelson 2010), specifying not ideal, utopian conditions for academic inquiry but "minimal standards ... essential to any community of scholars" (AAUP 1967). As the *lingua franca* of undergraduate education whose "heart and soul ... lies not in free speech but in ... collegial self-governance" (Haskell 1996: 54), academic freedom facilitates cooperation among colleagues who otherwise share little in common by foregrounding the unifying principles of our academic civil society.

The intellectual-cum-educational resources embedded in our disciplines

The expert-centered view of teaching as "a generic, practical, instrumental activity largely divorced from the serious intellectual work of research" discourages us from seeing the intimate connections between teaching and research in our own lives and across our academic communities (Rowland 2006: 71). Stephen Rowland suggests academic development forums to "[bring] teaching and research into a closer relationship" (ibid.: 13). Rowland believes that "when academics from different disciplines are given the space and encouragement to speak to each other about their work in terms that matter to them" (Rowland 2006: 69–70), they frequently discover connections among their disciplinary idioms that "can challenge and deepen both disciplinary thinking and educational ideas," e.g., a cell biologist and systems engineer who strike up a conversation about their differing notions of "feedback" and potential applications of these concepts (ibid.: 71). Such conversations unearth the tacit educational resources embedded within our respective disciplines (Garnett and Vanderlinden 2011).

The teacher and student within

The intellectual resources of "the self that teaches" are never limited to the knowledge and skills we acquire as Ph.D. students (Palmer 1998: 7). Palmer argues that our authority as teachers flows from "the teacher within" (ibid.: 30–31), a persona shaped profoundly by our experiences as students:

> Many of us were called to teach by encountering not only a mentor but a particular field of study ... [that] shed light on our identity as well as on the world. We did not merely find a subject to teach – the subject also found us.
>
> (Palmer 1998: 25)

Palmer's faith in our hidden wholeness as teacher-scholars underscores the potency of liberal education talk, among colleagues and within ourselves. As we become more aware of the questions and values that keep us alive as teachers and scholars, the "teacher within" can become a generative ally in our quest for more meaningful connections to the great things that inspire our learning and expand our capacity for community.

Conclusion

In moments of impending crisis, philosophical arguments may seem indulgent or beside the point. Yet liberal education stands in need of a ringing ethical, epistemological, and thoroughly practical defense today, as every college and university is pressed to justify its commitment to classroom courses taught by full-time faculty members over cheaper (and generally more expert-centered) alternatives. To the real and growing concerns about "limited learning" on today's campuses (Arum and Roska 2011), the liberal classroom offers a robust response. Arum and Roksa (2011) trace the limited learning phenomenon to what George Kuh (2003: 28) terms a "mutual disengagement compact" between instructors and students:

> There seems to be a breakdown of shared responsibility for learning – on the part of faculty members who allow students to get by with far less than maximum effort, and on the part of students who are not taking full advantage of the resources institutions provide.

The magic of liberal education lies in its power to reverse this symbiotic "breakdown of shared responsibility" by generating a virtuous cycle of mutual *re-engagement*. Indeed, a growing body of educational literature suggests that learning is enhanced along multiple dimensions when students act as co-explorers within polycentric learning spaces rather than receivers of instruction in expert-centered classrooms (Hake 1998, Campbell and Smith 1997, Finkel 2000, Fink 2003, Tagg 2003, Mazur 2009, Deslauriers *et al.* 2011).

Colleges and universities are flush with learned, creative thinkers endowed with troves of knowledge and gratitude from their own undergraduate experiences and who share an abiding interest in the liberal enterprise of helping young (and older) adults to own and develop their own minds. To elicit more educational value from these resources, we and our chief academic officers must recognize that liberal education – providing our share of the conditions for students' flourishing as free and responsible thinkers – is our core mission and most sacred duty as baccalaureate institutions. When we shrink from this challenge, we leave students ill-prepared to "grapple successfully with uncertainty, complexity, and conflicting perspectives and [to] still take stands that are based on evidence, analysis and compassion" (Nelson 1997: 71). We also leave ourselves and our institutions vulnerable to the charge that we are not educating students but exploiting them, by treating our undergraduate students not as moral agents and junior apprentices but as mere means to our institutions' revenue-generating ends.

Acknowledgements

I have benefited from many conversations on these topics with Ted Burczak, Kristin Klopfenstein, Ed McNertney, Lisa Vanderlinden, Emily Chamlee-Wright, Steve Horwitz, David Ellerman, and Lenore Ealy. I am especially grateful to Emily for encouraging my internal dialogue between the broad traditions of liberal education and liberal political economy.

References

American Association of University Professors (1915) *General Declaration of Principles*, New York: Columbia University Press.

American Association of University Professors (1940) *Statement of Principles on Academic Freedom and Tenure*, Washington, DC.

American Association of University Professors (1967) *Joint Statement on Rights and Freedoms of Students*, Washington, DC.

American Association of University Professors (1970) *Interpretive Comments on 1940 Statement of Principles on Academic Freedom and Tenure*, Washington, DC.

American Association of University Professors (1987) *Statement of Professional Ethics*, Washington, DC.

American Association of University Professors (2005) *AAUP Policies in the Classroom*, Washington, DC.

American Association of University Professors (2007) "Freedom in the classroom," *Academe*, 93(5): 54–61.

Arum, R. and Roksa J. (2011) *Academically Adrift: Limited learning on college campuses*, Chicago, IL: University of Chicago Press.

Association of American Colleges and Universities (2006) *Academic Freedom and Educational Responsibility*, Washington, DC.

Bakera, W. M., Luskb, E. J. and Neuhauser, K. L. (2012) "On the use of cell phones and other electronic devices in the classroom: Evidence from a survey of faculty and students," *Journal of Education for Business*, 87(5): 275–289.

Bok, D. (2008) *Our Underachieving Colleges: A candid look at how much students learn and why they should be learning more*, Princeton, NJ: Princeton University Press.

Bowen, H. R. (1980) *The Costs of Higher Education*, San Francisco, CA: Jossey-Bass.

Campbell, W. E. and Smith, K. A. (eds) (1997) *New Paradigms for College Teaching*, Edina, MN: Interaction Books.

Cornuelle, R. C. ([1965] 1993) *Reclaiming the American Dream: The role of private individuals and voluntary associations*, New Brunswick, NJ: Transaction Publishers.

DeMartino, G. F. (2011) *The Economist's Oath: On the need for and content of professional economic ethics*, New York: Oxford University Press.

Deslauriers, L., Schelew, E. and Wieman, C. (2011) "Improved learning in a large-enrollment physics class," *Science*, 332(6031): 862–864.

Dewey, J. (1916) *Democracy and Education*, Toronto: Macmillan.

Dewey, J. (1929) "My pedagogic creed," *Journal of the National Education Association*, 18(9): 291–295.

Ellerman, D. (2005) *Helping People Help Themselves: From the World Bank to an alternative philosophy of development assistance*, Ann Arbor: University of Michigan Press.

Fink, L. D. (2003) *Creating Significant Learning Experiences: An integrated approach to designing college courses*, San Francisco, CA: Jossey-Bass.

Finkel, D. L. (2000) *Teaching with Your Mouth Shut*, Portsmouth, NH: Boynton/Cook.

Fish, S. (2008) *Save the World on Your Own Time*, Oxford: Oxford University Press.

Gaff, J. G., Pruitt-Logan, A. S., Sims, L. B. and Denecke, D. D. (2003) "Preparing future faculty in the social sciences and the humanities," Washington, DC: Council of Graduate Schools and Association of American Colleges and Universities.

Garnett, R. F. (2009a) "Liberal learning as freedom: A capabilities approach to undergraduate education," *Studies in Philosophy and Education*, 28(5): 437–447.

Garnett, R. F. (2009b) "Hayek and liberal pedagogy," *Review of Austrian Economics*, 22(4): 315–331.

Garnett, R. F. (2011) "Rethinking the pluralist debate in economics education," *International Review of Economic Education*, 8(2): 58–71.

Garnett, R. F. and Butler, M. R. (2009) "Should economic educators care about students' academic freedom?" *International Journal of Pluralism and Economics Education*, 1(1/2): 148–160.

Garnett. R. F. and Klopfenstein, K. M. (2003) "Critical thinking as an interpersonal experience: Rethinking introductory courses across the disciplines," *Inquiry: Critical thinking across the disciplines*, 23(1): 11–16.

Garnett, R. F. and Vanderlinden, L. K. (2011) "Reflexive pedagogy: Disciplinary idioms as resources for teaching," *Teaching in Higher Education*, 16 (December): 242–249.

Ginsberg, B. (2011) *The Fall of the Faculty: The rise of the all-administrative university and why it matters*, New York: Oxford University Press.

Grossman, J. B. (1998) "Academic freedom: Threats and limits," in W. L. Hansen (ed.) *Academic Freedom on Trial*, Madison: University of Wisconsin–Madison, pp. 253–263.

Hake, R. R. (1998) "Interactive engagement vs. traditional methods: A six thousand-student survey of mechanics test data for introductory physics courses," *American Journal of Physics*, 66(1): 64–74.

Haskell, T. L. (1996) "Justifying the rights of academic freedom in the era of 'power/knowledge,'" in L. Menand (ed.) *The Future of Academic Freedom*, Chicago, IL: University of Chicago Press, pp. 43–92.

Hayek, F. A. (1948) *Individualism and Economic Order*, Chicago, IL: University of Chicago Press.

Hayek, F. A. (1979) *Law, Legislation, and Liberty, Volume III: The political order of a free people*, Chicago, IL: University of Chicago Press.

Kuh, G. D. (2003) "What we are learning about student engagement," *Change*, 35 (March/April): 24–32.

Lavoie, D. (1985) *National Economic Planning: What is left?* Washington, DC: Cato Institute.

Lavoie, D. (1995a) "The market as a procedure for the discovery and conveyance of inarticulate knowledge," in D. Prychitko (ed.) *Individuals, Institutions, Interpretations: Hermeneutics applied to economics*, Brookfield, VT: Avebury, pp. 115–137.

Lavoie, D. (1995b) "The 'objectivity' of scholarship and the ideal of the university," *Advances in Austrian Economics*, 2B: 371–403.

Mazur, E. (2009) "Farewell, lecture?" *Science*, 2(1): 50–51.

McCloskey, D. N. (2006) "The Hobbes problem: From Machiavelli to Buchanan," Unpublished paper, James M. Buchanan Lecture, Department of Economics, George Mason University, 7 April.

McLaughlin, E. J. (2013) "Teaching millennials: Bridging the schism between traditional instruction and active engagement of undergraduate students in a problem-based introductory finance class," *International Research Journal of Applied Finance*, 4(2): 263–270.

Nelson, C. (2010) *No University is an Island: Saving academic freedom*, New York and London: New York University Press.

Nelson, C. E. (1997) "Tools for tampering with teaching's taboos," in W. E. Campbell and K. A. Smith (eds) *New Paradigms for College Teaching*, Edina, MN: Interaction Books, pp. 51–77.

Nussbaum, M. C. (1997) *Cultivating Humanity: A classical defense of reform in liberal education*, Cambridge, MA: Harvard University Press.

Ostrom, E. (1990) *Governing the Commons: The evolution of institutions for collective action*, Cambridge: Cambridge University Press.

Ostrom, E. (2009) "Beyond markets and states: Polycentric governance of complex economic systems," Nobel Prize Lecture, 8 December, Stockholm University, Sweden, www.nobelprize.org/nobel_prizes/economics/laureates/2009/ostrom-lecture. html (accessed 4 July 2014).

Ostrom, E. (2011) "Honoring James Buchanan," *Journal of Economic Behavior and Organization*, 80(2): 370–373.

Palmer, P. J. (1990) "Good teaching," *Change*, 22: 11–16.

Palmer, P. J. (1998) *The Courage to Teach: Exploring the inner landscape of a teacher's life*, San Francisco, CA: Jossey-Bass.

Perry, Jr., W. G. (1970) *Forms of Intellectual and Ethical Development in the College Years: A scheme*, New York: Holt, Rinehart and Winston.

Rowland, S. (2006) *The Enquiring University: Compliance and contestation in higher education*, Maidenhead: Open University Press.

Saito, M. (2003) "Amartya Sen's capability approach to education: A critical exploration," *Journal of Philosophy of Education*, 37(1): 17–33.

Schrecker, E. (2010) *The Lost Soul of Higher Education: Corporatization, the assault on academic freedom, and the end of the American university*, New York and London: The New Press.

Strike, K. A. (1982) *Liberty and Learning*, New York: St. Martin's Press.

Tagg, J. (2003) *The Learning Paradigm College*, Boston, MA: Anker.

Vedder, R. (2004) *Going Broke by Degree: Why college costs too much*, Washington, DC: AEI Press.

Versényi, L. (1963) *Socratic Humanism*, Westport, CT: Greenwood Press.

Wieman, C. (2007) "The 'curse of knowledge' or why intuition about teaching often fails," *American Physical Society News*, 16(10), www.aps.org/publications/apsnews/ 200711/backpage.cfm (accessed 21 April 2012).

2 On "strongly fortified minds"

Self-restraint and cooperation in the discussion tradition

Sandra J. Peart and David M. Levy

Public reasoning is not only crucial for democratic legitimacy, it is essential for a better public epistemology that would allow the consideration of divergent perspectives. It is also required for more effective practical reasoning. It can bring out what particular demands and protests can be restrained in interactive public reasoning, in line with scrutinized priorities between a cluster of quite distinct demands. This involves a process of "give and take" which many political analysts, from Adam Smith and the Marquis de Condorcet in the eighteenth century to Frank Knight and James Buchanan in our time, have made us appreciate better.

(A. K. Sen 2012)

We are all subject to wishing that a thing be true or at least provisionally correct, so that our priors are confirmed. Indeed, John Stuart Mill recognized this in his 1843 *Logic*, a tour de force in making the case for inductive logic. Mill wrote:

> We cannot believe a proposition only by wishing, or only by dreading, to believe it. ... [Wishing] operates, by making [a person] look out eagerly for reasons, or apparent reasons, to support opinions which are conformable to his interests or feelings; ... whoever was on his guard against all kinds of inconclusive evidence which can be mistaken for conclusive, would be in no danger of being led into error even by the strongest bias. There are minds so strongly fortified on the intellectual side, that they could not blind themselves to the light of truth, however really desirous of doing so.
>
> (Mill [1843] 1981: 738)

Mill placed his faith in education – including, significantly, robust discussion – as at least a partial correction for this failing. In his view discussion was the means by which free individuals come to more fully understand what they believe. More than this, in the classical view of economics, the exchange of words, discussion, constitutes the means by which we come to moderate our selfish impulses and, increasingly, to cooperate.[1]

Accordingly, this essay explores some unappreciated benefits of discussion.[2] While educators frequently favor discussion as a means to encouraging engaged learning, they nonetheless rarely attempt to explain how or why these benefits arise. More than this, the role of economists from Adam Smith through Frank Knight and his student, James Buchanan, in explaining the benefits associated with discussion has been neglected both within economics and throughout the academy. In this tradition one accepts the inevitability of an individual "point of view" and the good society is one that can govern itself by means of an emergent consensus among points of view. In this chapter we demonstrate that beginning with Smith and continuing through the experimental economists and Amartya Sen, economists have expounded upon the rich moral and material benefits associated with discussion – benefits that contribute to a well-governed social order.[3] To emphasize the common themes in this neglected tradition, we shall refer to it as the "discussion tradition."

Discussion, the self and trade: Adam Smith

Perhaps the first and hardest bias is the bias that places the self at the center of the universe. Without language there is no other and hence no requirement for reciprocity or civility: the sense that one resides at the center of the universe simply persists. With language, we convey our sense of self to others, and we learn how others perceive our self and our sense of self. We also learn about others; we exchange ideas and emotions with them. The first lesson about discussion, then, is that language forms the basis for imaginative exchange, for the placing of one's self in another's shoes and for giving and receiving approval or approbation.[4]

For Smith, this first type of exchange, the exchange of approbation helps us become moral persons. As is well known, Smith distinguished between "praise" and "praiseworthiness" in *The Theory of Moral Sentiments,* and he held that we are all subject to the desire to be praiseworthy. While we may not always know how to obtain the approbation of others, we observe people's reactions to our acts and we come to understand what constitutes appropriate, or virtuous conduct by observing what is generally approved. We come to moderate our actions in order to obtain general approval. We come to understand that we are not the center of the universe and we behave accordingly:

> A very young child has no self-command; but, whatever are its emotions, whether fear, or grief, or anger, it endeavours always, by the violence of its outcries, to alarm, as much as it can, the attention of its nurse, or of its parents. While it remains under the custody of such partial protectors, its anger is the first and, perhaps, the only passion which it is taught to moderate. ... When it is old enough to go to school, or to mix with its equals, it soon finds that they have no such indulgent partiality. It naturally wishes to gain their favour, and to avoid their hatred or contempt.

Regard even to its own safety teaches it to do so; and it soon finds that it can do so in no other way than by moderating, not only its anger, but all its other passions, to the degree which its play-fellows and companions are likely to be pleased with. It thus enters into the great school of self-command, it studies to be more and more master of itself, and begins to exercise over its own feelings a discipline which the practice of the longest life is very seldom sufficient to bring to complete perfection.

(Smith [1759] 1976: 145)

The first significant benefit of (face-to-face) language, of discussion, in Smith's view is therefore that it induces moderation and perhaps even something we would today refer to as tolerance. It is through language, and the exchange of approbation over time, that we come to understand what is generally approved and we try to act accordingly. To the extent that we succeed, we become virtuous individuals. Importantly, for Smith all that is required for this is language and discussion – exchange of approbation: civility and virtue emerge from our general desire for approval.[5] In terms of governance, in the discussion tradition we are led to accept that ours is only one of many points of view in the search for consensus. Discussion is also a means by which our imaginative capacity is stretched to include at least partial understanding of the goals and arguments of others.[6]

But there is more to language for Smith than its role in generating virtue. In his account discussion also generates significant material benefits. As noted above, Smith famously held that without discussion there is no trade; with discussion there is. Without the ability to converse, creatures like greyhounds and mastiffs are therefore unable to obtain the material benefits attendant on language:

The strength of the mastiff is not in the least supported either by the swiftness of the greyhound, or by the sagacity of the spaniel, or by the docility of the shepherd's dog. The effects of those different geniuses and talents, for want of the power or disposition to barter and exchange, cannot be brought into a common stock, and do not in the least contribute to the better accommodation and conveniency of the species. Each animal is still obliged to support and defend itself, separately and independently, and derives no sort of advantage from that variety of talents with which nature has distinguished its fellows.

(Smith [1776] 1904, I.2.5)

In contrast, humans have access to language and that enables them to obtain the benefits of specialization, trade and cooperation:

Among men, on the contrary, the most dissimilar geniuses are of use to one another; the different produces of their respective talents, by the general disposition to truck, barter, and exchange, being brought, as it

were, into a common stock, where every man may purchase whatever
part of the produce of other men's talents he has occasion for.

(Smith [1776] 1904, I.2.5)

In this view, discussion is also the key means by which wealth is produced
and increased over time. In today's vernacular, it is via discussion that we are
able best to decide who should do what and when.

There is, then, an external economy in the realm of knowledge associated
with discussion among free people. One dramatic example occurred at a
celebrated dinner party hosted by Aaron Director with guests from the economics department at the University of Chicago. At this dinner, Ronald
Coase famously changed the minds of his colleagues on the question of
externalities and property rights. George Stigler described the conversation:

> When, in 1960, Ronald Coase criticized Pigou's theory rather casually, in the
> course of a masterly analysis of the regulatory philosophy underlying the
> Federal Communications Commission's work, Chicago economists could not
> understand how so fine an economist as Coase could make so obvious a
> mistake. Since he persisted, we invited Coase (he was then at the Uni-
> versity of Virginia) to come and give a talk on it. Some twenty econo-
> mists from the University of Chicago and Ronald Coase assembled one
> evening at the home of Aaron Director. Ronald asked us to assume, for a
> time, a world without transaction costs. That seemed reasonable because
> economic theorists, like all theorists, are accustomed (nay, compelled) to
> deal with simplified and therefore unrealistic "models" and problems.
>
> (Stigler [1988] 2003: 75)

It was this thought experiment that led to a deeper understanding of the role that
property rights (and other social institutions that reduce the costs of
exchange) play in fostering overall efficiency as individuals bargain with one
another in a market context. We call attention to the deep respect that the Chicago
economists and Coase had for each other. They discussed what divided them and
through this discussion they changed the course of twentieth-century economics.[7]

Discussion and learning: J. S. Mill

As noted at the outset, Mill believed that education was a means by which we
come to fortify ourselves against bias. While he was for the most part silent
on the source of such priors, Mill was convinced that we come to rid ourselves of false beliefs and better to understand true ones through discussion.[8]

In Mill's view, all people[9] are capable of being "guided to their own
improvement by conviction or persuasion":

> rectifying … mistakes, by discussion and experience. Not by experience
> alone. There must be discussion, to show how experience is to be

interpreted. Wrong opinions and practices gradually yield to fact and argument: but facts and arguments, to produce any effect on the mind, must be brought before it.

(Mill [1867] 1984: 306)

Silencing discussion "is an assumption of infallibility," the presumption of perfection.[10]

For Mill, we come to know a thing by knowing what is said about it:

> [T]he only way in which a human being can make some approach to knowing the whole of a subject, is by hearing what can be said about it by persons of every variety of opinion, and studying all modes in which it can be looked at by every character of mind.
>
> (Mill [1869] 1977: 232)

If, instead, we simply believe what we are told, we fail fully to understand the proposition and our belief might well be called "superstition."[11]

So, knowledge is better understood once experienced or discussed:

> [T]here are many truths of which the full meaning *cannot* be realized, until personal experience has brought it home. But much more of the meaning even of these would have been understood, and what was understood would have been far more deeply impressed on the mind, if the man had been accustomed to hear it argued *pro* and *con* by people who did understand it. The fatal tendency of mankind to leave off thinking about a thing when it is no longer doubtful, is the cause of half their errors. A contemporary author has well spoken of "the deep slumber of a decided opinion."
>
> (Mill [1869] 1977: 250)

It is important to know and perhaps to learn from one's critics, to develop a "steady habit of correcting and completing" our opinion "by collating it with those of others."[12] This thought forms the basis for assigning students randomly to a "point of view" and then asking them to argue a conclusion that may well be contrary to what they bring to the classroom. As they do so, they may come to better appreciate the weight of their opponents' arguments.

Arguments that try to silence discussion often, in Mill's view, hide behind a pronouncement that we must avoid discussing an extreme case. Like Smith, Mill recognized the problem of faction; discussion may not break down the barriers of factionalized or party interests. While discussion may not successfully penetrate and alter the minds of those whose views have been hardened by faction, it will, nonetheless be useful to the "calmer and more disinterested bystander," one who has yet to become factionalized:

> I acknowledge that the tendency of all opinions to become sectarian is not cured by the freest discussion, but is often heightened and

exacerbated thereby; the truth which ought to have been, but was not, seen, being rejected all the more violently because proclaimed by persons regarded as opponents. But it is not on the impassioned partisan, it is on the calmer and more disinterested bystander, that this collision of opinions works its salutary effect. Not the violent conflict between parts of the truth, but the quiet suppression of half of it, is the formidable evil.

(Mill [1869] 1977: 259)

Free discussion leads to moderation, although here Mill suggested that the incentives are asymmetrically aligned. In a twist on Smith's theme, Mill argued that those who speak against received wisdom must practice moderation more systematically than those who hold received opinions:

In general, opinions contrary to those commonly received can only obtain a hearing by studied moderation of language, and the most cautious avoidance of unnecessary offence, from which they hardly ever deviate even in a slight degree without losing ground: while unmeasured vituperation employed on the side of the prevailing opinion, really does deter people from professing contrary opinions, and from listening to those who profess them.

(Mill [1869] 1977: 249)

Teachers consequently for Mill had a special obligation to teach from different perspectives:

If teaching, even on matters of scientific certainty, should aim quite as much at showing how the results are arrived at, as at teaching the results themselves, far more, then, should this be the case on subjects where there is the widest diversity of opinion among men of equal ability, and who have taken equal pains to arrive at the truth. This diversity should of itself be a warning to a conscientious teacher that he has no right to impose his opinion authoritatively upon a youthful mind. His teaching should not be in the spirit of dogmatism, but in that of enquiry.

(Mill [1867] 1984: 249)

The discussion tradition that recognizes the inevitability of a point of view can be contrasted with a tradition that idealizes anonymity, where because scientific knowledge is presumed anonymous the scientist ought not to have a point of view. In one sense the issue is trivial. If everyone agrees then there is nothing interesting to discuss. More dangerously, however, those with power can easily stigmatize those without power on the basis that the powerful have no point of view but the stigmatized do. The "impartial" are therefore better than the stigmatized and thus are to be trusted with power. The fundamental moral issue is respect for personal autonomy carried by a reciprocity norm. One is aware of one's point of view and by reciprocity one accepts that all other moral agents are entitled to their own point of view. Open discussion is thus the signature of this mutual respect. Moreover, the respect for others carries with it a commitment to a seriousness that leaves open the possibility of being persuaded to alter one's point of view.

Fair play and language

In the twentieth century, a helpful treatment of the role of moral restraint in discussion is found in the papers collected by his students and younger colleagues in Frank Knight's 1947 *Freedom and Reform*. Knight's dictum that he attributed to Lord Bryce – democracy is government by discussion – (Knight [1947] 1982: 219, 402) has attained a status in recent years as a substantial improvement over the approach to "social choice" laid out by Kenneth Arrow ([1951] 1963). Arrow's initial formulation supposed that the preferences of the agents in the political process remained unchanged in the process of voting whereas, if discussion has any role to play in governance, it would seem to involve preference change (Buchanan 1954, Sen 1995). Here is Sen's recent judgment:

> By clarifying the role of that momentous engagement in a truly outstanding pair of articles in the *Journal of Political Economy* in 1954, Buchanan immensely enriched the subject matter with which social choice as well as public choice has to be centrally engaged. In contrast with Arrow's initial inclination – as he put it – "to assume ... that individual values are taken as data and are not capable of being altered by the nature of the decision process itself," Buchanan had to insist that seeing "democracy as 'government by discussion' implies that individual values can and do change in the process of decision-making" (Arrow, 1951 and Buchanan, 1954). It can be claimed that it is only through Buchanan's expansion of Arrow's departures that we can do justice to the Enlightenment enterprise of advancing rational decision making in societies, which lies at the foundation of democratic modernity.
>
> (Sen 2013)[13]

Sen's final sentence alludes to the issue of whether governance is an occasion for learning. Consistent with liberal tenants, Arrow had assumed that everyone's views count and he then demonstrated that, given participants with fixed, coherent desires, the only way to obtain coherence at a group level was to give up liberality and let the decision be made by a single individual (Arrow [1951] 1963). For decades after Arrow first published his formulation Buchanan protested against Arrow's assumption that nothing is learned in the democratic process. Buchanan challenged Arrow's assumption of fixed desires and Sen points us to Buchanan's objections in the passage above. The key problem, to which Sen draws our attention above, is that Arrow's formulation assumes there is no learning in the course of discussion.

Knight, who was Buchanan's teacher at Chicago, described how preferences might change in the course of discussion. People enter into discussion in part because they are discontented with themselves:

> In contrast with natural objects – even with the higher animals – man is unique in that he is dissatisfied with himself; he is the discontented animal, the romantic, argumentative, aspiring animal. Consequently, his behavior can only in part be described by scientific principles or laws.
>
> (Knight [1947] 1982: 282)

Real discussion, as Knight ([1947] 1982: 414–415) sees it, is rare because it depends on public-spirited participants:

> Genuine, purely intellectual discussion is rare in modern society, even in intellectual and academic circles, and is approximated only in very small and essentially casual groups. On the larger scale, what passes for discussion is mostly argumentation or debate. The intellectual interest is largely subordinate to entertainment, i.e., entertaining and being entertained, or the immediate interest of the active parties centers chiefly in dominance, victory, instructing others, or persuading rather than convincing, and not in the impartial quest of truth.

Knight saw the conflict in the discussion tradition between attempting to implement one's point of view by any means available and truth seeking. By requiring that economists in the discussion are truth seekers and allowing that ordinary people seek their own interests, Buchanan and Knight introduced a motivational heterogeneity – some people in discussion seek the truth, and others seek their own happiness. But the solution to this paradox is close at hand as long as we can accept ethical rules of conduct as constraints for all who enter into the discussion. In an extension of Buchanan and Knight, we have supposed that participants in the discussion bind themselves *ex ante* with rules of conduct that constrain how they argue their points of view.

Agreement on such constraints depends strongly on an awareness that those who participate in discussion generally have a "point of view." Viewing the contending parties' views as equally deserving of respect is a critical step in the argument. It seems unlikely that constraints on discussion will come about without an awareness that, without them, unwanted results will emerge. Smith's principle of moral reform held that before we change ourselves or society, we need to come to view our own actions from the vantage point of outside observers. If we see others offering biased advice and we think poorly of the practice, then there is hope for a reformation. It is helpful to notice that for Smith there is little distinction between individual and social reform (Levy and Peart 2013).

In Smith's account we view ourselves and our society from an outside vantage. This result is taken for granted when Knight describes humans as the unique dissatisfied animal. But he did not lay out any plausible process of reform. He could not have availed himself of *Theory of Moral Sentiments* since, when Knight wrote, *TMS* was known only to specialists. The greatest of these, Knight's colleague Jacob Viner, had offered the judgment at the University of Chicago sesquicentennial celebration of the *Wealth of Nations* that there was a deep inconsistency between it and Smith's early book (Viner 1927).

Thus, one of the most promising developments in the last four decades has been the recovery by economists of Smith's *Theory of Moral Sentiments*. The recovery of the *Theory of Moral Sentiments* and the overcoming of Viner's objections has had a considerable impact on the interpretation and the development of experimental economics. Many puzzles in the experimental results became coherent when viewed in light of Smith's *TMS*. To this line of research we turn now.

Discussion and cooperation: experimental evidence

The recovery of the *Theory of Moral Sentiments* by experimental economists (V. Smith 1998, 2003; Ashraf *et al.* 2005) brought about a sea change in how economists deal with the experimental regularities of cooperation and sharing. There is perhaps no stronger experimental evidence than the conclusion, confirmed in many experimental studies, that discussion strongly enhances cooperation. As guides to a large literature we point to a wide-ranging survey of the literature from 1992 and two meta-analyses, one from 1995 and one from 2010. Twenty years ago Elinor Ostrom and her colleagues (Ostrom *et al.* 1992) summarized a large body of empirical work, which addressed the neo-classical economic (Hobbesian) commonplace that language did not matter. They summarized the empirical findings:

1   In one-shot social dilemma experiments, communication alone leads to substantial improvements in outcomes.
2   In repeated social dilemma experiments, repeated communication alone leads to substantial improvements in joint outcomes.
3   In field settings of repeated social dilemmas, participants invest substantial time and effort monitoring and imposing sanctions on one another (1992: 405).

Three years later David Sally published a meta-analysis of the experimental evidence from 1958 to 1992 (Sally 1995). Sally noted that the standard model of rational choice had problems accounting for the observed regularities, and "This incongruity is widest with respect to the role of language in encouraging cooperation" (Sally 1995: 58). A meta-analysis in the 2010 *Journal of Conflict Resolution* summarized the results of experiments studying the impact of communication on cooperation as follows:

Among the most researched solutions to social dilemmas is communication. Since the late 1950s, it has been well known that communication enhances cooperation in social dilemmas. This article reports a meta-analysis of this literature ... and finds a large positive effect of communication on cooperation in social dilemmas ... This effect is moderated by the type of communication, with a stronger effect of face-to-face discussion ... compared to written messages ... The communication-cooperation relationship is also stronger in larger, compared to smaller, group social dilemmas. Whether communication occurred before or during iterated dilemmas did not statistically affect the communication-cooperation effect size.

(Balliet 2010: 39)

Smith provides a valuable guide to this body of research because, as noted above and unlike the economists of the next two centuries, Smith anchors trade in language. Twentieth-century economists who are also careful students of Smith's work have expressed puzzlement over his claim that dogs do not trade because they lack a language in which to support the concept for "fairness" (Levy and Peart 2013). While Smith has a reputation of individualism, there is no mistaking his concern for how membership in a group influences one's conduct. The group could be a family, neighborhood, college campus, commercial association or a nation; Smith analyzes the impact of many such groups on individual choice (Levy and Peart 2009). But perhaps the group to which he gives the most substantial attention is that of a religious body. His celebrated defense of religion independent of government is offered as a means of changing the terms of discussion among religious leaders (Levy and Peart 2009, 2013). Here, in a passage that deserves to be quoted at length, Smith offers evidence of an American "field experiment" on the nature of discussion. This is where we see Sen's "give and take" is most clearly expressed:

The interested and active zeal of religious teachers can be dangerous and troublesome only where there is either but one sect tolerated in the society, or where the whole of a large society is divided into two or three great sects; the teachers of each acting by concert, and under a regular discipline and subordination. But that zeal must be altogether innocent where the society is divided into two or three hundred, or perhaps into as many thousand small sects, of which no one could be considerable enough to disturb the public tranquility. The teachers of each sect, seeing themselves surrounded on all sides with more adversaries than friends, would be obliged to learn that candour and moderation which is so seldom to be found among the teachers of those great sects ... This plan of ecclesiastical government, or more properly of no ecclesiastical government, was what the sect called Independents, a sect no doubt of very wild enthusiasts, proposed to establish in England towards the end of the civil war. If it had been established, though of a very unphilosophical origin, it would probably by this time have been productive of the most philosophical good temper and moderation with regard to every sort of religious principle. It has been established in Pennsylvania, where, though the Quakers happen to be the most numerous, the law in reality favours no one sect more than another, and it is there said to have been productive of this philosophical good temper and moderation.

(Smith [1776] 1904, V.1.197)

In the statement we quoted earlier, Sen argued that Knight and Buchanan progressed a step beyond Smith's enlightenment project with their appeal to government by discussion. Smith holds clearly and distinctly that justice is central to a well-governed society. He also makes the case that factionalized religion presents a clear danger to social order because religious doctrine is the path by which the duty of justice is diffused. The danger is that the dictates of impartial justice will be suspended for the benefit of one's fellow sectarians (Levy and Peart 2013). The path away from that danger is, for Smith, to alter the terms of discussion.

Conclusion

If the foregoing insights, beginning with Smith and carried through Mill to Knight, Buchanan, and Sen are correct, do they provide any guidance for liberal learning? We take several lessons from the political economists who work in the "discussion tradition."

That tradition suggests there may be real and unappreciated benefits associated with discussion on college campuses. While many educators pay lip service to discussion, they less frequently provide evidence of the benefits of discussion. Three major benefits have been sketched above. Smith emphasized, first, the development of a moral sense that emerges as one begins to see oneself as a part – and only a small part – of the universe. Mill accepted this argument and added a second benefit: conversation is corrective. Discussion yields insight into bias and profound learning. The Knight–Buchanan–Sen tradition takes a step beyond Mill to suggest that through discussion one becomes aware and self-aware. One may change one's position in the course of discussion.

Experimental evidence confirms these insights and strongly suggests that discussion facilitates cooperation with others when private and group interests are not fully aligned.[14] Though parties may begin as (only) self-interested entities, they come to perceive their interconnectedness in the course of discussion. A well-governed society requires that people enter into the spirit of laws and cooperate when their material interests urge them in another direction. Experimental evidence confirms the importance of discussion in encouraging such cooperation. Thus, we can extend these findings to suggest that the benefits from discussion on college campuses are both moral and material, and in either event they are significant.

Discussion requires respect for others and their point of view. The same respect for others and their actions is required in Smith's account for considerations of justice to have motivational force. For Smith people come into the world with two foundational principles: an instinct to trade and an instinct to persuade, and in fact he conjectured that these are actually the same principle ([1776] 1904: I.2.2). The experimental evidence suggests that Smith's conjecture holds. Modern writers tend to think of governance and justice in terms of trade, i.e., whether material dealings are fair and equitable. But if Smith is correct, the question of whether discussions take place in a fair and equitable manner is prior.

Acknowledgements

We thank Hannah Mead for comments and corrections. The comments from the volume's editor have led to a major improvement.

Notes

1 The Mill passage we quote comes from the section of *Logic* that concerns fallacies. In this and in many other areas, it is helpful to read Mill and Richard Whately together. See Levy and Peart (2010).
2 Martha Nussbaum focuses on argumentation, as opposed to discussion, and she suggests that we must continue to support Socratic pedagogy on college campuses. See Nussbaum (2010: 46–61). We seek to broaden the focus to include all forms of communication.
3 Most recently, Deirdre McCloskey has argued that the material benefits associated with persuasion are significant. See McCloskey (2010: 385ff).
4 Language is the mechanism by which approval is conveyed, just as it is required for material exchange. We return to material trade below.
5 What can thwart this moderating influence of discussion, of course, is faction: the desire to obtain approval from one subset of the polity. When one belongs to a faction, one cares about approval from that group rather more than approval from everyone; consequently one might grandstand, showboat or behave poorly towards those who are not in the group, in order to obtain the group members' approval. Smith was well aware of this problem. We will return to factions below.
6 Our account is in line with that in Nussbaum (1997: 93) in which she links liberal education via imagination to an improved capacity for compassion. In the nineteenth century major figures in the discussion tradition, Mill and Whately, were important in the larger anti-slavery movement. See Peart and Levy (2005).
7 In an increasingly complex society in which knowledge is partial and local, many key innovations are similarly the result of discussion and collaboration amongst those who bring their separate expertise to the table.
8 What Mill called "false beliefs" might today be referred to as "implicit bias"; see Greenwald and Cooper (2006). Consistent with the argument below, Greenwald and Cooper maintain that such biases are malleable and they suggest that biases against "out group" individuals are reduced by inter-group interactions.
9 Mill provided the qualification that those who are child-like had yet to acquire this capacity. In his 1867 Inaugural Address at St. Andrews, Mill reiterated that "improvement consists in bringing our opinions into nearer agreement with facts; and we shall not be likely to do this while we look at facts only through glasses coloured by those very opinions. But since we cannot divest ourselves of pre-conceived notions, there is no known means of eliminating their influence but by

frequently using the differently coloured glasses of other people: and those of other nations, as the most different, are the best" (Mill [1867] 1984: 226).

10 "To call any proposition certain, while there is any one who would deny its certainty if permitted, but who is not permitted, is to assume that we ourselves, and those who agree with us, are the judges of certainty, and judges without hearing the other side" (Mill [1869] 1977: 223). For an egregious example of silencing an academic textbook, see Levy and Peart (2011). As we demonstrate there, Lorie Tarshis's textbook was silenced and Paul Samuelson's textbook thereupon obtained and maintained monopoly status. We have recently learned that F. A. Hayek refused to endorse William F. Buckley's continuation of the attack on the Keynesian economics textbooks. See Peart and Levy (2013).

11 "The fact, however, is, that not only the grounds of the opinion are forgotten in the absence of discussion, but too often the meaning of the opinion itself. The words which convey it, cease to suggest ideas, or suggest only a small portion of those they were originally employed to communicate. Instead of a vivid conception and a living belief, there remain only a few phrases retained by rote; or, if any part, the shell and husk only of the meaning is retained, the finer essence being lost. The great chapter in human history which this fact occupies and fills, cannot be too earnestly studied and meditated on" (Mill [1869] 1977: 247). See also Mill ([1867] 1984).

12 We might also hold conversations with people in the past: "To question all things; never to turn away from any difficulty; to accept no doctrine either from ourselves or from other people without a rigid scrutiny by negative criticism, letting no fallacy, or incoherence, or confusion of thought, slip by unperceived; above all, to insist upon having the meaning of a word clearly understood before using it, and the meaning of a proposition before assenting to it; these are the lessons we learn from the ancient dialecticians" Mill ([1869] 1977: 229–230).

13 John Rawls's dependence on Knight's *Ethics of Competition* (Knight [1935] 1951) at the step in *Theory of Justice* (Rawls [1971] 1999) at which governance is supposed to be a form of truth seeking, is discussed in Levy and Peart (2015).

14 This is consistent with the claim that universities may serve to develop social capital; see Trani and Holsworth (2010: 6).

References

Arrow, K. J. ([1951] 1963) *Social Choice and Individual Values*, New York: John Wiley.
Ashraf, N., Camerer, C. F. and Loewenstein, G. (2005) "Adam Smith, behavioral economist," *Journal of Economic Perspectives*, 19: 131–145.
Balliet, D. (2010) "Communication and cooperation in social dilemmas: A meta-analytic review," *Journal of Conflict Resolution*, 54: 39–57.
Buchanan, J. M. (1954) "Individual choice in voting and the market," *Journal of Political Economy*, 62: 334–343.
Greenwald, A. G. and Cooper, L. H. (2006) "Implicit bias: Scientific foundations," *California Law Review*, 94 (July): 945–967.
Knight, F. H. ([1935] 1951) *Ethics of Competition*, New York: Augustus Kelly.
Knight, F. H. ([1947] 1982) *Freedom and Reform*, Indianapolis, IN: Liberty Fund.
Levy, D. and Peart, S. (2009) "Adam Smith and the place of faction," in J. Young (ed.) *The Elgar Companion to Adam Smith*, Cheltenham: Edward Elgar, pp. 335–345.
Levy, D. and Peart, S. (2010) "Richard Whately and the gospel of transparency," *American Journal of Economics and Sociology*, 69: 166–187.
Levy, D. and Peart, S. (2011) "Soviet growth and American textbooks: An endogenous past," *Journal of Economic Behavior and Organization*, 78: 110–125.

Levy, D. and Peart, S. (2013) "Adam Smith on the state: Language and reform," in C. Berry, M. P. Paganelli, and C. Smith (eds) *Oxford Handbook on Adam Smith*, Oxford: Oxford University Press, pp. 372–392.

Levy, D. and Peart, S. (forthcoming 2015) "The ethics problem: Towards a second-best solution to the problem of economic expertise," in G. de Martino and D. McCloskey (eds) *Oxford Handbook on Professional Economics Ethics*, Oxford: Oxford University Press.

McCloskey, D. (2010) *Bourgeois Dignity: Why economists can't explain the modern world*, Chicago, IL: University of Chicago Press.

Mill, J. S. ([1843] 1981) *A System of Logic Ratiocinative and Inductive Being a Connected View of the Principles of Evidence and the Methods of Scientific Investigation*, in J. M. Robson (ed.) Collected Works of John Stuart Mill, Volume 8, Toronto: University of Toronto Press.

Mill, J. S. ([1867] 1984) "Inaugural address delivered to the University of St. Andrews," in J. M. Robson (ed.) *J. S. Mill, Essays on Equality, Law, and Education*, Volume 21, *Collected Works of John Stuart Mill*, Toronto: University of Toronto Press, pp. 215–258.

Mill, J. S. ([1869] 1977) On Liberty, in J. M. Robson (ed.) *J. S. Mill, Essays on Politics and Society*, Volume 18, *Collected Works of John Stuart Mill*, Toronto: University of Toronto Press, pp. 213–310.

Nussbaum, M. (1997) *Cultivating Humanity: A classical defense of reform in liberal education*, Cambridge, MA: Harvard University Press.

Nussbaum, M. (2010) *Not for Profit: Why democracy needs the humanities*, Princeton, NJ: Princeton University Press.

Ostrom, E., Walker, J., and Gardner, R. (1992) "Covenants with and without a sword: Self-governance is possible," *American Political Science Review*, 86: 404–417.

Peart, S. J. and Levy, D. M. (2005) *The "Vanity of the Philosopher": From equality to hierarchy in post-classical economics*, Ann Arbor: University of Michigan Press.

Peart, S. J. and Levy, D. M. (2013) "F. A. Hayek and the individualists," in S. J. Peart and D. M. Levy (eds) *F. A. Hayek and the Modern Economy*, New York: Palgrave, pp. 29–56.

Rawls, J. ([1971] 1999) *A Theory of Justice*, revised edition, Cambridge, MA: Harvard University Press.

Sally, D. (1995) "Conversation and cooperation in social dilemmas: A meta-analysis of experiments from 1958 to 1992," *Rationality and Society*, 7: 58–92.

Sen, A. (1995) "Rationality and social choice," *American Economic Review*, 85: 1–24.

Sen, A. (2012) "What happened to Europe?" *New Republic*, 2 August. www.newrepublic.com/article/magazine/105657/sen-europe-democracy-keynes-social-justice (accessed 4 July 2014).

Sen, A. (2013) "On James Buchanan," http://lijian267.blog.sohu.com/252974528.html (accessed 4 July 2014).

Smith, A. ([1759] 1976) *The Theory of Moral Sentiments*, D. D. Raphael and A. L. Macfie (eds) Oxford: Clarendon Press.

Smith, A. ([1776] 1904) *An Inquiry into the Nature and Causes of the Wealth of Nations*, E. Cannan (ed.) www.econlib.org/library/Smith/smWN.html (accessed 4 July 2014).

Smith, V. (1998) "The two faces of Adam Smith," *Southern Economic Journal*, 65: 1–19.

Smith, V. (2003) "Constructivist and ecological rationality in economics," Nobel Prize Lecture. www.nobelprize.org/nobel_prizes/economic-sciences/laureates/2002/smith-lecture.pdf (accessed 4 July 2014).

Stigler, G. J. ([1988] 2003) *Memories of an Unregulated Economist*, Chicago, IL: University of Chicago Press.

Trani, E. P. and Holsworth, R. D. (2010) *The Indispensable University: Higher education, economic development, and the knowledge economy*, Lanham, MD: Rowman & Littlefield.

Viner, J. (1927) "Adam Smith and laissez faire," *Journal of Political Economy*, 35: 198–232.

3 Teaching the art of speaking across ideological paradigms

Traci Fordham

> The qualifications for self-government in society are not innate. They are the result of habit and long training.
>
> Thomas Jefferson (1824)

> [E]very day in contemporary society we face conflicts rooted in the historical legacies of the social divisions of our country and ... at the same time, we embrace a pluralistic and democratic America that functions on deliberation, thrives on difference of opinion, and operates on principles of representation.
>
> Schoem and Hurtado (2001: 1)

> [W]hether we are concerned in traditional terms with the "breadth and depth" of academic learning or in more contemporary terms with helping students explore the implications and contestations surrounding the uses of knowledge, civic engagement claims a formative place in today's conceptions of academic excellence.
>
> Carol Geary Schneider, President of the American Association of Colleges and Universities (2003)

I wrote this essay during the U.S. government shutdown in October of 2013. Finger pointing, logical fallacies, diatribes, infantile accusations and posturing were pervasive – in mainstream press, on pedestrian social media, in the hallowed halls of academe. This is not to suggest that bifurcated, ill-informed political discourse is somehow novel. The ability to engage critically and empathetically with divergent positions, however, does seem to be increasingly less prevalent (and less valued) in popular media, in the classroom, and at work. The art of "doing" democracy requires of citizens a commitment to the common good and a critical rhetorical sensibility; an ethos that must be valued, nurtured, and practiced. One of the essential functions of liberal education is to provide opportunities for students to develop this civic ethos through learning the art of thinking and speaking across ideological paradigms.

Higher education in the United States has become ubiquitously consumer-oriented and the culture of corporatism permeates our institutions and learning spaces creating an environment that "stresses career training and competition among students, while urging faculty into narrower and narrower paths of disciplinary research" (Grattan *et al.* 2008: 7). We appear to be in a social moment of hyper individualism and entrenchment, which are antithetical to democratic praxis. Re-committing ourselves to the aims of liberal education is essential, especially when the liberal arts are increasingly under siege (Reed 2004).

What do students learn about democracy? How is it that they often come to think about democracy as a system of governance, as a type of machinery that appears to somehow stand outside of social intercourse? We do not spend a great deal of time, it seems, teaching our students (or ourselves) the art of "doing" democracy. Democracy, like all human creations, must be imagined (Anderson 1983), recreated, and tended; it is a fragile process that requires those who are committed to it to believe in it and practice it.

Civil society (and the civic ethos necessary to maintain these social systems) must be undergirded by the assumption that citizens hold divergent and often incompatible worldviews, interests, goals, and values. The sine qua non of democratic praxis is a committed citizenry engaging these different ideologies in robust and critical communication; the development of rhetorical and communicative competency is necessary for democracy to flourish. Every public space could be envisioned as a forum where deliberative democracy might be learned and enacted.

When we come to understand that democracy is not a system that exists outside of human interaction, but is a malleable, *social* process we can see that citizenship, too, is *accomplished* in communication with others. One "is" not a citizen; it is not an identity, nor is it simply a function of legally living in a given nation state. Citizenship is a skill, a set of understandings and behaviors that is taught, learned, performed, and negotiated. Democracy is enacted through citizenship and it is, at the very core about intentional engagement with difference, disagreement, and inequality at both micro and macro levels.

In a globalizing world, teaching citizenship has become even more necessary (and, not surprisingly, more difficult). A primary objective of liberal education is to help students to develop and practice citizenship. Institutions, administrators, and teacher-scholars might imagine this goal in different ways and through different means, however, its centrality must be a foundational tenet of our practice.

Citizenship as a critical literacy

Citizenship in both the legal and political dimensions of the term requires attitudinal, cognitive, and behavioral engagement. Educators generally agree that certain epistemologies and skills are the hallmarks of liberal learning. Conceptualized as a set of literacies, these epistemologies and skills include the ability to read well and understand the thesis and positions contained in a text, the ability to construct coherent arguments and ideas through the written word, the ability to listen carefully and critically to the oral and aural messages that surround us, the ability to create and transmit spoken and other aural ideas, the ability to understand and to design symbolic and representational meanings through numeracy and through corporeal and visual forms, and the ability to work in and through other, emerging genres and media (Fordham and Oakes 2013). All of these literacies concern themselves with various modes of communication, vehicles through which meanings and information are created and exchanged. Civic engagement is, then, a metaliteracy in that it requires the ability to critically understand and employ the most appropriate forms of communication in different contexts, for different audiences. Citizenship, as a set of skills and abilities, is therefore a *rhetorical* enterprise (ibid.).

Ideology, epistemology, pedagogy

Many students and educators alike, surprisingly, operate under the erroneous assumption that only *some* epistemologies, texts, or ideas are political; that there are select academic subjects or situations that stand outside of ideology. Sociology, for instance, is ideological; Molecular Biology, for instance, is not. One of the first steps necessary to teach (and learn) how to engage effectively across difference is to recognize that all knowledge and all ways of knowing are positioned and therefore ideological and political. Critical liberal education must involve a self-reflexive engagement with the ideological foundations of any curriculum, discipline, or course and should engage students in examining the histories and debates in the field or area of inquiry. Most educators agree that scholarship is a kind of conversation and sometimes this conversation is a lively or even contentious debate.

If all knowledge and ways of knowing are positioned and therefore political, it is incumbent upon educators to provide opportunities for students to analyze and critique the *processes* through which some epistemologies become privileged over others. Not all ways of knowing are given equal weight in every social context. How does a "canon," for instance, come to be taken as an essential body of knowledge in a given field or discipline? What dissenting voices or epistemologies have been silenced or deemed invalid? What matrices of inequality exist that prevent other forms of knowledge and ways of knowing from coming to be known more widely? Problematizing the very foundations of our disciplinary epistemologies can help our students to understand that liberal learning involves grappling with multiple, conflicting ideas and that all of these "truth claims" are positioned.

When we provide opportunities for students to deconstruct the very foundations of disciplinary and other forms of knowledge we create a context for them to critically engage their own worldviews and understandings. This is one of the most important civic literacies of all – the ability to be self-reflexive and to be open to new or different ways of seeing. When we understand that systems of knowledge (and the many discourses that undergird how we come to think and know) are historical, positioned, and transient we come to see that "un-learning" can be as significant a process as knowledge "acquisition." Asking students (and ourselves) to conduct an occasional "epistemological inventory" (e.g. *What did you once believe or know about X that you understand now in a different way?*) can assist them in cultivating the necessary habits of critical self-reflexivity. This pedagogical practice can also help to create an environment where students understand that their identities are not tied to their ideas or arguments; that subjectivities, like knowledge, itself, are fleeting and positioned:

> Education for critical consciousness or critical pedagogy, as it is sometimes called, requires a reformulation of the knowledge-as-accumulated-capital mode of education and focuses instead on the link between the historical configuration of social forms and the way they work subjectively. This issue of subjectivity represents a realization of the fact that who we are, how we act, what we think and what stories we tell become more intelligible within an epistemological framework that begins by recognizing existing hegemonic histories. The issue of subjectivity and voice thus concerns the effort to understand our specific locations in the educational process and in the institutions through which we are constituted. Resistance lies in self-conscious engagement with dominant, normative discourses and representations and in the active creation of oppositional analytic and cultural spaces.
>
> (Mohanty 1994: 148)

Critical discovery, a key component of civic literacy, occurs when as many questions as possible are entertained and explored in an environment of open, social inquiry. We must therefore present students in all areas of the curriculum with opportunities to individually and collectively identify and evaluate the positions, arguments, objectives, and strategies of the scholarship and other forms of knowledge they encounter and create – whether it is in Literature, Economics, or Physics.

Obstacles to and opportunities for critical, civic pedagogy

Critical pedagogies and the concomitant skills of thinking about and practicing communication across difference require a great deal of cognitive and behavioral effort. It is not for the faint of heart because, ironically, it ultimately requires a suspension of what one believes to be true (e.g. self, worldview, aesthetics, etc.). A civic literacy presupposes that there are multiple, and even seemingly contradictory ways to engage the art of living (Thayer 2012) and it requires openness to change (one's mind, worldview, aesthetics, etc.). There exist many factors in the sociocultural context, in higher education, and in the human condition that make the work of civic pedagogy challenging and difficult.

Education for plural democracy must involve discussions of difference. It is impossible to talk about difference, however, without discussing what "difference" is different *from*. This crucial distinction, or our frequent inability to make that distinction, is a major obstacle to diversity (civic) education.

Diversity is not a quality that an individual possesses nor is it simply a beautiful rainbow of difference. The human condition is a context of difference by definition, as people are distinct one from another in myriad ways. Culture provides the meanings and conditions of our differences, from the languages we speak, the foods we eat, the gods in which we believe (or don't), the relationships we create and maintain, and the values we hold. The human condition is also characterized, it seems, by the ascendency of certain ways of being and seeing over others. (How some beliefs and practices come to be "ascendant" is another issue for discussion. It may be important, however, for pedagogues to discuss with students the sometimes very violent and inhumane ways in which particular epistemologies and practices come to be learned.) Discussions of plurality or difference therefore cannot happen without discussions of hegemony and inequality.

Helping students to develop a critical civic ethos must be the responsibility of the institution, not of one discipline, department, or program. It is incumbent upon all educators to know *something* of the history of their professions and bodies of knowledge, as this awareness helps students to develop their own understanding of the historical, ideological, and contingent bases of knowledge. This is, in a very broad sense a type of civic *justice* work – acknowledging that there have always existed many ways of explaining the world and we are learning (and *not* learning) certain bodies of knowledge that have particular histories.

What place in say, a science curriculum does a discussion of inequality and social justice have? Any mathematician or physicist can explain the long and difficult road to the Enlightenment. While the Copernican paradigm shift, the now taken-for-granted assumption of a heliocentric universe fundamentally changed people's understanding of cosmology it was a revolutionary (!) concept in 1543. Galileo Galilei, Tycho Brahe, and others were, of course, deemed heretics and persecuted for advancing the Copernican theory. While discussion of the histories of Western scientific knowledge may not *seem* like social justice work, it is in that it exposes the ways in which all "discoveries" and taken-for-granted ways of knowing are components of a matrix of power, ideology, and discourse in any cultural and historical moment.

One significant obstacle to civic learning then, is that discussions of difference, inequality, and social justice have frequently become the educational objective of only select few programs or disciplines in the academy. When education for citizenship is made to be the labor of only a few departments or programs in an institution then it (logically, but erroneously) follows that *those* departments or programs are seen as ideological and the others as objective, often minimizing the legitimacy of the former. In the context of liberal education in particular, education for citizenship must be the transdisciplinary goal of all.

How, generally, is civic discourse performed in popular culture? How do we learn about communication across difference in the context of our mediated landscape? Many linguists and critical media scholars, such as Chomsky (2002), Shactman (1995), Tannen (1999), West (2005), and Hall *et al.* (1980) have opined about the declining state of public discourse in the U.S. Whether it be on the level of linguistic pragmatics – Shactman's argument that, due in large part to mindless, pedestrian media fare we have become a culture of inarticulate idiots (see *Jersey Shore*) or Tannen's thesis that, because of the hyper-sensationalizing of ... everything (from weather to Miley Cyrus) and the propensity of popular media to broadcast people engaging in nasty, insensitive, obnoxious talk we, as a society do not learn or value empathic, ethical communication. There is more social utility in telling someone to "talk to the hand" than there is to carefully and sensitively listening to an idea that might contradict your own. Even better if you can engage in a little ad hominem attack while you're at it. Add to this the "meme-ification," "tweetification," and "instagramification" (all my terms) of ideas via social media and we have an interesting set of challenges to the teaching and learning of engaged dialogue across difference. Exposing students to even the rudimentary notions of *ethos* or logical appeals (and logical fallacies) can be very helpful in demonstrating how ways of knowing are created and maintained. Also, it is crucial that we reinforce the idea that *critique* is the process of holding an idea or assumption up for scrutiny and deconstructing the premises that undergird it. The argument culture seems to have fostered a type of fear in us to engage in healthy, necessary, civil disagreement. Students often see critical engagement with material, different perspectives on an issue, and disagreement as "fighting" and are loathe to participate. Modeling productive scholarly conflict or providing examples of it is important.

Another obstacle to the pedagogy of civic communication (which is, ultimately *intercultural* communication) is the notion of "ideological imperviousness." Young adults in particular come to the higher education context with the very entrenched yet mistaken assumption that how they think and what they know and believe have been somehow created solely by them. They can be very resistant to the mere *idea* that their minds have been shaped by myriad, "invisible" social forces. Asking students to reflect upon the socially constructed and perpetuated nature of knowledge (which must underlie any attempt to communicate across ideological difference) is a difficult pedagogical enterprise. Ideology "works" at the level of the non-obvious. Ideas and practices that come to be naturalized, normalized, or taken-for-granted as inevitable are what constitute hegemony. Students frequently have difficulty deconstructing the ideologies, the taken-for-granted assumptions inherent in what they know or believe, yet they often have little difficulty identifying the ideological nature of *other* ways of being and seeing (e.g. Islam). Doing the pedagogical work of demystifying ideology is a necessary precursor to cultivating an environment where students can talk across or beyond these ideological differences. Cultural Studies, as a theoretical paradigm and as a methodological process, can be very helpful to this work (Hall 1997). It is also important to remind students (and ourselves) that *simply because knowledge is socially constructed* doesn't make it "wrong." In fact, what any culture believes to be right or wrong is established in discourse. Helping students to understand the social processes through which cultural beliefs and practices are created and maintained is crucial to pedagogies of difference.

Related to all of this is that in U.S. dominant culture we often value fashion over substance, and speed and efficiency over the sometimes laborious and time-consuming processes of thinking and deliberating. Teaching students how to engage complicated and contradictory ideas through oral communication cannot be relegated to a 15-minute exercise. People who are used to speed, efficiency, convenience, the perpetual compression of time, have difficulty listening, reading, and grappling with multiple sources of information. It is easier to get the "take-away," or to sit passively as an expert tells you in a 15-minute talk what you need to know. Collaborative learning is time-consuming, cumbersome, and difficult (Bruffee 1998).

Collaborative, dialogue-centered learning environments then are also complicated, unpredictable, and multidimensional (Burbules 1993). The pedagogies that are necessary to cultivate a civic ethos require imagining the work of a class (or lab or stage, etc.) in different ways. Educators must always think about the relationship between course content and pedagogical process, but one does not necessarily have to take precedence over the other. Focusing primarily on the "coverage" of content presupposes a linear and unidirectional model of communication: If you just tell students a lot of stuff, they'll just "get it." The entire notion of *covering* material reflects a teacher or sender model of pedagogy. Prioritizing process over content means that students may not be exposed to the necessary, foundational knowledge of a field or discipline. As liberal educators we must understand that we are not only teaching students *subjects*, we are also teaching them *how to learn* and therefore how to participate as informed citizens in the world. We must see process and content as complementary and inextricably linked. Liberal educators must be especially parsimonious regarding the learning goals for a course given that pedagogies of difference inevitably require more time and reflection.

The dominant culture of the U.S. is a hyper-individualized one (Neuliep 2011) where self-awareness, self-aggrandizement, self-esteem, self-discovery, "selfies" are seemingly more important than community, the common good, or relationality. The cult of the individual poses interesting challenges for teaching the art of civic communication since the latter is *necessarily* relational. A major obstacle to understanding another's perspective is one's own ego-bounded-ness (Marske 1987). Teaching communication across difference means helping students to see the non-singularity of self: We are all tied to myriad others – socially, economically, culturally, and globally. When students come to understand that their identities are created and maintained in social discourse and relationship they are more able to deconstruct their own, multiple subjectivities. Communicating across ideological difference means having the ability to de-naturalize one's own identity and social positions. This is tough, existential (and phenomenological) work in that, developmentally, most university students are just beginning the process of figuring out who they are and want to be. This work can be liberating, too, in that engaging young adults in the process of collaborative inquiry across ideological difference exposes them to many more options for being-in-the-world.

Another significant challenge to teaching the art of communicating across ideological difference has to do with people's propensity to cling tenaciously to an opinion or argument even if, under scrutiny it doesn't make sense or work. One's position on a given topic or issue does not *constitute* the self. An additional consequence of a hyper-individualized culture is our apparent difficulty in being *wrong* or in changing our minds. Civic pedagogies require helping students to disentangle identity from argument and give students opportunities to wrestle with diverse opinions and reassess their own ideas and positions.

Finally (and there are certainly as many challenges to as there are promises of this work), teaching students about communication is both tautological and paradoxical. In order to learn how to communicate more effectively, students must identify those communicative behaviors and strategies that may be problematic. We must therefore use the same "mind" to deconstruct as well as to improve itself. Even more perplexing is the fact that people do not generally think about communication unless they find themselves in some sort of interpersonal mess (Thayer 2009). Students *know* that they don't know, say, Physics. They don't know that they don't know Communication. So, teaching the art of thinking, listening, and talking across ideological difference means, most of all, helping students to un-learn whole ranges of problematic assumptions about processes of human interaction. When students see the possibilities of their lives expanding through the processes of un-learning, listening, and grappling with different and contradictory information, they can hopefully understand that these processes are what make strong democracy.

Dialogue-centered and deliberative pedagogies

At the core of liberal arts/civic pedagogy is (or should be) an understanding that human communication is not singular, unidirectional, or episodic. This more transactional model of communication is meaning- or learning-centered rather than message- or teacher-centered. Communication is the process of people rendering meaningful the data in their environment (Thayer 2009). How we render data meaningful is a function of myriad individual, social, and cultural factors. The consequences of this view of communication are enormous for pedagogues (and parents, and partners, and managers). When we understand that communication is *receiver-oriented* (ibid.), that what anything ultimately means (and the decisions and actions that come from these meanings) rests in the minds of interpreters, we are compelled to pay attention to the "hows" of learning, rather than to the "thats" of learning. We ask ourselves as communicators not *whether* someone understood a message that we tried to convey, but *how* someone understood the message. Understanding this more collaborative paradigm for communication can have a profound impact on how we imagine our contexts for teaching and learning.

Box 3.1 Learning-centered pedagogy

Pedagogies for civic literacy must involve a certain amount of transparency. Explain to students at the beginning of a course (or program or lab) that there will be some facts or data that must be memorized and there are other concepts or ideas in the class that are contested or continue to be under investigation in the scholarly community. Engage students from the onset with the difference between the number or quantity of "facts" that they internalize (e.g. the definition of a term or concept) and their ability to critically write or speak about ideas (e.g. how the concept became part of a disciplinary canon or how different scholars in the field operationalize or utilize this paradigm). Some assessment tools (e.g. multiple choice exams) are better at indicating that students have memorized and understood a term or idea – capturing the "that" of student learning – while other tools (e.g. an in-class debate) help students to practice and to demonstrate for teachers that they are able to articulate and analyze these ideas – the "hows" of learning.

Learning environments are created and maintained in the communication that takes place between participants. Our talk with one another creates our social spaces and enterprises. Different modes of communication, different genres of discourse, foster different kinds of environments. A formal lecture, for instance, where one person talks to a group of people who listen, is a very different communication situation than one where a group of people thinks and talks together. All modes and genres of communication bring particular exigencies to any situation and all modes and genres of communication have particular value in different learning spaces. One of the most important diagnostic/rhetorical skills that a pedagogue can possess and model is the ability to effectively employ the most efficacious communication strategy for a given learning goal. Sometimes a lecture is the best strategy; sometimes a debate is most effective, given a particular objective for a course or assignment. There are some communication situations, however, that are especially conducive to democratic practice. Dialogue and deliberation are modes that can help to cultivate, not only transformative learning, but are also especially critical to the development of civic literacy (Schoem and Hurtado 2001) and "deep democracy":

> Unlike "classical" democracy, which focuses on majority rule, Deep Democracy suggests that all voices, states of awareness, and frameworks of reality are important. Deep Democracy also suggests that the

information carried within these voices, awarenesses, and frameworks are all needed to understand the complete process of the system. The meaning of this information appears, when the various frameworks and voices are relating to each other. Deep Democracy is a process of relationship, not a state-oriented still picture, or a set of policies.

(Thayer 2012)

Helping students (and ourselves) to develop and practice civic literacy, the ability to think and communicate across ideological difference, involves the perpetual reiteration of the non-singularity of self, knowledge, markets, etc. Our selves, our social enterprises, and our institutions are contingent upon people working in consort. Deep Democracy (or Barber's (1984) notion of strong democracy) requires commitment and collaboration. How might educators teach, model, and help students to practice the kinds of rhetorical and communicative strategies that constitute citizenship?

Dialogue

While most educators understand the benefits of class discussions and of students working through ideas "out loud," most of us don't have a great deal of experience in creating and facilitating (let alone assessing the effectiveness of) the kinds of talk we want to have in our classes. What are some of the differences between conversation, discussion, dialogue, deliberation, and debate? These are all contexts of communication between people, yet they are distinctly different modes, involve different kinds of talk and strategy, and have different ends or outcomes. Conversations are typically low-stakes contexts of talk wherein participants meander in and out of various topics of mutual interest without a necessary outcome. In conversations, we don't usually think about what our strategies are or what we might want from the interaction. Conversations are the foundation of most of our social life. Discussions are a bit more focused and concentrated on a particular subject or question. In the classroom context, discussions may be highly orchestrated (i.e. involving set questions) or more organic. The pedagogue may (or may not) have an ultimate, desired outcome for the discussion, a place where s/he would like the discussion to "land." Debate, of course, is a formal context of articulating a position and making and countering arguments. Debate necessarily presupposes opposition and involves a taking of sides, listening for rhetorical or factual inconsistencies, and convincing an audience of the ultimate validity of a position. The communicative skills employed in a debate are not necessarily the ones utilized in a discussion.

Dialogue, broadly speaking, is a context wherein different participants identify their stand on an issue or question, listen carefully to the positions of others, and try to identify places of both divergence and commonality. Dialogic theories of communication, while not monolithic, understand dialogue to be a special context and practice of interaction. Dialogic approaches to communication are transactional and multivocal (Bakhtin 1981) and as a specific communication mode center on people thinking, talking, listening, and responding in intentional and engaged ways. "These qualities of thought and talk include willingness to risk change in one's own perspective and commitment to embracing and struggling with others whose worldviews may be radically different from and threatening to one's own" (Wood 2004: xvi). Theorists and practitioners of dialogue understand that because communication is complex, contradictory, and multivocal situations that ask for a more dialogic approach to thinking and learning will be messy and complicated – and potentially fraught. Dialogue-centered pedagogies acknowledge, understand, and *utilize* conflict and difference as these are the foundation of learning, transformation, and civic life. Dialogue-centered pedagogies help students to grapple with the inevitability and necessity of difference and tension and help them to think about and address them more effectively. The purpose of dialogue is not for one "side" to win; it is for all stakeholders to understand more deeply the complexity of an issue or question and to, hopefully, identify sources of commonality.

A dialogue-centered learning environment cannot be achieved without participants being willing and able to suspend judgment, to be critically self-reflexive, and to listen and respond with a goal to *understand* rather than to agree or disagree. As a potentially transformative process dialogue can lead to different ways of thinking, knowing, and acting – in and outside of a particular class.

Box 3.2 Facilitating dialogue

Incorporating dialogue into one's pedagogy involves valuing and utilizing oral communication, formally and informally, throughout the course. Dialogue typically includes the understanding that there exist multiple positions on a particular issue or question. A valuable in-class discussion prior to engaging in a dialogue might be to ask students to identify as many of the possible positions on an issue that they can (given their readings and other class discussions); students might even do this in groups. For homework, ask students to come to the class dialogue with their own position on an issue clearly articulated and argued, in writing. In this homework ask students to reflect upon why they have taken this position – what experiences, beliefs, and values might underlie this stance? Students should know that a dialogue is a special context of engaged communication and should be ready to listen for understanding, to acknowledge the opinions of others, and to carefully articulate their own positions and those of experts in the field, if appropriate. Dialogues should be approached with a collaboratively designed covenant or set of agreements about how people will interact. The teacher or facilitator might help students to generate this covenant, but s/he should allow the participants to create it. One student should be assigned the task of recording what people say and ask by putting key ideas on the board or on a slide can be helpful as students see knowledge "emerge" in dialogue. Dialogues should be facilitated – ideas, opinions, insights, moved along by a non-participant. This role can be played by the teacher or another student. Facilitators should be good listeners, able to reiterate or paraphrase what a participant has said and able to ask the kinds of questions that move a dialogue forward or that enable participants to clarify or to expand upon an idea. At the conclusion of the dialogue participants should be given an opportunity to reflect upon what they have learned, what they still question, and how their thinking has changed.

Deliberation

While the communicative/epistemological goal of dialogue is collaborative and mutual understanding, deliberative models of interaction presuppose areas or issues of profound difference or conflict. Like facilitated dialogue, deliberation involves a "neutral" facilitator, representations of the various "sides" or positions in a conflict situation, and a specific set of communicative agreements for participation in the deliberative process. The objective of dialogue-centered pedagogies is mutual understanding of ideas and positions; deliberation's aim is to reason collectively and to create common ground toward decision and resolution. This practice is especially germane to the development of a civic ethos in that it asks that deliberating bodies collectively construct some sort of recommendation on how to proceed. Deliberation does not require complete consensus (since that is never possible); it asks for reasoned arguments, the suspension of judgment, good faith attempts to understand, creative problem-solving, and a commitment to the process of community decision-making.

Box 3.3 Incorporating deliberation

Deliberative pedagogies can be employed in classrooms, residence halls, committee or faculty meetings, and with other groups associated with a college or university. The first, most significant step to creating a context for deliberation is to frame the question, issue, or source of conflict; issue-framing is the most important and most difficult part of the deliberative process. Who "identifies" the issue? Whose voices and concerns are included in how the issue is constructed? Whose problems or concerns are we deliberating? The most effective deliberative contexts are those wherein the participants themselves help to identify, define, and characterize the "problem" and then work to flesh out the various concerns and positions. An entire academic course could be constructed, for instance, around a deliberative model – where a context of deep division is the "subject" of the class (e.g. global climate change) and the semester is devoted to researching, interviewing, issue-framing, and deliberation. Students could be assigned to take on different positions throughout the semester. The final exam might consist of the written and oral "proposal" of a collective decision regarding this problem or issue. Student Affairs offices at colleges across the country, for instance, utilize deliberation as a way to identify and address trenchant campus issues such as binge drinking and sexual assault.

As Farland (2008: 91) notes:

> Deliberative approaches stand in stark contrast to the culture of professional expertise in which the role of the academic professional is to employ specialized knowledge in order to endorse a particular pragmatic or conceptual solution. Beyond the clear and concise presentation that we expect of students' oral and written arguments, the deliberative classroom invites students to situate and differentiate claims; to establish the logical soundness of arguments and evidence; and to justify the reasons for an action or belief.

While dialogue places multivocality and collaboration at the center, deliberation focuses more intentionally on traditional, rhetorical abilities of logic, reasoning, evaluating claims, and reaching common ground. Both approaches understand that communication, knowledge, and decision-making are social, collaborative processes, processes that are central to democratic praxis and civic engagement.

At every point in the curriculum there exist myriad opportunities to teach and to learn rhetorical sensitivity, civic discourse, dialogue, and deliberation. These epistemologies and skills need not be must not be limited to specific disciplines or contexts. Thinking, composing, speaking, listening, reading, writing, designing, performing, (etc.) – communicating – across ideological differences means the cultivation and practice of a set of epistemological and behavioral skills that are ultimately both inherent in and beyond any singular discipline. Teaching and employing critical rhetoric should then be a goal in every learning environment (Fink 2003) and an inextricable factor in the engagement of course content. Thinking rhetorically about one's discipline, subject, course, and curriculum in the context of liberal education and civic literacy means cultivating more democratic spaces for learning.

Beyond the examples offered above, how do liberal educators, people who are likely trained to do scholarship in a particular disciplinary area, create learning opportunities for students to practice democracy? Many academics do not have formal training in critical pedagogy or in methods of dialogue, debate, or deliberation and frequently see the most important aspect of their jobs as "covering" necessary course material. An important step in teaching the art of thinking and speaking across ideological difference is to understand that pedagogical strategy and curricular content are two aspects of the same process. One must "get at" subject matter somehow and much research suggests that having students talk about, discuss, and think collectively about course ideas helps them to learn the material more deeply (Mooney *et al.* 2005). Civic pedagogies must stem from the learning goals of the course itself. These pedagogies are not "teaching tricks" or convenient "best practices" that can be arbitrarily attached to discrete moments in a class; they must be the foundation of institutional and curricular practice and underscore a commitment to critical, liberal learning.

Collaboration, reflection, academic freedom

Teaching civic literacy – critical approaches to difference, then is not a singular or solo enterprise. Students must understand from the moment they enter a course (or, hopefully, matriculate at an institution), that their focused engagement in the process of learning is expected.

Box 3.4 Civic literacy as an institutional objective

Many colleges and universities across the U.S. have, as part of their mission, a commitment to educating students for citizenship. This mission cannot simply exist on a college or university charter; it is imperative that an institution's dedication to civic learning be apparent in all aspects of its policies, programs, recruitment material, and external communications. The more pressing question, though, is *how to cultivate in students the understanding of and commitment to liberal learning as civic learning*. One mistake that some colleges and universities make is to see student "orientation" as a short-term, one-time set of events that take place at the beginning of the first year, or to see orientation (enculturation) as a process of cultivating commitment to the institution itself. While developing student loyalty to the institution is necessary for retention (and for alumni giving), students' understanding of and commitment to the learning goals that are the very foundation of the institution are crucial to the development of civic literacy. *Citizenship, civic engagement, and social responsibility* are words, concepts, ideas, and practices that students should hear, discuss, understand, and come to value as part of their entire education experience at an institution. Ideally, all members of an educational institution that is committed to educating for citizenship in a plural democracy should be committed to these ideas and practices. Students embrace the values of their academic institutions when they see them performed and reinforced in syllabi, classes, the library, the curriculum, the residence halls, student government. When an institution itself employs collaborative decision-making strategies, deliberative problem-solving, and effective communication across difference, it establishes a model and an expectation of engaged citizenship and responsibility for its most important stakeholders: students.

Collaborative learning is a central component of democratic, liberal education, but it takes commitment on the part of all interlocutors – administration, faculty, and staff. Education for civic literacy requires holding one another accountable. Learning how to collaboratively engage ideas across ideological difference is *uncomfortable* and fraught because deep learning does not take place when one's own particular position or worldview is simply, perpetually confirmed. Students (and frankly, teachers) should expect to be "shaken up" with great regularity. It is troubling to read of the myriad examples across the spectrum of U.S. higher education where scholars who ask students to analyze their own positionalities are criticized, sanctioned, or worse. A fundamental aspect of democracy, of citizenship itself, is the right to articulate dissent and disagreement, to hold privileged ideas, laws, and practices up for scrutiny. This fundamentally *democratic* process of critique must be one of the hallmarks of liberal education. Faculty-scholars must be free to create environments where students can safely learn and practice conflict and critique through thinking, listening, and speaking. Institutions must understand that these pedagogical processes can be very difficult for students and that those moments of dissonance are the roots of deep learning and change.

Creating syllabi, assignments, and activities

In the end, a more democratic, collaborative learning environment is one where all participants feel free to orally articulate ideas, questions, and positions, where "thinking out loud together" holds a privileged place. It is a space where participants listen to one another in order to understand better, to broaden their perspectives and, perhaps have their own positions ultimately confirmed by others. Communicating across ideological difference is a long-term life skill – like numeracy or writing – and is as crucial in the Sciences as it is in the Humanities. How do liberal pedagogues initiate the creation of and help maintain these learning environments?

Pedagogy for civic literacy begins with the imagining of a course itself. Ideally, it is a fundamental learning goal of a major or program. The expectation that students will talk, discuss, debate, and deliberate should be apparent in the syllabus, in the teaching philosophy, and in the assignments and activities that move the disciplinary content.

Some of the assignments and activities may be more "formal" or "high stakes" (i.e. graded) and some may (should) be part of the regular business of the course (i.e. not graded); both are necessary to creating and maintaining a learning environment that enables the cultivation of a critical, civic literacy. Asking students to move beyond memorization of content and to identify and articulate different arguments, providing them with opportunities to listen to and understand divergent opinions, expecting students to verbally articulate a position with which they do not agree, and to entertain questions and participate in discussion and deliberation are all important components of this pedagogy.

Box 3.5 Who's in control?

Teaching the art of thinking, listening, and speaking across ideological difference requires of pedagogues a commitment to creating a learning environment that values process as much as the "acquisition" of disciplinary content. More collaborative or dialogue-centered pedagogies do not necessarily mean that the teacher completely relinquishes structure or control, however. Dialogue, deliberation, discussions, and debates should be carefully crafted and facilitated. Guidelines, expectations, time limits, "rules of engagement," and clear criteria for assessment are all ways in which teachers can structure these more collaborative practices. Communicating across ideological differences inevitably takes more time, involves more tangents, and is less predictable than a situation wherein a teacher simply tells students what to know. But if deep learning and the development of a civic ethos is the ultimate objective, then the messy process/practice of deliberative democracy is necessary and must be central to one's pedagogical philosophy.

Co-curricular pedagogies and university citizenship

Civic learning is not restricted to the classroom environment, nor is it simply the purview of service- or community-based learning endeavors on campus. The classroom (or lab or stage) is a civic space, as are all other areas of students' public life at the institution. Where are the other contexts in which we can help them to engage in deliberative, democratic practice? Advising, residence halls, student clubs and organizations, internships, and international education are all contexts where the practice of communication across difference can and should be encouraged, cultivated, practiced, and reflected upon.

All stakeholders in the academic enterprise, and in the liberal arts context in particular, are citizens in this public sphere. Teachers, administrators, and advisors are in the unique and special position to both model and provide opportunities for students to engage difference through dialogue and deliberation. Whether it be a town hall where all campus constituencies are invited to discuss a specific university conflict, the advisors to the Young Republicans and Young Democrats co-sponsor a deliberative dialogue, or different groups who might not otherwise interact are invited to create a symposium on a given campus or social issue, the co-curricular context can augment the learning and practice of civic literacies.

Liberal educators have the responsibility to demonstrate the importance of *practicing* the skills of communication across ideological difference – in all of our work with students, and with one another. Our comportment as citizens of our institutions is part of this inevitable mix. How do *we* engage difference in our professional lives? How do a libertarian economist and a progressive sociologist, for instance model civil, democratic dialogue across their many ideological and practical differences? How can we model our own common ground, beyond the inevitable differences in our epistemologies and approaches? Team teaching, cluster courses, common readings and seminars, faculty governance, open forums where we can practice the art of communicating across difference, can be significant learning experiences – for us and for our students.

Conclusion

A central component of this work is *hope.* Buber (1970), Bohm (1996), Rogers (1961), Gadamer (1989), Habermas (1984), Bakhtin (1981) – all philosophers of engaged communication and dialogue – believe/d in the capacity of humans to create understanding through engaged, public, empathetic, social intercourse. Citizenship and democracy are not identities or systems, respectively; they are sets of beliefs and behaviors that can be taught, learned, honed, and practiced. Central to a civic ethos is the willingness and ability to engage with difference. It requires rhetorical sensitivity, a critical self-reflexivity, the ability to entertain multiple and even contradictory sets of ideas and information simultaneously and a commitment to an ethic of communication that seeks to understand positions that might not be one's own.

Even in this social moment where political entrenchment, defensiveness, and callous indifference to diversity is commonplace, we can hope that the call to critical citizenship is one that liberal educators reclaim.

References

Anderson, B. (1983) *Imagined Communities: Reflections on the origins and spread of nationalism*, New York: Verso Books.

Bakhtin, M. M. (1981) *The Dialogic Imagination: Four essays by M.M. Bakhtin*, M. Holquist and V. Liapunov (eds) V. Liapunov (trans.) Austin: University of Texas Press.

Barber, B. (1984) *Strong Democracy: Participatory politics for a new age*, Berkeley: University of California Press.

Bohm, D. (1996) *On Dialogue*, N. Lee (ed.) London: Routledge.

Bruffee, K. (1998) *Collaborative Learning: Higher education, interdependence, and the authority of knowledge*, 2nd edn, Baltimore, MD: Johns Hopkins University Press.

Buber, M. (1970) *I and Thou*, W. Kauffman (trans.) New York: Scribner.

Burbules, N. C. (1993) *Dialogue in Teaching: Theory and practice*, New York: Teachers College Press.

Chomsky, N. (2002) *Media Control: The spectacular achievements of propaganda*, New York: Seven Stories Press.

Farland, M. (2008) "The deliberative writing classroom: Public engagement and Aristotle in the Core Curriculum," in J. Dedrick, L. Grattan, and H. Dienstfrey (eds) *Deliberation and the Work of Higher Education*, Dayton, OH: Kettering Foundation Press, pp. 89–112.

Fink, D. (2003) *Creating Significant Learning Experiences: An integrated approach to designing college courses*, San Francisco, CA: Jossey-Bass.

Fordham, T. and Oakes, H. (2013) "Rhetoric across modes, rhetoric across campus: Faculty and students building a multimodal curriculum," in T. Bowen and C. Whithaus (eds) *Multimodal Literacies and Emerging Genres*, Pittsburgh, PA: University of Pittsburgh Press, pp. 313–336.

Gadamer, H. G. (1989) *Truth and Method*, 2nd rev. edn, J. Weinsheimer and D. G. Marshall (trans.) New York: Crossroad.

Grattan, L., Dedrick, J. R., and Dienstfrey, H. (2008) "Creating new spaces for deliberation in higher education," in J. Dedrick, L. Grattan, and H. Dienstfrey (eds) *Deliberation and the Work of Higher Education*, Dayton, OH: Kettering Foundation Press, pp. 5–16.

Habermas, J. (1984) *The Theory of Communicative Action: Reason and the rationalization of society*, Thomas McCarthy (trans.) Boston, MA: Beacon Press.

Hall, S. (1997) *Representation: Cultural representations and signifying practices*, Culture, Media and Identities Series, Buckingham: Open University Press.

Hall, S., Hobson, D., and Lowe, A. (eds) (1980) *Culture, Media, Language*, London: Routledge.

Jefferson, T. (1824) March 27 letter to Edward Everett. www.monticello.org (accessed 20 December 2013).

Mohanty, C. T. (1994) "On race and voice: Challenges for liberal education in the 1990s," in H. Giroux and P. McLaren (eds) *Between Borders: Pedagogy and the politics of cultural studies*, New York and London: Routledge.

Marske, C. (1987) "Durkheim's cult of the individual and the moral reconstitution of society," *Sociological Theory*, 5(1): 1–14.

Mooney, K., Fordham, T., and Lehr, V. (2005) "A faculty development program to promote engaged classroom dialogue: The oral communication institute," in S. Chadwick-Blossey and D. R. Robertson (eds) *To Improve the Academy: Resources for faculty, instructional, and organizational development*, Bolton, MA: Anker, pp. 219–235.

Neuliep, J. (2011) *Intercultural Communication: A contextual approach*, 5th edn, Thousand Oaks, CA: Sage.

Reed, D. (2004) "Universities and the promotion of corporate responsibility: Reinterpreting the liberal arts tradition," *Journal of Academic Ethics*, 2: 3–41.

Rogers, C. (1961) *On Becoming a Person*, Boston, MA: Houghton Mifflin.

Schneider, C. G. (2003) "How civic engagement is reframing liberal education," *Peer Review*, 5(3): xi.

Schoem, D. and Hurtado, S. (eds) (2001) *Intergroup Dialogue: Deliberative democracy in school, college, community, and workplace*, Ann Arbor: University of Michigan Press.

Shactman, T. (1995) *The Inarticulate Society: Eloquence and culture in America*, New York: Free Press.

Tannen, D. (1999) *The Argument Culture: Stopping America's war of words*, New York: Ballantine Books.

Thayer, L. (2009) *Communication! A radical new approach to life's most perplexing problem*, Bloomington, IN: Xlibris Corporation.

Thayer, L. (2012) *Doing Life: A pragmatist manifesto*, Bloomington, IN: Xlibris Corporation. www.iapop.com (accessed 20 December 2013).

West, C. (2005) *Democracy Matters: Winning the fight against imperialism*, New York: Penguin.

Wood, J. (2004) "Forward: Entering into dialogue," in R. Anderson, L. Baxter, and K. Cissna (eds) *Dialogue: Theorizing difference in communication studies*, Thousand Oaks, CA: Sage, pp. xv–xxiii.

Part II
Place, community, and context
Cultivating the habits of self-governance beyond the traditional classroom

4 More than community-based learning

Practicing the liberal arts

Charles Westerberg and Carol Wickersham

Trapped in a pernicious dichotomy

The discourse surrounding the contemporary higher education landscape places the value and purpose of a college degree at issue. One need not look further than the storm of commentary surrounding the publication of *Academically Adrift: Liberal learning on college campuses* by Richard Arum and Josipa Roksa in 2011. From the leading higher education periodicals, to the popular press, to the president of the United States, the future and direction of higher education is on everyone's mind. In many respects, the conversation about the proper purposes and role of higher education has been a polarized one. On one side, we hear about higher education as an expensive and time-consuming credential for a specific job (McArdle 2012; Lawrence 2012). On the other, we hear that it provides the tools to lead a fulfilling and meaningful life (Edmundson 2013; Brann 1999). We see colleges debating whether to adjust their programs and curricula to attend more explicitly to the instrumental value that their institutions provide, or stick their heads in the sand and rely on large endowments and a reputation as the bastion of elite learning to help them weather the current storm (Chopp *et al.* 2013).

As faculty members at a liberal arts institution that neither has nor will have an expanding set of pre-professional majors (cf. nursing, criminal justice, social work, hotel and restaurant management, etc.), and is in the economic position of being largely tuition-driven, we believe that the current debate about the future of higher education is both wrong-headed and short-sighted. At the heart of our dissatisfaction with the current debate is the fact that scant attention is given to the role of higher education broadly, and liberal education specifically, as places where the forms and habits of effective civic participation are introduced, practiced, and reflected upon. We believe that the opportunity to encounter and practice civic responsibility is the ultimate value of liberal education to the society that it serves. These civic aims are neither purely instrumental nor purely a matter of intrinsic betterment. We argue that not only is liberal education an essential tool in the production of civic engagement, but that it is a precursor to achievement, responsibility, and contribution in a person's career and life. It is for this reason that we reject what we call the pernicious dichotomy between job-training and ideas for their own sake, disconnected from any practical purpose. After all, ideas are the basis upon which we make decisions on the job and in our broader lives as citizens. Louis Menand (2010: 57) has forcefully made this point by suggesting that, "The divorce between liberalism and professionalism as educational missions rests on a superstition: that the practical is the enemy of the true. This is nonsense. Disinterestedness is perfectly consistent with practical ambition and practical ambitions are perfectly consistent with disinterestedness."

Pursuing a path forward

In our own work at Beloit College, we have attempted to be true to the idea that liberal learning is indeed the path to self-governance and civic participation. The biggest way Beloit College has attempted to move beyond the dichotomy between learning a particular set of skills for a particular job and learning that is disconnected from any instrumental purpose whatsoever is by referring to our brand of liberal education as "the liberal arts in practice." We believe that the education we provide should put students in a position to achieve success in the contemporary occupational structure, while also making a public contribution to the society around them. In order to do this, students need to see themselves as being possessed of the personal agency and collaborative skills necessary to bring their vision of success to fruition. This sense of agency and capacity for collaboration are developed through opportunities to practice the skills they will need for success in life, both inside the classroom and beyond it; both in one's career and in broader civic life.

For this reason, Beloit College advertises its curriculum as a liberal arts in practice curriculum. We want our students to be practitioners of the liberal arts. We say that Beloit's curriculum requires practice, not only through one course or a requisite internship, but with a set of opportunities that connect knowledge with action throughout the educational trajectory. Practice is a powerful concept in that it can be defined in multiple ways. It can simply mean repetition toward mastery, but it can also refer to the application of an idea or method, or a habitual way of being in the world. We think that practitioners of the liberal arts synthesize knowledge and experience, are able to transfer it to new settings, and through reflection and self-assessment, build on prior experiences to ethically and thoughtfully confront new challenges and take full advantage of new opportunities.

The skills associated with being able to practice the liberal arts are in high demand in a job market where, according to a recent survey of employers by the *Chronicle of Higher Education* and American Public Media's *Marketplace* (*Chronicle of Higher Education* 2013). Employers place more weight on experience, particularly internships and employment during school, than they do on academic credentials such as college major or even grade point average. The important part of these findings for us is that we are interested in more than merely getting a job, and in more than simply being a liberal artist.

Instead, we argue that the two, liberal learning and preparation for success in a career, are linked in important and oft-neglected ways. Liberal learning is an essential tool for being both successful in a career and living life. Why do we have to choose one over the other? The small size and close collaboration between faculty, staff, and students that this size allows, make liberal arts colleges like ours ideal locations to take advantage of the unique opportunity to pair the two and to prepare students for lives of meaningful consequence. Central to the idea of meaningful consequence is the relationship between the kind of education we are describing and the ability to participate in collaborative self-governance.

Our commitment to the liberal arts in practice arises out of a belief that opportunities to learn are not the singular province of classroom learning. Instead, a student's education in the classroom can be enriched beyond it, that the important learning we do in the classroom is tested and challenged beyond it. Of course, this is a two-way street. Students come to the classroom having done a lot of learning, and their experiences and knowledge from outside the classroom are equally tested and challenged within it. In this chapter we will explicate how our approach to putting the liberal arts in practice can be a case study of how to resolve the pernicious dichotomy between being an institution that prepares students only for particular jobs, and an institution that eschews all instrumental value for students. We will focus on the significance of the context where learning takes place for student readiness for and attitudes about civic engagement, and the importance of being able to reflect on the learning that is happening in various contexts, so students are able to transfer knowledge and skills to new and future settings. The current state of the discussion around liberal education seems to be missing a major piece of what makes it so valuable. By highlighting students' experiences with putting the liberal arts into practice we seek to demonstrate that in order to have a complete education, attention needs to be paid to the context in which their learning will be applied.

In the end, we will argue that this process of being able to connect multiple contexts, transfer knowledge between them, and critically self-reflect on lessons learned is an important antecedent to being able to civically engage in productive ways, and that this need not be seen as being in opposition to career success. Seeing liberal education as a vehicle for self-governance is a way to resolve the tension between these polarized approaches to higher education, and allows us to reject the pernicious dichotomy that presently grips the popular discourse concerning the future of higher education.

Why context matters

One important way to make the connections we are talking about is to engage in community-based learning. Classroom and community-based education differ in several important respects. Before explicating these differences, it is important to note that we are broadly defining the term community to mean contexts outside of classrooms, laboratories, or studios, where faculty are in control of the pedagogical variables. Thus, a community may be geographically located beyond the campus perimeter, or it may be on the non-academic side of campus – an athletic field, work study site, or campus club, or it may be a study abroad site halfway around the globe or a virtual community. These contexts share an important commonality: the fact that the variables involved in learning and successfully acting are largely given by the community, not chosen by the instructor or student. This emphasizes one of the most important aspects of communities as loci for student learning: their exquisite murkiness. Community contexts force students to new levels of critical thinking as they sort through what they need to attend to and what they can afford to ignore in order to apprehend the lessons that are there for them. Critical thinking requires the ability to consider options, prioritize and contextualize information. Critical thinkers both raise and answer questions. At times they problematize and complicate constructs, at other times they simplify, depending on contexts. Critical thinking is a progressive skill, which when mastered, puts the student in charge. In contrast, classrooms provide faculty with control of the environment and the ability to continuously frame the focus of inquiry, increasing the complexity as students advance. This means students engaged in community-based learning need to get a grasp on what they already know and how that knowledge can be transferred to new contexts. This requires an examination of basic epistemological constructs. In other words, students need to develop a certain level of metacognition, becoming aware of what they know and how they know it so that they can rightly judge whether previous knowledge is congruent with new situations. All of this requires a healthy measure of honest self-appraisal which develops through guided practice. An Arab proverb sets out the task:

> The one who knows not and knows not that he knows not is a fool; shun him.
> The one who knows not and knows that he knows not is ignorant; teach him.
> The one who knows and knows not that he knows is asleep; wake him.
> The one who knows and knows that he knows is wise; follow him.

An example of such learning was evident for a Beloit College junior who was asked to help a health clinic write a grant to extend the availability of breast and cervical cancer screenings to low-income women as a part of his internship. At first he was completely overwhelmed. He had no experience in grant writing, but once he began engaging in the task he realized that his courses taught him how to analyze demographic data and also how to write persuasively. He could adapt and transfer these skills. Furthermore, he noted many similarities between the grant proposal process and scholarship applications – and he had a lot of experience in this arena. On the other hand, when he had to gather stories from the community he realized the limits of his cultural competence and social capital. As a young, white, male student, he quickly realized he was not the one to run focus groups about intimate topics with middle-aged, minority women; he needed to find collaborators and he did.

The habits of judgment and humility

This short illustration points out two key ways in which contextual education can extend and deepen learning. It provides the opportunity to strengthen shaky confidence; and it can demonstrate the need to put the brake on it. Practice in community situations helps students to develop the facility to sort out when to take initiative and when to hold back, as they become deft at appropriately transferring knowledge between contexts. Because college students have been in school for 12 to 16 years, they generally tend to identify the classroom, reading, and writing assignments as the only way learning occurs. Students often experience education as a single teacher-driven vehicle in which they are passive passengers. Community-based learning forces students into the driver's seat, defining both their destination and the route. In other words, they must develop the ability to take initiative or agency. And in order to develop agency, students must hone the habit of judgment, meaning the ability to compare and select among competing priorities in order to make decisions. To do this, students must appropriately transfer knowledge from one context to another, discerning when situations are congruent or dissonant, and thus adapting and editing old understandings to fit new situations. The prior knowledge they bring to bear might be derived from inside or outside the classroom, thus requiring students to become conscious of unconscious reservoirs of knowledge so they can make appropriate transference. This asks them to become aware of things that they know but take for granted, or that have become inert from lack of use. For instance, athletes who have learned teamwork and strategy on the field can use those skills as members of a scientific research team, or work study students who have learned professionalism in the college dining hall become alert to how these dynamics play out when they are an intern in a senator's office.

Appropriately transferring knowledge from one context to another requires the ability to identify a spectrum of possibilities and make informed but not prescribed choices, rather than replicate correct procedures. In this way transference differs from application, as it is often understood in vocational or professional education. It is the difference between strictly following a recipe and creating a feast from what is found in the cupboard. In other words creative and critical thinking, as well as a storehouse of factual and theoretical information, is required. Thus, the goal of higher education becomes the process of helping students fill a toolbox and learn how to judge which tool to use, tailoring an appropriate approach to the particular context that is presented. Of course, this takes practice, as well as the willingness to test assumptions and learn from mistakes. The practice necessary to become adept at transfer is why field experience alone is not enough. Community or con-textually based education must include both repetition and reflection before, during, and after the experience, guided by faculty and supervisors who are farther down the road than the student. The result of this practice is not merely a skill, it is the habit of judgment which appropriately links general concepts with the particulars of a specific context through comparison and discernment.

While developing student agency is a primary goal for community-based learning, there is an essential and counter-balancing goal of helping students develop a capacity for collegiality, with the concurrent ability to recognize that others are essential to the learning they are doing. While many institu-tions pride themselves on developing student leadership capacities, few make explicit the corollary of how learning requires following – and most importantly of all – how to discern when to lead and when to follow. Similarly, while many emphasize the need for critical thinking as necessary for good judgments, few discuss the necessity of suspending judgment, which is often needed in ambiguous situations. In other words, students need to be able to identify their own ignorance, which requires humility and the relinquishment of personal agency in deference to the communal wisdom of a group. In community contexts, these lessons may be brought home as students quickly discover that they do not know as much as they thought they knew. In his essay "Professing the Liberal Arts," Lee Shulman points out that the process of putting knowledge into practice helps students recognize the limits of their knowledge. "A great problem of liberal learning is the confidence with which our graduates ima-gine they understand many things with which they have only superficial acquaintance and glib verbal familiarity. Thus, they can throw around phrases like 'supply and demand' or 'survival of the fittest' with marvelous agility, albeit without substantial understanding" (Shulman 1997: 162–163).

For instance, Oscar, a sophomore sociology student, believed he under-stood the dynamics of racism because of the theories he had explored in classes; however, when he began working with a racially diverse group of teens in a summer recreation program, he quickly realized that, while the theories provided insight, they glossed over much of the rough complexity of the experience. What helped Oscar most were the insights garnered from a 13-year-old African-American participant in the program. This young teen helped Oscar identify purposeful activity in a situation that he had formerly experienced as chaos. As Oscar put it, "Until he pointed it out, I did not understand how much my background colored (pun intended) the way I was interacting with the youth."

In a report by the National Research Council, this ability to discern meaningful patterns is one of the key attributes that separates experts from novices. Experts are possessed of both an extensive data base (many tools in their toolbox) and an awareness of the deep underlying principles (under-standing of how the tools work), thus, "(e)xperts' knowledge cannot be reduced to sets of isolated facts or propositions but, instead, reflects context of applicability: that is, the knowledge is 'conditionalized' on a set of circumstances" (Bransford *et al.* 1999: 31).

In order for a novice to learn from an expert, the novice must have the humility to acknowledge the limits of his or her knowledge in order to be receptive to the expert's teaching, and this can be especially difficult if the expert is 13 years old. The ability to synthesize understandings from multiple sources takes intelligence and imagination, but more critically it takes the humble acknowledgement that teachers come in many, and often uncredentialed, guises.

In Beloit College's brand of community-based learning, we call this receptivity "the learning stance." Simply stated, the learning stance posits that every person you meet has the potential to be a teacher, whether they have a Ph.D. or are a third grader. The only question is whether the student is humble enough and perceptive enough to absorb the lesson. Paradoxically this also requires students to take agency as they assume responsibility for shaping their learning goals and outcomes. Students try on various lessons for size, guided by mentors whose perspectives may be congruent, complementary, or clashing, and are informed by the trial and error inherent in practicing a new skill. As they critically reflect on these experiences, intentionally looking for connections between classroom and community, students grow more adept at transferring and translating knowledge between contexts.

One can conceptualize the habits or virtues of judgment and humility as complementary and in tension with each other. They are two essential lessons to be derived through the practice of transferring knowledge between the classroom and other contexts. Judgment drives the development of agency as students learn to take individual initiative. And as counterpoint, humility allows students to develop the habit of collaboration, which can often require the restraint of agency. Both virtues require discernment to know when to step forward and when to step back. Of course, these virtues are not in competition, rather they are interrelated and mutually reinforcing. For instance, a student who was working with a non-profit agency to help create a human growth and development curriculum for adolescents became enthusiastic about other communities' success in using humor and role-playing workshops. He took the initiative to research options, but in conversation with the director of the program, realized that there was the need to create buy-in from various constituencies if the workshops were to be well received. Because he was a senior with a lot of experience in community-based learning, he was able to discern the need to step back, listen, and learn from the students, their parents, the non-profit board and staff, and the school administration. His awareness that he had a good idea was tempered by the concurrent awareness that he needed more information from a variety of sources before he could translate his understanding of the benefits of the approach in a way that the community would welcome. His balance of agency and restraint, judgment and humility worked to further his learning and towards the exercise of productive civic engagement.

Instituting a structure for practicing the liberal arts

These insights have been foundational in Beloit College's incorporation of experiential, context-based education as an essential part of a twenty-first-century liberal education. Beloit continues to build on its legacy of context-based education, which garnered national attention beginning in 1965 when its curriculum, referred to as "The Beloit Plan," included a required semester off campus. Since the 1980s, Beloit College's commitment to experiential education has continued to be reflected in its prioritization of study abroad and internship programs. In 2011, Beloit adopted a new curriculum that reinserted a context-based requirement for students that asks them to extend their learning beyond the traditional classroom. Additionally, the current curriculum explicitly infuses contextual education in all disciplines, across the campus and throughout all four years of study. The privileging of context-based learning, it is important to note, is not simply a reaction to the current climate in higher education and its calls for job-training. Rather it is a continuation of the belief that context-based education develops the capacities necessary to exercise judgment and humility, and serves to develop the capacity for collaborative self-governance.

This holistic approach to liberal education is undergirded by advising relationships with students, which are geared toward encouraging students to regard education as taking place everywhere and all the time. Students are asked to integrate and articulate the experiences they have – curricular and co-curricular, during the academic year and outside it – as a part of their larger educational project. The classroom, the residential sides of campus, and the wider community are all meaningful locations where the lessons of liberal learning are absorbed and applied. Thus, the student practices the learning stance both on campus and off, rejecting various dichotomies that tend to reinforce student passivity, which, at its worst, manifests itself in the questions, "Will this be on the exam?" and "Can I use this in the 'real' world?" If students view their education primarily as a means to a credential, professors are viewed primarily as gatekeepers. On the other hand, if students see no connection between the ideas dissected in their classrooms and their lives or the urgent problems of the world, they may put those ideas on a mental shelf and leave them there to be admired from time to time like precious knick-knacks. In both cases, students experience learning as peripheral to the life they are actually living, neither informed by nor informing daily routines, let alone social ethics or civic involvement. Once the credential is obtained, the student can stop learning or once the press of daily needs crowds in, precious ideas may be set aside as a luxury. By helping students practice making connections between their learning and their lives, their education is not inert; rather, it grows and flourishes from experience to experience.

In order to structurally advance our approach to liberal education, Beloit has developed an administrative support structure we refer to as the Liberal Arts in Practice Center. The pieces that make up the Liberal Arts in Practice

Center include: academic advising, community-based learning, career development, and the college's entrepreneurship program. All of the offices housed in the Liberal Arts in Practice Center exist to support students in learning the skills necessary for collaborative self-governance. In order to articulate how a Beloit education will result in being possessed of the tools to support self-governance, a model has been developed to guide students in seeing the trajectory that their education can follow (Figure 4.1). The model is designed to help students conceptualize the developmental and individualized trajectory by which they can acquire the capacity of individual agency and become an adept practitioner of the liberal arts. Students enter the process in various ways, and at various points, depending on their previous experience and their academic and professional goals. Each step is informed by the curricular requirements and builds on contextual experience that invites students to deeper levels of analysis and engagement. All the while the student is developing the complementary capacities of agency and collaboration, as they chart their own course in partnership with others.

During their first and second years, students are encouraged to experiment and cultivate their interests in preparation for their junior year where they are required to engage in an academically grounded beyond-the-classroom experience supervised by their advisor. This experience might be fulfilled through designated courses available in most disciplines, the study abroad program, or through more individually designed internships, research projects, or collaborations. The beyond-the-classroom requirement is, in turn, designed to inform a senior capstone project that synthesizes and articulates the arc of their liberal education.

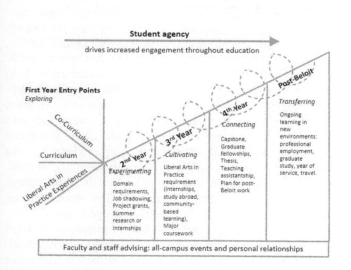

Developmental Outcomes:
- Effective Communication
- Critical Self-Assessment
- Collaborative Action
- Ethical Work
- Cultural Competency
- Information Literacy
- Professionalism

Figure 4.1 The liberal arts in practice developmental mode

Beloit College has articulated the liberal arts in practice as the way we do business and has put structures into place that make explicit to internal and external audiences how collaborative self-governance can be supported and facilitated. In this way, the institution itself engages in the practice of the learning stance, whereby faculty come to see their teaching enhanced and complemented by colleagues residing in all parts of the campus, as well as by community partners in the local community and around the world. Articulation of this kind also helps faculty to be looking for opportunities to make the connections between previously taken for granted student experiences, and to provide examples and modeling of the transfer that lies at the heart of putting the liberal arts into practice.

One of the most visible manifestations of Beloit's commitment to the rejection of the pernicious dichotomy between impractical classroom learning and purely instrumental, job-training focused education has been the creation of the aforementioned Liberal Arts in Practice Center, which geographically and philosophically straddles the juncture between the student affairs and academic affairs hemispheres of the campus. The creation of the Center signals the college's intent to provide an integrated, holistic education. The Liberal Arts in Practice Center houses seven different programs, all of which interface with the wider community in different ways. For instance, the offices of Community-Based Learning and Career Development exist literally side by side and closely collaborate to help students see their academic and professional goals as two sides of the same coin. A good example of how this works is a capstone course called "Translating the Liberal Arts," which is co-taught by the director of Career Development and a faculty member. This course focuses on helping students to be able to articulate the experiences that they have had during their college years and the ways that liberally educated students can make contributions in a wide array of settings, based on the skills they have developed. Academic Advising is also lodged within the Liberal Arts in Practice Center, and is viewed as one of the primary means faculty and staff use to guide students in taking ownership of the whole of their college experience and to help them see it as a part of a long-term educational enterprise. In order to support this more robust approach to advising, one day is set aside each semester, free from courses, as an Advising Practicum. The day is organized into workshops led by faculty, staff, alumni, community leaders, and advanced students on a wide variety of issues that inform and equip students to take control of their education. For instance, information about study abroad, internships, résumé writing, study skills, and informational meetings about various disciplinary initiatives are offered by departments. The workshops are geared to the various developmental levels in students' college careers.

Comparative literature and sociology major, Abby, eloquently articulated her understanding of how her liberal arts in practice education is both developmental and synthetic. Describing her experience as a student coordinator of a volunteer tutoring program at a local elementary school, which provided her an opportunity to reflect on education at large, she said:

At Todd [Elementary] I have had the privilege of working with first graders who are just learning to read. I watch as students begin to conceptualize "reading" ... [and] I've been contemplating my own education anew. Each day students and teachers arrive in the room with distinct needs, preconceptions, desires, and goals. I've been considering all the things I've learned from my classes that weren't spelled out on pieces of paper or in lectures: the dynamics of contributing to a group, or the nuances of self-presentation, for example. In some bizarre (and yet expected, even common-sense) way the longer I've been in school the more time and space I need to digest what I learn and consolidate it into my understanding of the world.

At Beloit (let me just speak for the institution real quick) we support the philosophy that the material we learn in our courses is just one (really expensive) part of a daily education. The dichotomy between the "academic" and "real" world blurs under scrutiny, and instead we see that the texts and contexts of our lives are interwoven. Being at Todd Elementary School has reminded me that nothing I learn is value-free, and that in order to really own my education, I have to take the time and space to investigate how all the parts of my life are interacting.

Similarly, Marcia, a senior in psychology, reflects on how her experiences during a summer internship at a mental health clinic position her to integrate her academic and community-based education:

While it seems education is not a substitute for real life experience in a field, it can complement experience quite well, and the classes I have taken in past years at Beloit have helped to inform my experience thus far ... The principles taught in a [sociology] class help facilitate the understanding of social and cultural influences on the clients at [the clinic] – they have been very helpful in interpreting counseling settings. While the knowledge I have gained from psychology courses has been helpful as well, even more so are the skills in organization and time management I have acquired in the college setting. The combination of my position as a liberally minded Beloit College undergraduate has helped the transition into being a full member of the [mental health] community, informed by past learning as well as social experience.

These two seniors articulate their understandings of how the education they have received at Beloit College equips them for productive and ethical civic engagement. They are exquisitely conscious that their education involves reflecting on action in light of ideas and vice versa so that they can make connections and appropriately transfer information from one context to another. As they stand at the threshold of graduation, they are ready to take charge of their learning. No longer novices, they are now full-fledged, abundantly engaged alumni ready to contribute to the common good.

Some examples of students practicing the liberal arts at Beloit College

Several key initiatives have helped to shape, test, and infuse the liberal arts in practice throughout the Beloit College educational enterprise. Four examples, drawn from across the academic divisions of the College, serve as illustrations: the Duffy Community Partnerships, the Sustainability Fellows program, a Labs Across the Curriculum initiative, and faculty collaborations with our pre-college Help Yourself program. Each has benefited from significant outside investment by alumni and corporate and foundation support, as well as in-kind donations of expertise from the community. These examples illustrate some of the myriad ways that grounding the liberal arts in community practice promotes the transfer of knowledge necessary for civic engagement.

The Duffy Community Partnerships

Now ten years old, the Duffy, as it is fondly called, is an academically focused, hands-on, community-based sociology course which places 15 selected students per semester in various field sites and then draws them together to analyze their experiences in the context of course readings in a weekly seminar. The overarching question of the Duffy is "What makes a good society?" The students strive to answer this by examining the dynamics of institutional sectors that their community contexts represent: government, business, social service, agriculture, education, religion.

The Duffy purposely places students in situations to assume "the learning stance" at field sites that double as "classrooms" where everyone a student encounters has the potential to be their teacher; the only trick is to figure out what the lesson is. The learning stance seats the locus of learning squarely with the student, but also assumes respectful collaborative learning, thus predisposing the student to learn the habits of humility and judgment. In the Duffy Partnerships, this progress is measured through a series of reflective, analytical field notes that direct students to connect classroom texts with community contexts, but does not direct them as to what connections to make or how. Students complete either five or ten sets of notes, depending whether they are enrolled for one semester of the course or two.

Garrett was a senior majoring in economics and management when he became a Duffy student. He already had considerable experience as an intern in two prominent financial analysis and marketing firms on the East Coast. His Duffy placement was with a Midwest, blue-collar manufacturing company which has important contracts with the U.S. military. His first sets of written reflections disclose his discomfort. He was appalled by the lack of professionalism of the engineers and business managers of the company who never wore neckties and used humor he thought crude. Furthermore, these professionals ate their sack lunches with the machinists on the shop floor. Garrett was resistant and judgmental, wondering whether his placement, or even the site itself, would yield anything productive. He complained that there was nothing to learn from such an unprofessional company. The turning point in Garrett's Duffy education came quite late in the semester when he was allowed to follow along for the day with one of his supervisors who was hosting a customer who happened to be a navy admiral. The supervisor introduced the admiral to several of the workers on the shop floor and Garrett realized that the social capital accrued through sack lunches and jokes, as well as the fact that many of the workers had experience in the military, allowed them to converse easily. Garrett wrote:

> More information was transferred there on the shop floor smelling like diesel oil and filled with loud, clanging machinery than I'd seen in presented fancy powerpoint charts in fancy boardrooms. The general got his questions answered. The machinists made suggestions that made sense. The company secured the contract and everyone went out for a beer. I have to admit I was wrong. If the General can learn from the machinists, maybe I should, too. And I think I need to lose the tie.

These notes point to connections that Garrett was making between his academic texts and the context on the factory floor, for earlier that week the students had explored the concept of social capital drawing on essays from Robert Putnam (2000) and Francis Fukuyama (2000). As an economics student, he found resonance with Fukuyama's analysis of the dynamics of social capital, grounded in the coinage of trust and culturally determined, rational decision-making. These readings illuminated his ignorance of the sophisticated dynamics that had been in full view all semester. In the seminar, he was able to articulate how all of these elements came together in an epiphany as he made a quantum shift in understanding by seeing competence and professionalism in a situation where he had seen incompetence and crudeness previously. He was humbled and his newfound humility made him a receptive learner.

Garrett's experience also illustrates community-based learning as a developmental process. The learning stance posits that everyone a student meets has the potential to be their teacher; the key word is potential, which the student must actualize for him or herself, accompanied by teachers and texts. In this way, the virtues of humility and judgment meet, as students humbly recognize their need to learn and exercise judgment in seeking out the lesson in any particular context. Student growth in the habits and virtues of agency/collaboration; judgment/humility – qualities needed for effective self-governance and civic engagement – are clearly evident in the trajectory of the Duffy reflections.

Sustainability Fellows program

A second Beloit College community-based learning opportunity is the Sustainability Fellows program, directed by a professor of biology. This summer program, now three years old, has engaged 31 students with 14 majors in 13 different projects. Students learn from faculty mentors and community partners on research projects that investigate and promote environmental, economic and social sustainability. Similar to the Duffy Partnerships, the Sustainability Fellows program seeks to promote appropriate transfer of knowledge between academic and community contexts. For example, students work with the College's physical plant staff conducting research to inform recommendations for reducing energy or water use, and they work with community groups on habitat restoration, community gardens, and environmental education.

Recognizing that this is a developmental process, a Sustainability Learning Outcomes Rubric (Figure 4.2) was created based on the American Colleges and Universities' Valid Assessment of Learning in Undergraduate Education rubrics (Rhodes 2010), to assess student progress. The evidence from an analysis of reflective essay responses from 31 students demonstrated that over the course of eight weeks students made significant strides toward the learning goals of the program. Students reported that the program improved their quantitative and analytical skills, increased their confidence when faced with practical tasks, and made them more focused with respect to their future academic and career plans. One student summed up her experience in the program by saying, "I think the best part of the Sustainability Fellows Program is the amount of independent, self-motivated, hands-on work that you get to do. I really enjoyed making my own connections and discovering important things." This end-of-program assessment is intriguing, given that the program director points out that the route to achieving this view is not always smooth. She notes that early in the program students often articulate frustration with the lack of clear goals, or rather, with the expectation that they set their own goals and design their own research. One senior geology major articulates the change in her perspective from seeing the experience as linear, where learning X leads to being able to do Y, by saying, "The way I thought about sustainability shifted … I no longer saw environmental protection as the ultimate goal, but understood that to have a stable society in the future, we needed to ensure economic development and equity."

Over and over again, the students reiterated how the program helps them to make connections between their narrowly focused research projects and larger civic issues. A senior economics major and geo-chemistry minor put it this way, "From crawling into hard to reach spaces to sitting in a conference room negotiating the parameters of a business deal with … a multibillion-dollar corporation, experiential learning has taught me that doing is a very powerful form of learning."

What we know from the various liberal arts in practice endeavors students have undertaken in recent years at Beloit is that students who begin to practice reflecting on what they do, in the sense of repetition toward mastery, often find that reflection becomes a "practice" in the sense of a habitual and foundational orientation toward the world. These Sustainability Fellows are in the process of moving from rookie status to becoming varsity level liberal arts practitioners.

	1	2	3	4
Sustainability Knowledge *Demonstrates clear understanding of the environmental, economic, and social dimensions of sustainability*	Shows limited understanding of sustainability as "green living."	Identifies various aspects of sustainability and connects them to specific sustainability-related activities.	Articulates the conceptual basis for sustainability-related activities.	Uses conceptual basis for sustainability in the development and implementation of specific activities.
Transfer *Adapts and applies skills, abilities, theories, or methodologies gained in one situation to new situations (1,2)*	References in a passing way the use of skills, abilities, theories, or methodologies gained in one situation in a new situation.	Demonstrates or explicitly explains the use of skills, abilities, theories, or methodologies gained in one situation in a new situation.	Adapts and applies skills, abilities, theories, or methodologies gained in one situation to new situations to contribute to the understanding of problems or to explore issues.	Adapts and applies skills, abilities, theories, or methodologies gained in one situation to new situations to solve problems or explore complex issues in original ways.
Reflection and Self-Assessment *Shows sense of self as a learner, building on prior experiences to respond to new and challenging contexts (1,2)*	Describes own performances with general descriptors of success and failure.	Articulates strengths and challenges (within specific performances or events) to increase effectiveness in different contexts (through increased self-awareness).	Evaluates changes in own learning over time, recognizing complex contextual factors (e.g., works with ambiguity/risk, deals with frustration, considers ethical frameworks).	Envisions a future self by making plans that build on past experiences that have occurred across multiple and diverse contexts.
Sustainability Leadership *Demonstrates independence and team leadership in sustainability activities (2)*	Has experimented with some sustainability activities but shows little internalized understanding of their aims or effects and little commitment to future action.	Has clearly participated in sustainability-focused actions and begins to reflect on how these actions may benefit individual(s) or communities.	Demonstrates independent experience and team leadership in sustainability action, with reflective insights or analysis about the aims and accomplishments of individual actions.	Demonstrates independent experience and shows initiative in team leadership in complex or multiple sustainability activities, accompanied by reflective insights or analysis about the aims and accomplishments of individual actions.
		"Talks the talk"	"Walks the walk"	"Leads others in 'walking the walk'"

Parenthetical numbers/words indicate source of entry:
(1)Beloit College. 2012. Liberal Arts in Practice Impact Rubric, Beloit College, Beloit, Wisc.
(2)Rhodes, Terrel, ed. 2010. *Assessing Outcomes and Improving Achievement: Tips and Tools for Using Rubrics.* Washington, DC: Association of American Colleges and Universities.

Figure 4.2 Sustainability rubric

Labs Across the Curriculum

In 2010, Beloit College received a grant from the Mellon foundation to embark on what Beloit College president, Scott Bierman, described as a "hands-on, outcomes-based field and lab experiment" that would apply a laboratory model to courses in every discipline, but most especially in the humanities, particularly those traditionally taught as lectures or seminars. This propelled many faculty to design courses that required students to engage in beyond-the-classroom learning. The process of conceiving or reconceiving courses was instrumental in helping faculty to make connections between what they had traditionally taught in the classroom and how concepts and ideas could be transferred into field settings. Examples of these courses have included philosophy students using familiar picture books to teach abstract concepts to elementary school children, dance students learning about running a repertory company by taking their show on the road to local schools, and modern languages students having live video conversations with fellow students in Kaifeng, China.

Two courses in the history department made explicit connections between liberal education and civic engagement. In a course focused on archival research, the faculty member and the college archivist jointly supervised students in hands-on projects with community materials from the college archives. These projects were designed to complement a more traditional theoretical examination of public history. The students visited and learned from the staffs of heritage sites, such as museums and archives, in preparation for a capstone project that brought together the foundations of the history major with practical skills learned in the "laboratory" settings. Though not funded by the Labs Across the Curriculum initiative, a course on "Citizenship in United States History" was pedagogically similar in its emphasis on concurrent theoretical and practical learning. Students read, wrote about and discussed texts from the ancient world and Colonial America through modern times, while spending several evenings tutoring adults who were preparing to take the United States citizenship exam, all the while making connections between their texts and the community context. For example, through their interactions with people going through a process to become a citizen, students began to see how their readings and discussions could help to inform their understanding of the significance of citizenship, and drove home the point that one's views about the importance of citizenship vary depending on whether one is counted as a citizen or not. They also came to appreciate the interplay between abstract concepts of citizenship and bureaucratic mechanisms for becoming a citizen.

Help Yourself workshops

Our final example is drawn from an interface that reaches across all of the College's academic disciplines. The Help Yourself program is a 26-year-old

Beloit College program for middle and high school students in the surrounding community who are members of populations traditionally underrepresented in higher education: first-generation, low-income, and/or ethnic minority students. For the past three and a half years, the College has built a more intentional bridge to this program, which involves professors embedding an assignment within their course directing students to design and implement a workshop for the younger Help Yourself students. These workshops served the dual purpose of offering enrichment workshops for the Help Yourself students through exposure to college course content while offering Beloit College students a beginning step in their liberal arts in practice trajectory. All of the elements of practicing the liberal arts come into play as the college students have to select what they want to convey and how they want to convey it. As the older students struggle to identify what might be meaningful to younger students and why, they are also articulating it for themselves. The director of the Help Yourself program guides and informs the work of the college students by asking them to examine their assumptions about the younger students, including their social and academic levels and the similarities and dissimilarities in cultural backgrounds. She prepares the college students to learn from the younger students as well as teach them.

The workshops have explored a wide diversity of subject matter. For instance, in a course on abstract algebra students designed a simulation game called "alien math" in which high school "space explorers" landed on a planet and had to figure out their math system based on the patterns of symbols they discovered. In a workshop led by anthropology students on osteology, middle school students learned how forensic scientists figure out race, gender, and age as they measured bones alongside the college students. A few of the other courses that have benefited from this connection include: music theory, writing 100, introductory Chinese, sociology of the family, fundamentals of acting, and nanochemistry.

Reflection papers following the workshop provide insight into how even these relatively small exercises in practicing the liberal arts can lead to significant student development with respect to seeing how liberal learning connects to self-governance and civic engagement. Following a workshop facilitated by students in an introductory level Chinese course, the professor observed that, by practicing teaching, his students realized how much they need to know in order to feel confident. The workshop also helped his students to locate their insecurities with the subject matter and, thus, they were better able to evaluate how well they understood the basic foundations of Chinese. In addition, he felt his students realized how difficult it is to communicate knowledge you are acquiring to another audience. All of these are first steps in putting the liberal arts into practice.

In all of these instances, students learned about the dynamics of civic engagement through the complementary pedagogies of classroom and beyond-the-classroom learning, deriving depth and nuance that neither approach could offer independently. Some important take-aways from these examples include the receptivity of the students and faculty who have tried these pedagogies on for size. The process has been one of starting small and allowing success to speak for itself. Additionally by systematically gathering student reflections, the College is able to more objectively analyze whether student enthusiasm for this approach to learning is borne out through assessment. Generally, students find it obvious that the various sectors of their lives should and do inform each other and they are appreciative of the invitation to make this explicit and intentional. Faculty who have been more thoroughly steeped in academic mores often find themselves more invested in one side or the other of the dichotomy. Now, well into our third year of practice with this model, we are finding that faculty are coming to see an integrated educational model as beneficial, even in their more traditionally taught courses. Students who approach their education as an opportunity to make connections tend to more vigorously engage with course material, deepen their level of analysis, and make more nuanced arguments. While it is true that not all faculty embrace this less traditional approach to liberal education, many who were initially resistant have found that there is value added by incorporating beyond-the-classroom components to their courses. Even faculty who are not participating are coming to recognize the benefits of seeing the complementarity of classroom and beyond-the-classroom work.

Escaping the dichotomy?

In this chapter, we have sought to move beyond the dominant discourse that higher education institutions must choose between instrumental and liberal aims. Instead, we have tried to demonstrate that liberal education can play a significant and valuable role in fostering a healthy and efficacious civil society. We have provided one college's day-to-day approach to educating students in such a way as to help them acquire a depth of knowledge in a major area of study, take full ownership of their education, and bring to their everyday lives a sense of purpose and consequence. It is important to recognize that this approach is more than a collection of individual programs; rather, what we have described is a set of components that are part of a holistic model of what it means to be a liberally educated person who is equipped to act ethically and thoughtfully in a world that is crying out for more such people. Instead of viewing this as work that is carried out by a single program or office, we have articulated how we have infused the actual practice of liberal education throughout academic departments, staff departments, and student life across the institution. As our pedagogical focus on connection, transfer, and reflection becomes increasingly naturalized throughout the institution, the dichotomy between education as job preparation versus education for its own sake is increasingly revealed as an artificial and distracting construct. Students are aware that the global challenges before them will require all the skills and knowledge that their generation can bring to bear. They know that as individuals they face stiff competition on the job front and as a cohort they face the interconnected public issues of economic disparity, climate change, and violence. They cannot afford a disconnection between what they know and what they will do. Therefore, they are seeking an education that will equip them to lead fulfilling lives and make public contributions. By putting the liberal arts into practice, they are being prepared to do exactly this: developing the liberal virtues of judgment and humility and, through constant practice, mastering the art of making connections in order to appropriately transfer knowledge from one sphere to another. All that remains is to keep practicing.

Institutions of higher education ignore these realities at their peril. Even if construed narrowly in terms of institutional survival, universities and colleges can read the demographics and the market and realize that there will be stiff competition for enrollment: thus, a both/and approach that appeals to a larger constituency is in their best interest. This requires a rejection of the strident either/or stand-off currently in play. We make the case that there are much more fundamental and ethical reasons to reshape the structure and stance of the institution, for we are equipping future global citizens to face the challenges that we all must face together. We must practice the liberal arts by wedding our clearest analysis and most profound theories to a pragmatic willingness to redirect resources and rehabilitate outmoded mechanisms. This will require thinking differently about expertise, credentialing, and privilege across and beyond our institutions. As educators we must recognize we are all in this together, at least to some limited degree or on some higher plane; we must cooperate as well as compete. Our civic duty demands it.

References

Arum, R. and Roksa, J. (2011) *Academically Adrift: Limited learning on college campuses*, Chicago, IL: University of Chicago Press.

Brann E. (1999) "The American college as the place for liberal learning," *Daedalus*, 128: 151–171.

Bransford, J. D., Brown, A. L., and Cocking, R. R. (1999) *How People Learn: Brain, mind, experience, and school*, Washington, DC: National Academy Press.

Chronicle of Higher Education. (2013) "The employment mismatch – special reports," http://chronicle.com/article/The-Employment-Mismatch/137625/#id=over view (accessed 20 December 2013).

Chopp, R., Frost, S. and Weiss, D.H. (2013) *Remaking College: Innovation and the liberal arts*, Baltimore, MD: Johns Hopkins University Press.

Edmundson, M. (2013) "Humanities for humanity's sake," *Washington Post*, 11 August, B04.

Fukuyama, F. (2000) "Trust: Social virtues and the creation of prosperity," in D. E. Eberly (ed.) *The Essential Civil Society Reader*, Lanham, MD: Rowman and Littlefield, pp. 257–266.

Lawrence, L. (2012) "Bachelor's degree: Has it lost its edge and its value? Undervalued and overpriced, the beleaguered bachelor's degree is losing its edge as the hallmark of an educated, readily employable American," *Christian Science Monitor*, 17 June.

McArdle, M. (2012) "The college bubble: Mythomania about college has turned getting a degree into an American neurosis. It's sending parents to the poorhouse and saddling students with a backpack full of debt that doesn't even guarantee a good job in the end," *Newsweek*, 160(12): 24.

Menand, L. (2010) *The Marketplace of Ideas*, New York: W.W. Norton.

Putnam, R. (2000) *Bowling Alone: The revival and collapse of American community*, New York: Simon and Schuster.

Rhodes, T. (2010) *Assessing Outcomes and Improving Achievement: Tips and tools for using rubrics*, Washington, DC: Association of American Colleges and Universities.

Shulman, L. (1997) "Professing the liberal arts," in R. Orrill (ed.) *Education and Democracy: Reimagining liberal learning in America*, New York: College Board Publications, pp. 151–173.

5 Developing the art of self-governance

Teaching the role of place in associative life

Emily Chamlee-Wright, Adam Goodheart and John L. Seidel

The central premise of this volume is that institutions of liberal learning are sites in which the art of self-governance is being nurtured and developed, and that a deeper understanding of this role can enable us to advance the art of self-governance even further. Liberal arts colleges founded in the shadow of the American Revolution, such as our own institution, Washington College, were palpably aware of the connection between liberty and the prospects for self-governance, on the one hand, and the project of liberal education on the other. Recounting Washington College's founding, the institution's first president, William Smith, confidently asserted that "LIBERTY will not deign to dwell, but where her fair companion KNOWLEDGE flourishes by her side" (Smith 1784: 4). Like many of his contemporaries in the first years of national independence, Smith was preoccupied with the question of how to render Americans fit for self-governance. As the historian Drew McCoy has written, "Many of the Revolutionaries were inspired to hope that the American people might … conform to the classical notion of virtue and thus become the special kind of simple, austere, egalitarian, civic-minded people that intellectuals had dreamed of for centuries" (McCoy 1982: 70). Yet they simultaneously worried that the nation's fragile experiment in democracy might eventually, like all previous republics, devolve into demagoguery and anarchy, especially after George Washington and the other unifying, inspirational figures of the founding generation had passed offstage.

For Smith, as for Thomas Jefferson, James Madison, and others, the solution was education, but not of the kind traditionally found at Oxford and Cambridge, nor even at American universities established during the colonial period. Those institutions traditionally focused on such subjects as theology, ancient history, and classical languages, with the goal of educating young gentlemen for careers in the ministry or lives of cultivated leisure. In the new republic, Smith proposed, colleges must offer curricula of broader relevance, comprising more recent history (including that of America itself), modern languages, science, and similar fields. These, he wrote, would be effective at "forming a succession, of sober, virtuous, industrious citizens" who would "do always the greatest good whether to ourselves or fellow-creatures, of whatever country, sect, or denomination they may be, [and] act a just and honest part in our social capacity." In an essay imagining his ideal institution, Smith described its physical setting not as an isolated grove of academe or enclosed college quadrangle, but rather as a hilltop "public garden" where professors and students would gather outdoors, observing both the untamed wilderness and the turrets and spires of a nearby city. In other words, this would be an institution with a strong sense of place, open to both the human and natural worlds (Smith 1803: 175–178, 217).

When, in 1782, the opportunity arose for Smith to apply these ideals in the creation of an actual college, its physical setting was somewhat different than he had imagined: on a hilltop overlooking a small town on Maryland's rural Eastern Shore. But the planned curriculum at Washington College hewed close to his original vision in most respects (Smith 1784). Notably, too, its mission was decidedly secular, and its founding documents explicitly eschewed any religious affiliation or religious litmus test for students, faculty, or administrators (Goodheart 2012). At this point of American history, there was no question as to the importance liberal learning would play in promoting self-governance through a tolerant and open civil society.

Within Smith's writings, a formula of sorts is being proposed. Knowledge and liberty are conjoined. Without knowledge, we can only be subjects, not self-governing citizens. Citizens have to be willing to and capable of navigating their individual affairs and common pursuits. Such is the essence of liberty. In turn, in order to exercise one's liberty, one must exercise intellectual agency – the capacity to challenge received wisdom, and the confidence that solutions can be found. Further, in these passages are inklings that a self-governing people would have to exercise the norms of associative life, such as the values of toleration.

Identifying the links that connect knowledge, liberty, and the habits conducive to self-governance, we contend, is just as important today as it was in the moments following the American Revolution. Arguably, the central goal of liberal learning is not to acquire a particular core of knowledge, but is instead to develop intellectual agency. Intellectual agency emancipates us from dogma. A freed mind is thus a prerequisite for self-governance.

Self-governance also requires a structure for and norms of associative life. The prospect of self-governance relies on there being an underlying institutional structure that allows for freedom of association, a sphere of autonomous behavior, and a sphere in which voluntary cooperative behavior is permitted. In addition to these necessary conditions, however, self-governance relies upon informal norms and habits of association. If citizens are to attend to matters of common concern we require a common understanding of how such things get done, such as a widely shared understanding of how, when, and where such matters get discussed, who has authority to command our attention to such matters, mental templates of how effective action has taken place in the past, and so on. Such norms and habits can, of course, be learned and practiced within community without critical reflection. By the time we enter college or university we have all been steeped in some tea of associative life. For some of us that tea is a rather thin brew; for others it is rich with complexity. But what is also true is that by the time we enter college or university, the norms of associative life can also be the subject of reflection and analysis. This is in part the promise of liberal education – that we are challenged to examine critically what is customary and familiar to reveal its functional logic, its virtues, and its shortcomings.

The intellectual habits conducive to self-governance are many, but those that are most closely tied to the mission of liberal learning are (a) learning to "read" civil society as an open text, with new insights ready to be discovered about the ways in which associative life works generally, and how it worked or is working specifically within a given context; (b) learning to look for and recognize both the seen and unseen structures that shape civil society; and as a consequence of these intellectual habits, (c) identifying ways of engaging in effective civic action.

But all this requires close attention. While it is possible to read any particular civil society context from a detached clinical standpoint, a more intimate proximity between investigator/learner and subject creates opportunities for discovery unavailable to a more distanced perspective. As any qualitative researcher knows, embedding within a given context puts the investigator/learner in closer proximity to the subject under investigation and gives access to small clues that often lead to leaps of insight. Arguing the merits of qualitative research methods, Chamlee-Wright (2011: 164) points out that:

> there is a two-way dialog between the investigator and the subject (Gadamer 1975). In response to our questions, the subject sometimes "speaks" in general terms, revealing broad patterns. But the subject can also "speak" in cryptic terms, revealing what might be small clues to a different and perhaps better question. But in order to gain the most we can out of this "conversation," we need to be close enough to get at the meanings behind the general pattern – to understand why and how a pattern emerges, and not just that a pattern has emerged. We need to be close enough to ask the subject or phenomenon under investigation new questions and see where the clues lead.

Part of the pedagogical advantage in connecting our students to place is that if they form an attachment or affinity for the local community, its history, environment, and culture, and so on, they may be more internally motivated to engage and learn. But an affinity for a particular place is only part of the pedagogical advantage of place-based learning. The principal advantage is that students learn how to read a complex social text and experience what it is to discover something new. This experience fosters confidence in their own sense of intellectual agency, enabling them to transfer and replicate that experience to other contexts, such as other investigative sites and eventually the communities in which they settle.

Further, connecting students to place puts them in closer proximity to the complex norms governing associative life. When guided by one or multiple disciplinary lenses, when mentored by experienced "readers" of these complex social texts, students come to identify the patterns and structures that facilitate and/or impede associative life. As we discuss below, by calling attention to the ways in which place is connected to associative life we help students identify both the seen and unseen structures that shape civil society, for good or ill. And once identified, such connections can become the subject of critical reflection, for example, reflection on how place plays a part in the success or failure of civic action. In doing so, we deliver on liberal education's promise, which is to develop engaged and effective citizen leaders capable of self-governance.

The power of place as a lever for education

The concept of leveraging place for pedagogical advantage is certainly not new. Place-based education has been a growing movement among education scholars, most notably in primary and secondary education (Ball and Lai 2006; Brooke 2003; Gibbs and Howley 2000; Graham 2007; Gruenewald 2002, 2003a, 2003b; Lieberman and Hoody 1998; Petts 2007; Smith 2002; Smith and Williams 1999; Theobald and Curtis 2002; Wiggenton 1985, 1991). Place-based education has also influenced higher education as service learning and community-based learning efforts within colleges and universities expand (Lewis 2004; Reardon 1995, 1997).

Embedded within the literature and practice of place-based education is a tension around what its primary purpose is. As Lewis (2004) points out, some place-based education scholars and practitioners argue that the primary purpose is pedagogical – that place offers the student opportunities for engaged and active learning that foster critical thinking, opportunities to develop and hone investigative skills, and so on. For others, particularly those working within the critical tradition of pedagogical theory such as Freire (1970) and hooks (1984), the place-based educator's primary role is to foster social change and community empowerment. Critical place-based pedagogy emphasizes the importance of identifying and challenging social structures that reinforce patterns of dominance and subordination within local communities.

Within this latter group are critics of education reform that promotes universal standards, testing, and accountability. Such efforts, critics charge, have removed the citizen's role in place-making from the public educational system (Gruenewald 2003a; Gibbs and Howley 2000).[1] According to Gruenewald (2003a: 620):

> Place-conscious education ... aims to work against the isolation of schooling's discourses and practices from the living world outside the increasingly placeless institution of schooling. Furthermore, it aims to enlist teachers and students in the firsthand experience of local life and in the political process of understanding and shaping what happens there.

Gruenewald and others advocate for place-based pedagogies because this is how young citizens learn to care for and adopt sustainable practices within their communities. If consistently employed, Gruenewald (2003a) argues, place-based education increases the likelihood that communities can engage in sustainable practices that preserve the richness and openness of the environmental, cultural, and local political context.

It is important to recognize that neither emphasis excludes the other. Approaches that lean toward honing the investigative skills of the student, for example, can also be oriented toward a service-related outcome, and pedagogies primarily focused on strengthening community can certainly and often do include a research component. That said, the particular position the instructor takes along this spectrum will shape the manner in which she frames the learning goals her students are expected to achieve. For example, the former might emphasize engagement with the academic literature and on research design, whereas the latter might favor engagement with a local community organization and program design. Just as importantly, the position the instructor takes along this spectrum will ready the gaze of the student in particular ways, and any particular gaze will carry with it both advantages and disadvantages.

Arguably, pedagogies that emphasize learning outcomes related to developing students' investigative skills have an advantage of developing general critical thinking skills that will extend beyond the local context. The potential downside of this approach is that communities take on the role of laboratory, with its members being positioned as research subjects. In a context where the college or university looms large in its size, economic and political power relative to the local population, such a gaze can feel, at the very least, tiresome over time, and at worst objectifying, i.e., community members come to feel like the rats in the researcher's maze.

Similarly, there are both potential benefits and pitfalls to approaches focused primarily on empowering community. At their best, these approaches allow faculty and student researchers to become engaged partners in the process of community development. We see this particularly in primary and secondary education efforts to connect students to place, as students are both learners and members of the local community. In practice, however, service activities have the potential to become ends in themselves, leaving behind the effort to advance critical thinking.

Critical pedagogies certainly ward against this danger, particularly when working with college-age student researchers. College students are by their very nature almost always transient outsiders. Given their age and their outsider status, and armed with a critical theoretical lens, they are more likely to be able to identify structures that impede some groups from contributing to and benefiting from civic life. This is a clear advantage when it comes to training students to see the unseen structures of place that shape associative life. But this approach can also be problematic. Equipped with the lens of critical theory, faculty and student investigators may view their role as dismantling structures that impede social justice. Yet community members may read actions aimed in this direction as patronizing attempts by outsiders to "fix" what is wrong with their community, making productive collaborative partnership less likely. The tension is exacerbated if the college–community relationship is marked by racial or socio-economic class differences, in which the local community sees faculty and student investigators as elite outsiders who are part of a problematic power dynamic that shapes their community.

In keeping with Lewis (2004: 97), the approach we describe below offers a "nuanced third path" in which faculty, students, and community members connect to place first by identifying assets within the community that can serve as vehicles for fostering intellectual agency, such as historical archives, publicly and privately held lands and waterways conducive to ecological study, and people within the community accustomed to working with student researchers. This connection to place sensitizes students that the place they are entering into has a story – the community is the way it is for multiple and complex reasons and that understanding at least some of these reasons is a necessary step before one can offer an effective social critique or propose a path for positive social change. No matter how well intended, any actions aimed toward social justice, ecological sustainability, and so on, will likely be misdirected absent this grounding.

One way to characterize this early stage of the process is that it is ambitious in terms of pedagogy but modest in terms of engagement with and impact on civic life – ambitious pedagogically as it is an arena in which the discoveries are not preordained and intellectual agency has an opportunity to unfold; modest in terms of community impact in that students simply have not yet learned enough. Ironically perhaps, it is in this sense that an investigative stance can be more respectful of community than an advocacy stance, in that the first aim is to understand.

As they progress through programmatic opportunities students earn increasing responsibilities in developing more complex research designs, guiding other students, and engaging with the community. As part of this approach, students learn and employ research practices that involve community members in ways that emphasize their humanity and their capacity to teach, for example, by inviting community members to share their stories. In line with the approach advanced by Reardon (1995, 1997), community members can become co-researchers identifying assets embedded within the community. And if social change is an element of the project, that change is driven from the inside, with community members shaping and driving those efforts as active participants in constructing the narrative, not as "social service clients" being acted upon by self-presumed experts (McKnight 1987; Kretzmann and McKnight 1993).

What follows are programs within two academic centers at Washington College that leverage place in a developmental fashion to foster the growth of intellectual agency and the intellectual habits conducive to citizen leadership and self-governance.

Illustrating the power of place

History, historical narrative, and place

Chestertown, Maryland, is a place where the past is very much present. A casual visitor – or a newly arrived first-year student at Washington College – sees streets lined with red-brick colonial mansions and turreted Victorian houses, as well as sailboats lying at anchor along the Chester River waterfront, once a bustling eighteenth-century port. The town's surrounding region of the Eastern Shore of Maryland can likewise seem like a land that time forgot: tiny crossroads villages nestle amid rolling cornfields, and ospreys nest along lazy tidal streams emptying into the Chesapeake Bay.

Yet those who notice only quaint houses and pretty landscapes miss most of the picture. A more complex and challenging history lies submerged, albeit often just barely submerged, beneath the landscape. An old building is a container of many lives, many generations, many stories. A rural hamlet might have been founded by newly emancipated African Americans or by seventeenth-century watermen. The fields and rivers, eternal though they may appear, have undergone vast transformation since the time – fairly recent in the scale of human history – when they were farmed and fished by Native Americans. In turn, understanding such social and ecological changes (or, in some cases, the lack thereof) provides deep background for addressing current problems: the persistence of race- and class-based inequality, for instance, or the continuing degradation of the natural environment.[2]

In 2000, largely in response to these rich historical surroundings, Washington College established the C. V. Starr Center for the Study of the American Experience, an interdisciplinary institute dedicated to exploring the nation's past and present through a variety of entry points: not just traditional history, but also art, literature, music, politics, and other fields. Headquartered in a circa-1746 riverfront building known as the Custom House, which once served as a maritime gateway to far-flung ports of call, the Starr Center too was conceived as a portal into the world beyond campus. It sponsors lectures, forums, exhibitions, and performances; hosts prominent authors as residential fellows; and places undergraduates in paid summer jobs at the Smithsonian, the National Archives, the Library of Congress, and other cultural institutions.[3]

But the Center's most distinctive asset has been its physical setting, which encourages a "boots-on-the-ground" approach to studying the past. Guided by faculty and staff, Washington College students venture beyond campus to dig through attics and courthouses in search of papers and artifacts; to explore and document buildings and landscapes; and to conduct oral-history interviews with local residents. Beyond simply the predictable result of making history seem more vivid, this approach lets students contribute valuable, original knowledge to local and regional conversations about the past – conversations that almost always end up touching present-day concerns as well. This new knowledge sometimes exposes inconvenient, and even controversial, truths.

Traditional historical scholarship often attempts to organize and simplify the past, seeking broad social, economic, or political patterns that explain the diverse experiences of millions of people. Place-centered history, on the other hand, complicates the past. Although limiting one's scope to an individual family, village, or farm might at first seem narrowing, it actually challenges students to unravel the tangled web of stories, relationships, contingencies, and motivations that make up human life as it is actually lived.

The Starr Center's approach to place-centered history is perhaps best illustrated by a seminar that the institute's director has taught at Washington College periodically since 2005. "Chestertown's America" examines America's past, from prehistory to recent times, through the lens of the town and its immediate surroundings. Although the course's temporal scope is broad, its syllabus is organized around a series of assignments (both individual and collaborative) that require participants to delve deeply into very specific historical moments and sites.

On the first day of class, students are taken on a surprise "mini-field trip" to three different sites as an introduction to the course's pedagogical method. To start with, they visit an eighteenth-century painting owned by Washington College that depicts the landscape of Chestertown and its environs, portrayed in great detail from the vantage point of an outlying plantation.[4] Spending about half an hour scrutinizing this single image, the students try to tease out every bit of information that the painting offers – inevitably coming to focus on a complicated vignette of enslaved African Americans in the picture's foreground. Next, they are led to two vans that take them to the nearby county courthouse. Here, they break up into small teams and examine early volumes of handwritten wills and estate inventories, seeking references to the human "property" owned by local masters – and then view an inventory from the estate depicted in the painting, executed in 1798 (just a few years after the artwork) and listing each enslaved person by name and dollar value. Finally, returning to the vans, they are driven to a nearby farm – which they soon realize is the plantation shown in the picture, its main house and surroundings little changed since the eighteenth century. Thus, in the span of two and a half hours, they have begun studying local history from a variety of vantage points: through visual art, archival documents, economic and legal history, and the built and natural environment. Moreover, they have begun to grasp the deep-rooted nature of race-based inequality in their own community, a point driven home when the vans return to campus through a neighborhood of low-income public housing occupied almost exclusively by African Americans.

Over the course of the semester, students in "Chestertown's America," relying solely on local resources, learn to interpret the architecture of a historic house, to mine information from back issues of newspapers, and to decipher and interpret eighteenth- and nineteenth-century manuscripts. In many cases, the sources that they are using and the stories that they are telling have been completely untouched by previous scholars – which also effectively prevents the students from relying on "Google research," compelling them instead to venture far afield in search of information. They are also given opportunities to share their work with a wider audience than just the instructor and classmates, and to produce research that has real value beyond the classroom and even beyond the confines of academia. In fact, each time that the course has been offered, it has led to discoveries that sparked public conversations at the local and regional – and in one instance, even national – level.

In 2005, for instance, students were assigned to unearth the true story of the Chestertown Tea Party, a 1774 incident in which, according to many secondary sources, local patriots hurled contraband tea into the Chester River. Since the mid-twentieth century, the occasion has been commemorated and reenacted at an annual festival presented as the community's flagship event of the year, rallying local pride, drawing thousands of tourists, and bringing considerable business to area merchants. But the undergraduates in "Chestertown's America" made a rather unwelcome discovery: There was no evidence that the supposed Revolutionary-era protest had actually occurred. Eighteenth-century sources did not mention it at all, and the earliest written reference was in an 1899 book presenting an unreliable, largely fanciful history of the town. When the students' findings were revealed in the press, considerable public debate ensued, raising questions that had no easy answers: How do we establish historical certainty? At what point does long-accepted myth take on significance – even a kind of truth – of its own? And should public interest trump scholarly accuracy (Vozella 2005; Wyatt 2005; Goodheart 2005)?

As it turned out, these questions were themselves incorporated into the local narrative. The festival's organizers produced a film investigating the controversy, a movie that has subsequently been screened during each year's celebration – thus giving the town a more nuanced and challenging awareness of its own past. The "Chestertown's America" students' findings have been referenced in several recent scholarly and popular books (Dudley 2010; Cummins 2012, Colbert 2012). And the sophomore who led the research later went to graduate school in history and is now a social studies teacher in New Jersey, where she reports using the same place-centered approach in her own lesson plans.[5]

Three years after the Tea Party controversy, a different cadre of "Chestertown's America" students were involved in another discovery, this time involving a trove of family papers found in the attic of an old plantation house on the Eastern Shore. Class members took the lead in investigating the documents, some 30,000 pages spanning the 1660s through the late twentieth century and including everything from slave records to Civil War letters. Their effort to rescue and conserve the collection, which was in imminent danger of being destroyed, drew widespread media coverage. It also led to a long-term partnership between the Starr Center and the Maryland State Archives, which now houses the collection. Washington College students have continued to work with the State Archives to digitize the papers and create finding aids, sharing their finds on a public blog (Blair 2008; Wyatt 2008).[6]

When the course was taught in 2013, class members helped with the creation of a new museum and cultural center in Chestertown. The Charles Sumner Post of the Grand Army of the Republic is one of just two African-American Civil War veterans' lodges surviving in the United States, and a local non-profit had secured funding to renovate the building and open it to the public. Working in pairs, students in "Chestertown's America" researched and wrote biographies of individual soldiers from the post for inclusion in the museum and publication online by the Maryland State Archives. The teams were given the names of their assigned soldiers ceremonially in the old building itself – which reinforced their sense of responsibility to the long-departed men who, despite the heavy burdens of poverty, racism, and wartime wounds, always carried themselves as heroes. Delving deep into nineteenth-century census records, newspapers, federal pension files, military rosters, regimental histories, slave lists, manumission papers, and land deeds, the students retrieved and reconstructed the life stories of people whose very existence had been largely forgotten. Initially doubtful that they could fill up even the required minimum of twelve pages, some of the students ended up turning in biographies thirty or forty pages long.[7]

This time, as with the Tea Party, some inconvenient truths came to light under the class's scrutiny. One of the soldiers, Oscar Crozier, a bugler in the legendary 54th Massachusetts (chronicled in the movie "Glory"), had been proudly held up as a local hero whose life story could be a centerpiece of the new museum and an inspiration for local schoolchildren. The student team researching Crozier discovered that shortly after his return from the Civil War, he served a prison sentence for knifing his lover in a drunken rage (Brown 2013; Mansbridge 2013). Post-traumatic stress? Cold-hearted murder? In any case, as the class wrestled with such questions, it became clear that the lives, deeds, and ordeals of actual "heroes" (whether past or present) do not often fit into neat heroic formulas, that scholarly investigation sometimes involves discoveries that are unwelcome or even ugly, and that even a subject as seemingly abstruse as a Civil War soldier's biography can draw the researcher into a complicated maze of moral reckonings.

In each of these three cases, the students' work had a real-world impact that would have been unlikely with more traditional assignments in a college history class, such as an essay about the causes of the Civil War or even a more general research paper about the experiences of African-American soldiers. A local focus requires the students to investigate previously untouched sources, to literally get their hands dirty working with dusty volumes of nineteenth-century records. It also demands that they interact with community members: conducting an oral history interview, persuading a courthouse clerk to retrieve documents, phoning the owner of an eighteenth-century house and asking permission to come over and look around. Beyond the strictly academic lessons to be learned, students develop a sense of agency, discovering their own ability to generate research and writing that is not just well executed, but also makes truly original contributions.

To assess the long-term impact of this approach, students who took the course in 2005, the first year it was offered, were asked to evaluate it from their present-day perspective. Some students report that they were impacted profoundly in that the experience helped to shape the course of their careers. Here, however, we emphasize the ways in which the course shaped what and how they learned.

Many former students reflected upon the tactile, hands-on nature of place-based pedagogies. As one former student observes, handling historical objects created a heightened sense of responsibility to get the history and people's stories within that history right:

> Perhaps the most powerful experience of the class, and really one of the most powerful experiences of my life, was when we went to the court-house in Chestertown and looked at the slave manumission papers. Reading them showed me more powerfully than any other book or document that historians have a huge responsibility to the subjects they study. These are people we're talking about, and historians have to get their stories right.[8]

Further, place-based pedagogy enabled this student to make a deeper connection. "Getting to know a place like we did inevitably leads us to invest in it. Chestertown wasn't just a place on the map anymore; it became one big question."

Many students also reflected on how the approach taken in the course gave them authority to "touch the past," to challenge the dominant narratives that had been passed down, and to develop intellectual agency:

> In studying the history of the town, I better understood the racial divisions that could be seen in where people lived, what they earned, where they worked. [The course taught] me that I could go out and touch the past, that it wasn't locked away in a book or a vault. It taught me that a historical marker is not the final authority on an event, but a starting point. It taught me about healthy skepticism as a necessary tool. I use it not only in writing a narrative history book that I will soon complete, but also in the daily television news writing I'm engaged in.[9]

Similarly, the course allowed students to "develop an appreciation for understanding the complexity of the place where [they] live" and in turn, "apply that knowledge to other communities and places." For this student, by delving into the particulars of place, "The past and present was no longer a line of disconnected events. Instead, my understanding of places, events (and now buildings and objects) changed to see things as an interconnected, complex, never ending, and fascinating cycle."[10]

Finally, responses from former students suggest that local histories help students put better-known national history into context:

I had been lucky enough to travel often with my family before starting college, but learning about how history affected the people of Chestertown was often more telling and connective than the historically grandiose tourist spots. For example, we had stood on the steps of the Lincoln Memorial, where Martin Luther King, Jr. gave his immortal speech. But when I learned about how the drugstore in Chestertown had removed its counter seats in the 1960s to prevent a sit-in from taking place – and saw the place in the store where the stools used to be – it conveyed the challenges that African Americans faced in ways that King's words could not.[11]

In addition to Chestertown's America, Washington College's Starr Center applies a place-based learning approach to many of its other programs as well. An ongoing oral-history project sends students out to document the diverse cultures of the Chesapeake region and the area's racial and civil rights history. Each year, a dozen newly arrived freshmen spend several days aboard a reconstructed eighteenth-century schooner on the Chester River, exploring the waterway and learning about its past and present. Students have helped produce a multimedia walking tour of the Chestertown waterfront, focusing on the paradoxes of slavery and freedom in the era of the American Revolution. They have created an exhibition on human trafficking that links the eighteenth-century African slave trade with current-day exploitation of sex workers and farm laborers in the region.

All of these programs are about learning to observe and interpret not just historical realities, but also the human experience in a broader sense. In certain respects, humanists can examine the past more easily than the present; although the passage of time erases some knowledge, it also reveals things unknown to the original actors. When students read the private diaries and memoirs of a male plantation owner, a female slaveholder, and an enslaved African–American who all lived near Chestertown in the 1820s, they gain knowledge and perspective that the writers themselves lacked. If, in the process, they also learn to strive for a multivalent understanding of the present-day world, they will surely become not only better scholars, but also better citizens.

The social and environmental ecology of place

Washington College made a conscious choice in naming its Center for the Environment and Society (CES) and defining its mission. As a small liberal arts college with no graduate programs in the environmental sciences, it would not compete with research centers at larger state institutions. Instead, it would leverage the natural strengths of the liberal arts by creating a center with a deliberate interdisciplinary mission. It would use not just natural science, but the humanities and social sciences to engage students in the critical problems facing our nation's largest estuary, the Chesapeake Bay. "The Bay" is perhaps the most intensively studied body of water on earth, but it remains deeply troubled, with water quality problems, expanding dead zones, and declining fisheries. Its problems are not so much problems of science, but "problems of people." Since its inception, the Center has been aimed at better under-standing the role of society in this equation, harnessing multiple disciplines to help solve seemingly intractable problems of this place.

In an estuary such as the Chesapeake, any serious environmental program must have one foot on the land and the other in the water, thus CES pro-grams range widely. CES manages two research vessels – a 46 ft. boat certi-fied by the U.S. Coast Guard and a 27 ft. boat that allows access to shallower water.[12] On land, CES operates the nearby Chester River Field Research Station (CRFRS) on the 5,000 acres of Chino Farms (all in conservation easements). The property has more than two miles of river frontage, an active farming operation (with conventional crops, organic farming, and precision agriculture), 240 acres of restored eastern coastal prairie, additional acreage in forest and restored oak and pine savanna, and a bird banding station.[13] The research vessels and the research field station provide rich opportunities for laboratory instruction, senior thesis research, and faculty–student colla-borative research. Further, CES provides approximately 90 internship and jobs to students each year, allowing students to work alongside professionals and community volunteers in habitat restoration, wildlife management, and research. Over the course of four years, students have the opportunity to increase their level of responsibility, ultimately supervising other students and managing projects by their senior year. Driven by the needs of local business, government, and non-profit partner organizations, many projects involve sig-nificant research with a defined scope of work, a budget, a timeline, and clear deliverables, allowing students to accrue experience in a professional setting.

As a model for engaged, liberal learning that leverages place as a means for fostering the habits of self-governance, the "Chesapeake Semester" deserves particular attention. This immersive curricular experience is structured to align with the mission of CES itself, recognizing the primary environmental challenge in the Chesapeake Bay (and many other estuaries) as a problem of how human social, economic, and political systems intersect with one another. The objective of the Chesapeake Semester is to help students recog-nize this complexity and to see interdisciplinary study as a powerful tool in understanding the nature and scope of environmental problems and in craft-ing workable solutions. This is achieved by combining class work with an intensive and far-reaching field component.

Launched in 2009, the program was partly a response to faculty desire to use our rich local resources for field study without the frustration of being constrained by the need to return to campus in time for other classes or extracurricular activities. Further, faculty desired greater opportunities for team teaching and interdisciplinary inquiry. The CES's solution was to design a four-course program that would constitute a student's entire academic load for the fall semester, freeing them from normal scheduling constraints. The program would also allow for interdisciplinary team teaching. With a course on the natural science of the estuary, a social science course, and a humanities course, the program encompasses each of the academic divisions of the college. The fourth course is an integration course, designed to break down the walls between disciplines, to integrate material from the other courses, and to show how multiple viewpoints enhance our understanding of issues. Each course has a faculty leader or coordinator, with 14–17 faculty members from different departments in each division taking on lectures, discussions, or labs.

An explicit objective of the Chesapeake Semester is to get students out of the classroom and to range widely around the watershed, meeting the people and seeing the places of the Chesapeake. The strategy is to alternate periods of intensive classroom work with themed "journeys," taking the program on the road for more than eight weeks throughout the 16-week term. This schedule allows concentrated preparation for the field experiences, followed by time to debrief and absorb the experience before moving to new topics.

Over the course of the semester, the curriculum follows a carefully designed trajectory: an orientation week; two weeks in class becoming familiar with the program requirements and preparing for the 12-day Journey 1 (History and Sense of Place); a week and a half in class; the ecology themed, 11-day Journey 2 (Mountains to Ocean); another week and a half in the classroom; a two-week Journey 3 (Comparative Experience in Peru); a week in class; Journey 4 (Fisheries, Agriculture, and Development Pressure), which is a series of short trips designed to explore critical public policy issues; and finally two weeks of discussion, reflection, and work on final projects. We describe the orientation week and Journey 1 at some length as they demonstrate the pedagogy we use throughout the term that integrates lessons of place and civic life.

The orientation week is designed with two critical objectives. The first is to create an intensive experience in which students get to know one another and the core faculty and staff, breaking down barriers and fostering a team approach to the semester. The second goal is to start an intensive immersion into "place." We begin with two days at the Chesapeake Bay Maritime Museum, an important partner in the program, with a knowledgeable staff with access to critical cultural resources. Students explore museum exhibits with curators, building an overall sense of the Chesapeake Bay and its distinctive cultures. They eat at a local crab house with several watermen (the local term for fishers). They then rise at 5:30 a.m., setting off with two local watermen, "trot-lining" for blue crabs. This gets the students used to a demanding schedule from the beginning. Later that day, they explore vernacular watercraft, go behind the scenes in the museum collections, and sail with Captain Wade Murphy on the *Rebecca Ruark*, one of the few remaining skipjacks on the Chesapeake Bay.[14] "Capt. Wadey" is a true waterman, one of the last great skipjack captains. Garrulous, opinionated, and a natural comedian, Capt. Wadey has turned to tourism to make a living in the face of declining oyster stocks. By book-ending this day with two experiences on the water, the first with crabbers who are still trying to make a living from the fishery, and the second with Capt. Wadey, who has turned to an alternative and is not shy about sharing his opinions, the students are able to put a human face on an iconic element of the estuary's population – the watermen.

Over the first 48 hours of orientation, students get the clear sense that this is not the normal semester, and the barriers begin to break down. The third day capitalizes on this by taking the students to an outdoor school for team building exercises and climbing low and high ropes courses. The aim here is to build a sense of team cohesion and interdependence, while pushing indivi-duals out of their comfort zone (a recurring theme throughout the semester).

The remainder of the week zeroes in on a feature of Chestertown that the students *think* they know: the Chester River. In kayaks, we explore the upper reaches of the Chester – shallow, narrow, with a gravel bottom and clear water that is quite unlike the mud bottom and brown water with which the students are familiar. Their path takes them past dense stands of wild rice and arrow arum, plant foods used by wildlife and Native Americans, and they kayak through arched bowers of trees before emerging into wider stretches of river flanked by farm fields. The next day, the team canoes the middle stretch of the river, from Chestertown to about seven miles downstream, fishing and exploring geology along the way. In early afternoon, they transfer to the skipjack *Elsworth* and the *Annie D.*, a buy boat (designed to buy the catch from watermen while they were on the fishing grounds and take it back to market, extending the boat's time in the fishery). These vessels take them farther downstream, toward the mouth of the river where they anchor for the night. As night falls, sleeping bags are laid out on the deck.

By 7:30 the next morning, the group is headed to meet another waterman, pound-netter Dickie Manning, Jr. Pound nets divert fish swimming along the shore into an enclosure, or pound, lined with a net. Working from a small boat, the pound-netter draws in the net, like closing a purse, and the water shimmers with a seemingly inexhaustible supply of fish, crabs, and other wildlife. But it is hard work, from driving the stakes that hold the nets, to pulling in on the net, dipping out the fish, and culling the catch. It is made more difficult when an engine dies or gear breaks, and it brings students closer to the razor's edge profit margin that is the waterman's reality. A small portion of Manning's catch usually goes into our boats, supplementing the students' catch for consumption on the *Elsworth* and *Annie D.* as they motor back to Chestertown later in the day.

While onboard the skipjack *Elsworth*, students meet Capt. Andy McCown, an educator and raconteur extraordinaire who also has worked in the fisheries. Capt. McCown reads poetry and short stories about the Chester and the Chesapeake Bay, such as Gilbert Byron's "These Chesapeake Men" (Byron 1942: 19), introducing us to the people who make their living on the waters of the Che-sapeake, to their boats and their quarry, the natural resources of the estuary. The readings remind us to see, to hear, to feel, and in opening up our senses, open up some deeper part of our consciousness in appreciation. Byron's (1942: 23) "My People" reinforces the notion that we should not be satisfied with seeing the exterior of people in this region, but probe deeper so that we might see beneath the "mahogany faces" of people who are "barnacled and rough" to "find them tender as the peeler crab, as soft and sweet as the oysters they shuck, a hard shell their only protection, from a world gone mad."[15] This mix of literature, history, place, and the natural world is compelling, particularly when experienced on the deck of boat in a secluded cove, rather than a classroom.

These readings are among the first of many experiences of deep "listening" in which students are challenged to dive below the surface of what is easily seen to what is hidden from the casual observer's view. In doing so, students come to see that the issues they encounter involve real people, not abstractions. Over the course the semester, we teach techniques of the ethnographic interview – another form of deep listening – emphasizing that a seemingly common language can disguise very different cultures. Throughout the semester, students complete what Annie Dillard (1974) describes as "stalking assignments," developing in the student awareness of what is happening both externally as well as internally with self-directed observations. In listening and observing, we talk about the necessity of openness and the desirability of leaving opinion and preconception behind whenever possible. This openness to new ideas and different viewpoints comes through to our many contacts and informants. Like most people, they want to be heard, and this approach builds trust and develops social capital (Flora and Flora 1996) for our students and our program.

Journey 1, History and Sense of Place, further develops the physical and cultural stage for the semester. Students embark on a clockwise circuit of the Bay, moving forward in time as they travel around the estuary. The deeper history – or prehistory – starts with Bay formation and the arrival of people on the continent and to the region. Earlier subsistence modes such as hunting and gathering are given immediacy as students camp, roaming the woods and foraging for food with an experimental archaeologist. Dinner is venison and plants gathered from the woods. Teamwork puts food on the table. The circuit runs down the Delmarva Peninsula to the mouth of the Bay. The route follows the high ground, running along the divides between watersheds, replicating ancient Indian trails, another reminder of the lasting importance of geography. On the other side of the Chesapeake, much of our route follows I-95 and the Fall Line, a line of erosion-resistant rock that divides the coastal plain from the piedmont. As the upstream limit of tidal waters, the Fall Line also was the head of navigation for ocean-going ships, and these trans-shipment points became natural locations for towns (e.g., Richmond, Washington, Baltimore).

Although it is difficult to compress the rich experiences and discussions of a two-week exploration, some highlights and themes are particularly relevant to the nexus of place, learning, and civic engagement. Our physical journey follows a timeline, moving from the seventeenth century in the Tidewater. Jamestown and Williamsburg inspire discussions of freedom (its meaning and its uneven application), of the powerful interplay between culture and environment, and of how English customs and traditions were transformed by conditions in the New World. We move into the late eighteenth century as we enter Annapolis with its baroque town plan revealing hidden messages in the urban landscape. We explore Miller's (1988) reading of the town plan as a political statement linking church and state in an effort to re-establish crown control of the province after more than half a century of governance by the religiously tolerant Calvert family. This provides students with a template for examining other landscapes for clues to power relationships. Baltimore's port, canals, and railroads move us to the nineteenth- and twentieth-century Industrial Age, enabling us to explore the linkages between seemingly unrelated technologies and the human environmental footprint. Through the colonial period, for example, fisheries were restricted to local markets due to the perishability of the food. As steam power exploded onto the scene, shipment times decreased, while food preservation technologies (canning and refrigeration) improved. Within a short period, the catch from the Chesapeake Bay was within range of burgeoning populations in the Midwest via railroads and of distant ports by steamboat. Exponentially expanding markets led watermen to adopt ever more efficient extraction technologies (power dredges, purse seines, etc.) to meet the demand – and over-fishing was one result. Oyster harvests went from a peak of 20 million bushels in the 1880s to less than 200,000 bushels by the end of the twentieth century. A similar relationship between transportation, food preservation technologies, and increasingly efficient extraction can be seen in agriculture, and has left its mark in today's larger field sizes, the loss of hedgerows, and monocultures of grain. These revelations set the stage for conversations later in the semester about common property resources, natural resource regulation, and the tensions between individual rights and governance issues related to common pool resources.

We have gone into some detail on the Orientation and Journey 1 itineraries because they set the stage for and model much of what happens over the course of the semester. The Orientation makes clear our expectation of early mornings and long days. We let students establish the rules of engagement with the course and one another. Invariably, they create a compact that is more stringent than what we might have tried to impose on them as faculty. The places we visit during the Orientation and Journey 1 frame a general context for our study of the estuary, introduce a wide variety of teachers (curators, educators, and watermen) and underscore the point that history is a potent and active force in our contemporary human and ecological communities.

An inherent tension exists in pedagogies of place – a tension between a pace that is at once deliberately slow (relative to the customary classroom lecture) and one that is deliberately compressed and catalyzed in its immersive intensity. As Yi-Fu Tuan (1977: 183) observes, it takes time to know a place. Though:

> abstract knowledge *about* a place can be acquired in short order if one is diligent ... the "feel" of a place takes longer to acquire. It is made up of experience, mostly fleeting and undramatic, repeated day after day and over the span of years.

Taking Tuan's point seriously, we intentionally slow down by stretching out the teaching and exploration across the entirety of the day, trusting that unscripted conversations can have greater impact than the well-rehearsed lecture. At the same time, a pedagogy of place accelerates the process by which students move from *knowing about* a place and gaining a *sense of place* that moves beyond the abstract and superficial.

The place-based pedagogy established in the Orientation and Journey 1 also establishes what Westerberg and Wickersham[16] refer to as a "learning stance" – an openness to the possibility that they may have their mind changed; an openness to recognizing that "teachers" can come from unexpected places and in a dizzying variety. The learning stance is particularly important as we continue through the remaining field studies, meet with increasing diversity in terms of culture, perspectives, and interests, and grapple with complex and often polarizing public policy issues.

For example, Journey 2 (Mountains to Ocean)[17] emphasizes the ecological effects of climate change on isolated island communities like that on Smith Island, which is accessible only by boat.[18] The island is home to a dwindling population of just over 300 people, almost all of whom make their living on the water. Although the islanders debate the reasons (most are skeptics when it comes to climate change), Smith Island has lost over 3,300 acres to erosion or sea level rise in the last 150 years, more than half of its area. They are close to the water in ways more than physical; as one waterman put it, "the Bay is our provider, protector, jailer and tormentor" (Lutz 2006). Questions of community resilience and sustainability, climate change, cultural survival, resource management, economics, and equity abound in this place. The intersections of culture and environment are rendered more complex as we journey to Peru for the comparative field experience. Here we examine creative community-based solutions to over-fishing and sustainable agriculture.

The final journey focuses explicitly on environmental policy issues facing the Chesapeake, examining the competing interests involved in regulating fisheries, agriculture, and development. The first step in approaching each issue is to meet members of the various constituencies, including watermen in the "wild" fisheries, seafood buyers, laborers in a crab-picking house (many of whom are migrant workers from Mexico), researchers at the University of Maryland's Horn Point marine laboratories, aquaculture companies, policy makers, and regulatory personnel in government.

The various actors do not see eye to eye, and they raise thorny issues about common resources, individual vs. group rights, access, the role of capital in fisheries, and the potential loss of traditional culture. These diverse perspectives set the stage for discussions about Hardin's (1968) "tragedy of the commons," and alternative schools of thought for how to avert it, from increased government regulation, to private ownership and leasing of water resources, to self-governance models of collective management (Hardin 1968; Demsetz 1967; Smith 1981; Berkes 1989; Ostrom 1990; Wilson *et al.* 2007).

Similarly, so that students understand agricultural issues from a variety of vantage points, we visit farms of various sizes, from a large, "24/7" dairy operation with a heavy reliance on automation to a small, grass-fed dairy that also produces grass-fed beef. We visit large-scale grain farms (ubiquitous on the Eastern Shore) that support Delmarva poultry producers, as well as small organic farms. And we focus on the poultry industry itself. With its confined lots and heavy production of nutrient-rich litter, the industry is under fire from many environmentalists. In the morning, students may meet with Jim Perdue, owner of one of the major poultry integrators. That afternoon, they meet with two brothers who manage a family-run poultry farm. They go inside the "chicken houses," see how manure is managed, and review the paper trail documenting nutrient management that is required by government regulation. The next day they meet with the director of a law clinic that is suing Perdue and a family poultry farm for nutrient pollution.

Its important to note that each person or group we meet is likeable and convincing. This pattern serves two valuable pedagogical functions. First, the fact that the characters we encounter are likeable and convincing forces students to avoid shortcuts around critical thinking (e.g., "I don't have to listen to him because he's a poultry farmer who doesn't care about the environment") and instead helps them maintain the "learning stance" (e.g., "Perhaps I can learn something from him even though I don't agree with his viewpoint"). Second, the fact that the characters we encounter are likeable and convincing forces students to develop the intellectual agency they require to sort it all out – to draw independent conclusions that are informed by theory, empirical research, and deep listening.

Conclusion

We argue above that liberal learning fosters, among other things, the intellectual habits conducive to self-governance. In particular, we argue that a liberally educated person is one who has the intellectual agency to "read" civil society as an open text – its conclusions not set or preordained. We argue that the liberally educated person is someone who is trained to recognize both the seen and unseen structures that shape civil society, and as a consequence of these intellectual habits, can identify ways of engaging in effective civic action.

In this chapter we explore the ways in which place-based pedagogy serves these ends of liberal learning. By inviting students into inherently complex place-based contexts, students have the opportunity to encounter, for example, inconvenient historical truths that require them to sharpen their investigative skills, see beyond the dominant narrative, exercise critical judgment, and communicate their findings to a potentially reluctant public. Place-based pedagogy intentionally complicates the investigative terrain, requiring students to develop their intellectual agency by calling upon multiple disciplines to address the intersections between ecological, historical, political, cultural, and economic forces that shape the local environment.

In addition to cultivating the skills of critical listening, reading, and thinking, place-based pedagogy also develops the skills of *sympathetic* listening, such that students adapt their learning stance in ways that leave them open to learning from diverse and unlikely "teachers" within the community. Cumulatively, it is these dimensions of place-based pedagogy that leave students better equipped to practice the art of association.

Notes

1 For an alternative perspective arguing that state educational standards can be consistent with the goals and principles of place-based education, see Jennings *et al.* (2005).
2 As early as the 1750s, Washington College's founder recognized the role of historical awareness in forming social consciousness. "The study of history," William Smith wrote, "teaches [youth], as citizens of the world, to do impartial justice to the virtues of every people and nation" (Smith 1803: 220–221).
3 For more about the Starr Center and some of its place-based programs, see Skinner (2012).
4 *A View of Chestertown from White House Farm*, oil on panel, circa 1795, collection of Washington College. Image online at www.washcoll.edu/centers/starr/revcollege/firstcollege/birthofwc.html (accessed 31 December 2013).
5 Erin Koster, email communication, 2 January 2014.
6 Similar stories about the documents appeared in dozens of newspapers, from the *Boston Globe* to the *Bangkok Post*.
7 The biographies are online via the Maryland State Archives at http://slavery.msa.maryland.gov/html/casestudies/usct_ktcs.html (accessed 10 January 2014).
8 Email communication, 30 December 2013. This student, who asked to remain anonymous, is now a professional historian.
9 Email communication from Jack Bohrer, 27 December 2013. Bohrer is now a journalist and is at work on his first book.
10 Email communication from Amy Uebel, 5 January 2014. Uebel is an artifact conservator and college instructor.
11 Email communication from Kaity Bergert, 9 January 2014. Bergert recently completed graduate study in the history of decorative arts.
12 The research vessels are equipped with sidescan sonar, marine magnetometers, and acoustic seabed classification systems.
13 Two Center staff work as full-time field ecologists at CRFRS, and CES coordinates the research of a variety of external partners from universities and state and federal agencies.
14 A regional icon, skipjacks were designed at the end of the nineteenth century for oyster dredging, in response to local environmental conditions and the constraints of shrinking wood supplies and declining boat-building skills.
15 That Gilbert Byron was once a Washington College student himself and a native of Chestertown provides the students with a tangible link to the writer, as well as the place.
16 See Westerberg and Wickersham's contribution to this volume (Chapter 4).
17 Journey 2 follows the water from the Appalachians and the Susquehanna drainage into the Bay, and then takes students across the Delmarva to the coastal islands of the Atlantic.

18 The bulk of the residents are of English origin, many from families like the Evanses and Tylers, who arrived in the 1600s. Their remoteness over several centuries has given them a unique culture, from their manner of speaking to their reliance upon community and a brand of Methodism that arrived in the early 1800s.

References

Ball, L. B. and Lai, A. (2006) "Place-based pedagogy for the arts and humanities," *Pedagogy*, 6(2): 261–287.

Berkes, F. (ed.) (1989) *Common Resources: Ecology and community based sustainable development*, London: Belhaven Press.

Blair, E. (2008) "In a crumbling house, a trove of everyday history," *All Things Considered*, National Public Radio, 3 July. www.npr.org/templates/story/story.php?storyId=92190792 (accessed 16 January 2014).

Brooke, R. (2003) *Rural Voices: Place-conscious education and the teaching of writing*, New York: Teachers College Press.

Brown, R. (2013) "Oscar James Crozier: Veteran, convict, family man, human," http://msa.maryland.gov/megafile/msa/speccol/sc5400/sc5496/051700/051755/images/oscar_crozier_by_rachel_brown.pdf (accessed 16 January 2014).

Byron, G. (1942) *These Chesapeake Men*, North Montpelier, VT: Driftwood Press.

Chamlee-Wright, E. (2011) "Operationalizing the interpretive turn: Deploying qualitative methods towards an economics of meaning," *Review of Austrian Economics* 24: 157–170.

Colbert, J. (2012) *It Happened in Maryland*, Guilford, CT: Globe Pequot.

Cummins, J. (2012) *Ten Tea Parties: Patriotic protests that history forgot*, Philadelphia, PA: Quirk Books.

Demsetz, H. (1967) "Toward a theory of property rights," *American Economic Review*, 52(2): 347–379.

Dillard, A. (1974) *Pilgrim at Tinker Creek*, New York: Harper's Magazine Press.

Dudley, W. S. (2010) *Maritime Maryland: A history*, Baltimore, MD: Johns Hopkins University Press.

Flora, C. B. and Flora, J. L. (1996) "Creating social capital," in W. Vitek and W. Jackson (eds) *Rooted in the Land: Essays on community and place*, New Haven, CT: Yale University Press.

Freire, P. (1970) *Pedagogy of the Oppressed*, New York: Continuum.

Gadamer, H. G. (1975) *Truth and Method*, G. Barden and J. Cumming (trans. and eds) New York: Seabury Press.

Gibbs, R. J. and Howley, A. (2000) "World class standards and local pedagogies: Can we do both?" *ERIC Digest*, no. ED 448014.

Goodheart, A. (2005) "Tea and fantasy: Fact, fiction, and revolution in a historic American town," *The American Scholar*, 74(4): 21–34.

Goodheart, A. (2012) The Birth of Washington College, http://revcollege.washcoll.edu/firstcollege/birthofwc.html (accessed 24 June 2012).

Graham, M. (2007) "Art, ecology, and art education: Locating art education in a critical place-based pedagogy," *Studies in Art Education*, 48(4): 375–391.

Gruenewald, D. (2002) "Teaching and learning with Thoreau: Honoring critique experimentation, wholeness, and the places where we live," *Harvard Educational Review*, 72(4): 514–541.

Gruenewald, D. (2003a) "Foundations of place: A multidisciplinary framework for place-conscious education," *American Educational Research Journal*, 40(3): 619–654.
Gruenewald, D. (2003b) "The best of both worlds: A critical pedagogy of place," *Educational Researcher*, 32: 3–12
Hardin, G. (1968) "The tragedy of the commons," *Science*, 162: 1243–1248.
hooks, b. (1984) *Feminist Theory: From margin to center*, Boston, MA: South End Press.
Jennings, N., Swidler, S., and Koliba, C. (2005) "Place based education in the standards based reform era: Conflict or complement?" *American Journal of Education*, 112: 44–56.
Kretzmann, J. and McKnight, J. (1993) *Building Communities from the Inside Out*, Chicago, IL: ACTA Publications.
Lewis, T. (2004) "Service learning for social change? Lessons from a liberal arts college," *Teaching Sociology*, 32: 94–108.
Lieberman, G. and Hoody, L. (1998) *Closing the Achievement Gap: Using the environment as an integrated context for learning*, Poway, CA: Science Wizards.
Lutz, L. (2006) "Life on Smith Island," *Bay Journal*, online version, www.bayjournal.com/article/life_on_smith_island_ebbs_and_flows_to_a rhythm_all_its_own (accessed 6 December 2013).
Mansbridge, J. (2013) "The Boogie Woogie Bugle Boy of Company B," http://msa.maryland.gov/megafile/msa/speccol/sc5400/sc5496/051700/051755/images/oscar_j_crosier_esq_by_jamie_mansbridge.pdf (accessed 16 January 2014).
McCoy, D. (1982) *The Elusive Republic: Political economy in Jeffersonian America*, New York: W.W. Norton.
McKnight, J. (1987) "Regenerating community," *Social Policy*, 17: 54–58.
Miller, H. (1988) "Baroque cities in the wilderness: Archaeology and urban development in the Chesapeake," *Historical Archaeology*, 22(2): 57–73.
Ostrom, E. (1990) *Governing the Commons: The evolution of institutions for collective action*, Cambridge: Cambridge University Press.
Petts, J. (2007) "Learning about learning: Lessons from public engagement and deliberation on urban river restoration," *The Geographic Journal*, 173(4): 300–311.
Reardon, K. (1995) "Creating a community/university partnership that works," *Metropolitan Universities*, 5: 47–60.
Reardon, K. (1997) "Participatory action research and the real community-based planning in East St. Louis, Illinois," in P. Nyden, A. Figert, M. Shibley, and D. Burrows (eds) *Building Community: Social science in action*, Thousand Oaks, CA: Pine Forge Press, pp. 233–239.
Skinner, D. (2012) "Majoring in history: A visit to Chestertown, Maryland," *Humanities*, 34(3): www.neh.gov/humanities/2013/mayjune/feature/majoring-in-history.
Smith, G. (2002) "Place based education: Learning to be where we are," *Kappan*, 83 (8): 584–595.
Smith, G. and Williams, D. (1999) *Ecological Education in Action: On weaving education, culture, and environment*, Albany, NY: SUNY Press.
Smith, R. J. (1981) "Resolving the tragedy of the commons by creating private property rights in wildlife," *CATO Journal*, 1(2): 439–468.
Smith, W. (1784) *An Account of Washington College, in the State of Maryland*. Philadelphia.
Smith, W. (1803) *The Works of William Smith, D.D.*, Philadelphia: Hugh Maxwell and William Fry.

Theobald, P. and Curtiss, J. (2002) "Communities as curricula," *Forum for Applied Research and Public Policy*, 15(1): 106–112.

Tuan, Y. (1977) *Space and Place: The perspective of experience*, Minneapolis: University of Minnesota Press.

Vozella, L. (2005) "Not about to bag the Tea Party," *Baltimore Sun*, 23 November.

Wiggenton, E. (1985) *Sometimes a Shining Moment: The Foxfire experience*, Garden City, NY: Anchor Press/Doubleday.

Wiggenton, E. (ed.) (1991) *Foxfire: 25 Years*, New York: Doubleday.

Wilson, J., Yan, L., and Wilson, C. (2007) "The precursors of governance in the Maine lobster fishery," *Proceedings of the National Academy of Sciences*, 104: 15212–15217.

Wyatt, K. (2005) "Say it ain't so: Chestertown's famed Tea Party may be figment of imagination," *Star-Democrat*, 18 December.

Wyatt, K. (2008) "Maryland plantation attic holds 400 years of documents," *Washington Post*, 22 June.

Part III

The generative power of social abrasion and social spaces

6 The essential role of abrasion in developing healthy institutions of liberal learning

Heather Wood Ion

Social learning through abrasion

How can we, as educators, establish the conversations that inspire and equip our students to become contributors to a community of truth and to recognize themselves as agents of discovery and cooperation?

In the small town of my childhood, school students knew that their grades were published in the local paper for all to see. Often teachers were encountered in many different contexts outside the classroom. There was no escape from the neighbor's watchfulness, or the scoutmaster's admonitions. When I entered a huge, urban university thousands of miles from that town, I anticipated anonymity and freedom from constant involvement of every adult in every child's life. When the results of the first exams in freshman year were posted – with names – on the bulletin board, and people in the dining hall commented on my grades that evening, I recognized how wrong my expectations were.

During those undergraduate years, I learned that there is constant negotiation between our private and public lives and roles, and that this negotiation was supported by a vigilant faculty who were eager and determined to help us become "citizens of the world." For them that meant that we would work against wars they had known, discrimination they had suffered, and deprivations they had endured. Further, we would do so thoughtfully, reflectively, as the bearers of the traditions they hallowed. Above all, those teachers, who had emerged from the Depression and from World War II, wanted us to eschew the trivial and the immediately satisfying and instead explore the questions of what it means to be human and what it means to take responsibility for our lives. For them, as for many faculty today, teaching was a profoundly moral calling, with constant demands for responsibility and engagement.

Of course many realities of higher education are quite different today. The Family Educational Rights and Privacy Act (FERPA), for example, no longer allows for public notice of academic performance, no doubt to the great relief of those who seek the anonymity I had hoped to find during my university days. And yet, the privatizing of academic information has likely contributed to the sense that there is no essential link between our private and public lives and roles.

Further, the contemporary emphasis on institutional assessment has fundamentally changed the landscape of higher education. Some of the impulses driving the "assessment movement" are understandable, with calls for greater institutional accountability for student retention, persistence to graduation, and attention to the financial challenges of acquiring a college or university education. But good intentions have often been derailed as the assessment industry has taken on a life of its own. The basic prevailing assumption seems to be that the purpose of a liberal education is to get the student a job. The purpose of curricula, as Bill Gates admonished, is to address the needs of business (Parry *et al.* 2013). Rankings of colleges and universities are based upon costs – both of tuition and of faculty salaries – institutions having the highest costs are ranked above those with lower costs. The emphasis seems to be on resource pressures and the "inputs" to the system, even though mass production systems are not the traditional, or cultural model of education (Bennett 2001).

Stressing quantifiable outcomes and supposed measures of efficacy, the arid vocabulary of the assessment movement portrays a college education as having little to do with the humanistic tradition of learning for its own sake, or for the pleasure of welding imagination and experience, so as to better contribute to one's own culture (Palmer and Zajonec 2010: 57). Nor do these foci develop students committed to constant, disciplined learning. For most liberal arts graduates, what is most striking in this current work on assessments, is the application of numeric, and often, economic models of measurement and return on investment. Einstein's question "Can What Counts be Counted?" seems more than usually pertinent.

Further and most important for a volume dedicated to understanding the role of liberal learning in fostering the art of self-governance, rarely does this work on assessment and outcomes explore the associational life of the student and its role in the ecology of learning.[1] Much of what is learned in college is learned by association or proximity, and is often not due to the conscious design or intention of the faculty, or even the student. The social learning that takes place informally during these years is every bit as important as the content, subject, or skill acquired by the requirements. By "social learning" I am referring to the phenomenon by which individuals and groups observe the behaviors of others and in consequence modify their own behavior. The social learning that takes place within the context of an intellectual community has a particular quality, as it takes place through shared curiosity, shared purpose, or shared activities. We know from various longitudinal studies that peer groups significantly influence intellectual and personal development, and especially the formation of social identity (Para 2008). Only a fraction of time in college is spent in the classroom or with tutors.[2] The majority of students spend their time with other students. Some of this time is directly related to academics, but some is intentional participation in a chosen activity (sports) or a chosen group (fraternities and sororities). Unstructured social engagement may be no less important to student life.[3] All forms of social learning involve interaction with others, and frequently that interaction is revelatory of unsuspected talents and unexplored attitudes. We owe it to our students to know where, when, and how they learn, as well as what they are told to learn.

When parents send their sons and daughters to college, they often express hope that they will acquire polish, that other student's love of learning will "rub off," that "rough edges" will be smoothed. This is social abrasion, the subject of this chapter. Abrasion is the scraping away by friction, when separate entities come in contact with each other. In our material world we use abrasion to make things appear or function more to our liking. We prevent abrasion by lubricants if we do not want its effect. We attempt to control it in nature by dams that divert water or by installing instruments that warn us of movement. In human relations we most often judge abrasion as unwanted, possibly painful, as destructive rather than constructive, even as we value its consequences. In American society we place a high value on competition, which is intentional conflict, often limited in scope, and on specialization that uses abrasion to achieve precision and focus. While we may use words such as "destroy" and "crush" when talking of competition, we also use words such as "refine" and "improve" when speaking of the specialization and collaboration that happens within it. Social abrasion takes place through mutual association and mutual exploration. We hone our skills, sharpen our thinking, and polish our presentations.

Karl Popper wrote that scientific knowledge was achieved through conjecture and refutation, thus the testability or verifiability of science is another form of abrasion. Perhaps the most obvious institution, dependent on positive or social abrasion, is Her Majesty's Loyal Opposition, the minority parties in the British parliamentary system, which are bound by the same loyalties to the democratic process as the governing party, but whose responsibility is to contest proposals and contribute constructive comment on policies. The Opposition members abrade the majority's platform through criticism and comment, but only rarely interrupt the process of governance itself by bringing about a vote of no confidence. Constructivist learning theories also rely on abrasion: Mistakes are learning opportunities, and what the student knows is abraded by experience, problem-solving, and the integration of feedback.

John Holt, writing of childhood learning, described three kinds of discipline:

- The discipline of Nature – if one block is not exactly on top of another, her tower will fall; if he closes his eyes when he swings, he does not hit the ball.
- The discipline of Superior Force – if she plays in the street, she may be hit by a car, if he hurts the dog, he will be punished.
- The discipline of Culture, or what people really do – a child senses the network of agreements, customs, habits, and rules that bind the adults around them together, and strives to imitate all these ways of being; toddlers are quiet in church when the adults are quiet.

(Holt 1972: 100–114)

In this chapter I am interested in what Holt calls the discipline of culture; as we consider the informal and formal norms and structures that transform an individual into a social being. We ask what happens when the environment changes and with it the network of agreements, customs, habits, and rules. This is the dynamic that ensues when a person comes to college. How does adaptation to such change impact learning? How can institutions support the ecology of learning in which the abrasion created in the confrontation with new ideas, customs, habits, and rules is constructive, and contributes to the development of a responsible and civil social identity?

Associational life in liberal education

To better understand the role of abrasion, we must first explore what we understand about associational life and learning. From the 1919 report *Voluntary Organizations and Adult Education* (1919 Report, Ministry of Reconstruction 1919) to the present, the educative power of associations has been understood regarding *informal* education, but very little attention has been paid to this educative power within the institutions of formal learning (Smith 2012). Much of the work on informal association derives from Tocqueville who stressed the influences of local institutions in teaching skills of shared learning and shared choice for common purposes. Mary Parker Follett (1998) stressed that early on the center of our consciousness is transferred from our private life to our associative life. She argued that gatherings in community brought forth the needs, desires, and aspirations of the partici-pants in ways that lead to taking personal responsibility for communal life. From John Dewey ([1938] 1997) forward, researchers have stressed the necessity of communal or associational participation for moral development. A college or university, particularly one that encourages students to spend some time in residence, is such a local environment.

Colleges describe themselves as chosen communities, requiring commitment from participants. Community aspirations and service to that community are distinct from institutional needs.

From Pomona College in California:

> Throughout its history, Pomona College has educated men and women of exceptional promise. We gather students, regardless of financial circum-stances, into a small residential community that is strongly rooted in Southern California yet global in its orientation. Through close ties among a diverse group of faculty, staff and classmates, Pomona students are inspired to engage in the probing inquiry and creative learning that enable them to identify and address their intellectual passions. This experience will continue to guide their contributions as the next genera-tion of leaders, scholars, artists and citizens to fulfill the vision of its founders: to bear their added riches in trust for all.

Bishop's University states, "We value the opportunity to learn from and with each other, in our classrooms, laboratories, libraries, theatres, residences, dining and sports facilities, as well as in the broader community." What is stated implies recognition that learning by members of the community, in association with each other, takes precedence over the intentional or formal transfer of knowledge by designated experts. The institution is structured to serve the moral purpose of this community. Pomona's phrase "to bear their added riches in trust for all," for example, expresses a goal that graduates will feel that they serve the commonweal.

How then do these institutions socialize students to these modes of thought and values? How are the private identities and values of a diverse incoming student body connected to the associational values articulated here? How does the experience of this socialization to the values of liberal arts colleges impact the social identities of graduates over time? What role does abrasion play as incoming students are polished and honed by their college experience?

Associational life begins as an infant begins to acquire skills, beliefs, and habits of relationship. Socialization has been extensively studied, so it is only necessary to remind ourselves that this is a process of learning. Language acquisition and conversation have been called a "negotiation of meaning." We know that language is itself an associational activity. Childhood play helps us learn that we are actors capable of mastery. The various contexts of our activities – family, day care, school, church, community – support our experiments with identity. We have many opportunities as children to engage with others in ways that help us discover who we are and who we wish to become. We watch, we imitate, we adapt, we reflect, and we experiment. Our families or our schools may pressure us, early, to choose an identity – "what do you want to be when you grow up?" – but as the environments in which we live change (such as, from elementary to middle school), so does our social learning. Choice of activity is also illustrative of our choice of association, and this may be illustrated as early as kindergarten.

By the time the high school student begins to research colleges, associational habits may strongly influence decision-making. Think for instance of an Eagle Scout who has persisted throughout adolescence with a demanding engagement apart from formal schooling. His regard for associational benefits will be very different from that of a child who has been discouraged from such commitments by parents who stressed academic achievement above all other activities. A shy young woman who has discovered her own talents and abilities through high school drama may be seeking other stages as she looks at college opportunities. Above all, the aspiring college student may want to abrade the ties that bind her to dependence on prior identities even as parents and teachers urge her to choose an environment where they think she will "succeed" based on exactly those same prior identities. As parents, some of us may fear how greatly our child will change as they leave us; some will eagerly look forward to participating in this change. Some assume that these changes will not corrode the bonds of affection.

Our students are then given a college tour, and a sales relationship is begun, often with the parents (as payers) viewed as the customer, not the student. In one of the many guides to college admissions, Cristiana Quinn states, "That is a primary mission of liberal arts colleges – to have students go on to advanced degrees" (Quinn 2012). Choice, once again, will be influenced by goal and purpose, but few parents on a first college tour with their high school student will be thinking of advanced degrees. In examining the opportunities for learning, both curricular and social, parents may be looking at class sizes, the diversity or homogeneity of the student body, the physical environment, and the resources available to support their son or daughter, given predicted increases in cost. At the same time, the student may be wondering – will I fit in? How hard is it going to be? What clubs or activities exist? Do I really want to live *here?*

If they were thinking in terms of social learning and social abrasion, parents' questions might be: Does this environment feel similar to what we know? How are conflicts handled? Does my daughter seem more or less anxious here than at another college? How much student participation is encouraged? Will my son be able to maintain ties with our church, ethnic group, culture? Will my daughter be exposed to danger? Do the students and teachers I meet seem to care about each other? What disciplines and traditions are emphasized here? Do I truly think my son can thrive here? Are these adults the mentors I want my daughter to identify with?

Abrasive experiences can be transformational and profound, such as the challenge a white middle-class student may feel being exposed to critical race theory for the first time. Abrasion can also be experienced in the mundane, such as the disappointment of not getting one's preferred course schedule. One of the keys to resilience is the ability to reframe experience, so that as expectations are abraded, an individual can reframe and reflect upon what has changed, and set new or different expectations for the new environment. Abrasion will also be present when the student recognizes new responsibilities, or the consequences of failure. Very quickly, a key component of social learning will become dominant when the freshman observes others and decides who, and when, to imitate or engage. Perhaps these choices will abrade past habits, but the opportunities available will evoke or provoke new choices.

Simultaneously when classes start, enrollment in activities and organizations begins. The possibility of associational life on campus is available to students. As stated in student life materials at Henry Ford Community College, "Student activities complement formal classroom instruction and enhance the overall educational experience by helping students develop leadership skills, communication skills, organizational techniques, as well as an increased understanding of self and others." Penn State's Office of Student Activities Learning Outcomes articulates its goals for informal association in five dense pages, but is summarized as follows:

> Students will:
> Develop critical and reflective thinking abilities
> Exhibit responsible decision-making and personal accountability

Appreciate creative expression and aesthetics
Exhibit the ability to work effectively with those different from themselves
Demonstrate a commitment to social justice
Demonstrate an understanding of group dynamics and effective teamwork
Develop a range of leadership skills and abilities such as effectively
  leading change, resolving conflict, and motivating others
Develop an understanding of knowledge from a range of areas.

These outcomes are expected from associational activities, not classroom activities. These outcomes are expected without structured instruction, on the basis of shared activities. Does the Office of Student Activities Learning Outcomes monitor student associational activities in order to know if desired outcomes are being achieved? If not, then, we might ask what is informal about such activities in such a context, for they seem integral to the campus experience.

Within the classroom, the teacher has many opportunities to model and facilitate the critical and reflective abilities advocated here, and in so doing uses positive abrasion. The friction of diverse opinion, diverse methods, and diverse perspectives reminds us again of Popper's conjectures and refutations. The teacher cultivates a safe environment in which participants can explore opposition, cooperation, and reciprocity. Habits of mind can be challenged in classroom debates without a challenge to the student's sense of self. Outside the classroom, we must remember that the student chooses association, perhaps without critical reflection, but because of affective ties, thus abrasion within the classroom plays an essential role in pushing some students outside their comfort zones.

Many undergraduates point out that the presence and engagement of teachers builds trust, especially in early weeks and months of the freshman year. A student values the teacher who knows her name, but reports, from large public colleges, suggest that this is rare in the undergraduate experience. When a professor is part of the welcome a student receives, she can be viewed as a witness to the student's growth, rather than an occasional actor who only appears rarely. The effect of witnessing and trusting is significant, but until now has largely been unexplored.

Nancy L. Rosenblum (1998) argues in *Membership and Morals* that associative life provides the "discipline of culture" referred to by John Holt. She observes that associational life cultivates the disposition to cooperate, and as such transmit shared morality (ibid.: 29–59). In many models of participatory learning, whether service- or place-based, social mediation and shared purpose become vehicles of moral development. Informal associations also further moral development, but without intention evident in formal classrooms or designed learning environments. Think of the adaptations involved in having a roommate for the first time, or in learning from a roommate of a different culture. Positive abrasion occurs as diverse individual perspectives and interests are applied to shared purpose.

As a student discovers communities of choice, prior identities and loyalties may be challenged and abraded. This is not necessarily destructive to learning, and it may enhance willingness to explore and experiment. Here it is important to note the associative experience of gaming, which many young people choose. Gaming can require similar responsible commitments as for example in the Boy Scouts. Traditional in-person table games involve reliability, cooperation, shared creativity, and acceptance of shared accountability. Online gaming communities can be complex social environments in which trust and informal rules must be built when players do not have the opportunity to meet face-to-face and it is openly acknowledged in such communities that social learning does take place. Nolan Bushnell, one of the founders of video gaming, speaks of the need for educational environments to maintain the levels of passionate enthusiasm. He hopes that most of the drudgery of repetitive tasks can be removed from classrooms by creating educational games. He believes that this frees the teacher to act as a catalyst for student development (Bushnell 2011).

On the other hand, the psychologist Sherry Turkle points out that with much of social media technology, we trade connection for conversation, and lose the dynamic of real conversation where we learn about the complexity of each other and ourselves. She warns against the distancing caused by expectations of control through technology, and the illusion of mechanical companionship instead of the reality of friendship. Her trenchant summary of the impact of texting, "I share therefore I am" (Turkle 2012) evokes the realization of need for social abrasion. Involving students in challenging participatory learning experiences can become an antidote to solitary and isolating texting and virtual worlds.

The poet Wendell Berry (1987) says that, "It may be that when we no longer know which way to go that we have come to our real journey. The mind that is not baffled is not employed. The impeded stream is the one that sings." Baffling the mind, impeding the stream so that it might sing reminds us of the joy, the sheer fun, of learning, of creativity, of scholarship. Although we think of abrasion as destructive, we rub a chilled patient to bring him or her warmth. The personal encounters of social learning often create heat, which can spark imagination, provide illumination and insight to a despairing student. To accomplish this we must be sure our learning environments avoid homogeneity, homeostasis and, above all, self-referential myopia. Our classrooms should be disruptive, baffling, and infectious. They can only be so if they are filled with caring, trust, and clarity. Our students, who are conditioned to immediacy of feedback, from technical environments, must learn patience, because it is necessary for discovery. We must offer them the experience of creative destruction to which they can be open only when they can trust us to accompany them on the journey of creative construction (Warren 2001; Brooks 2011). If liberal education's task is to develop engaged and effective citizens capable of self-governance, our teaching must be both engaged and effective. If our task is to help our students become autodidacts in pursuing wisdom, then our teaching must generate passion and demand constant rigorous self-reflection.

Creating harmony through discord

> Music, to create harmony, must investigate discord.
>
> (Plutarch)

Students worry about participation in various activities, and the choices related to that participation. We must ask ourselves as educators whether we, in our own preoccupations with academic persistence and institutional loyalty, are imposing our own conceptual confusion on students, rather than inviting exploration of their confusions. How do we know if our varying methodological or pedagogical experiments have impact on choice when students are experiencing so much complexity? When students are apprenticed to us for mastery, is it not our relationship that influences their learning?

There is a framework, currently applied in healthcare and community action, that may be useful and provocative as we think about the environments supporting positive abrasion and social learning. That is, the framework of the Leading Causes of Life, created by Dr. Gary Gunderson, professor at Wake Forest University (Gunderson and Pray 2009). While the title borrows language from public health, it subverts the industry's common measurement by failure rates and the prevailing focus on pathologies. The core causes of Gunderson's initiative have been identified as:

- Connection – we define ourselves in relationship with others and with our world.
- Coherence – we seek meaning from experience, our brains form and seek patterns.
- Agency – we must act on our own behalf, we are capable of action influencing our lives.
- Generativity – we bridge, with gratitude and responsibility, what came before and what will come after us.
- Hope – imagination helps us construct the lives we want to live and the legacies we want to leave.

Surely we want undergraduate environments to encourage and evoke vitality for students, faculty, and the community. Looking at associational engagements within the framework of these Leading Causes, we must define our tasks as going beyond assessing goals that enable persisting merely to graduate, or qualification for economic benefit. We must create an environment in which our students come to us as seekers wanting to find a sense of self, a sense of belonging, and a sense of purpose for their lives. We know our contact with them is constrained by institutional goals and structures, and that our influence upon them can be constrained by our own purposes and behaviors. If the goal of an educational entity is to graduate persons with particular, testable skills, the learning environment still must expand their ability to acquire necessary competence to be applied in different environments and for different purposes. Even if the goal of the entity is to promote loyalty to its own community, it must avoid all forms of self-righteousness, and allow students to evaluate their feeling of loyalty and fidelity to the community. The community must simultaneously encourage each student's capacity to identify with other communities, as well.

As we examine the meaning of Connection as a Cause of Life, we must avoid two presumptions: one that connection is defined as technologically facilitated; the other, that connection means intimacy and friendship. Many of us allow what we oppose to define who we are and what we do. We often feel connected to those we oppose with greater passion than to those with whom we agree. Connection is scalable, including the mother/infant dyad, partnership, and membership of species. Nicholas Christakis and James Fowler (2009) have shown the ubiquitous complexity of our social webs of connection, observing that the constraints on connection include place, status, access, affinity, and action. They believe that to know who we are as humans, we must know how we are connected. This takes us beyond our individual associational lives in which we choose to act with others, to the emergence of community and the truth that the whole is greater than the sum of the parts. If friction with "enemies" helps us to define ourselves, one may also examine how we are formed by the resonance we find with teachers and peers. How from these connections, both chosen and accidental, do we become more vital, more alive, and more self-aware? In an undergraduate environment most students first have an opportunity to become reflective about the impact of connection on their development. In pioneering times, the necessary duty to contribute to survival brought this awareness about early in childhood.

Coherence, the next of the Leading Causes, is perhaps most familiar in the academic world. Finding meaning is the quintessential intellectual pursuit, and discovering patterns is what our brains are made to do. How do we make sense of our lives? How do we find a sense of belonging and meaning as we construct the narrative of our lives? Whether these questions are viewed as pragmatic or spiritual, they must frame our pedagogy and construct an evocative and encouraging community for our young. Coherence helps us manage complexity. One of the tasks we as teachers have is to convey positive abrasion, and not a brutal pruning that confines growth to one imagined mode. In baffling and vital classroom discussion, we can explore and find coherence. We must not leave students to find reassurance in easy cynicism that insists there are no *real* meanings.

The third of the Leading Causes is Agency. To experience Life, human beings must act, and they do. Many students were scheduled to "do" before they could choose what to do, and many view action as their identity. As students discover their own capacities for intellectual agency, as well as the various responsibilities concomitant with adult agency, they also discover that agency provides a form of thought. It requires choosing the various options of action, as well as a choice about the application of energy: How much or how little will we do? Will this term paper be turned in late? Will I do more than is required for this class because I like the subject/teacher/timing? Will I get involved in social justice because it will look good on my résumé? Deeper questions regarding agency may emerge during the college years: What must I do in my life? What actions will I/must I refuse? What do I stand for? What actions truly matter to me?

Without agency, we become either passive or dependent; we are no longer vital participants. This is true of institutions and communities as well. When they no longer exert a capacity for agency they atrophy and dependence corrodes their identity. A college that no longer acts on behalf of its vision or moral position, but passively, or fearfully, adheres to financial habits that sustain its status quo, can neither teach agency to students, nor represent a sense of agency in its faculty. Generativity is among the most pertinent of the Leading Causes to the academic world. The university serves to generate educated learners on behalf of society. At a practical level, the academy continues to generate reflection, understanding, and appreciation of the past for the sake of the future. Students are challenged to apply what is learned to as yet unknown experience. Bridging past and future in multiple ways, colleges strive to generate new ideas and new capacities within a tradition, as well as to generate new traditions within a constantly refreshed community of seekers. Even when faculty and students do not look to the past with gratitude or to the future with generous optimism, nonetheless they are in an adventure of generativity. Together they explore what can emerge from their interaction, their abrasions.

Hope is the fifth cause in Gunderson's framework. He means *informed* hope, not wistful longing. This is the practical hope that entices young people to college in the first place. It is entangled in all other causes, and provides the underlying illumination for our lives. Most of us teach because we hope, most of us strive to learn because of hope. Yet, hope is dangerous if separated from the other Causes of Life. Hope needs connection, coherence, agency, and generativity to remain thoughtful and disciplined. Without those complexities, hope can lead us off the cliff. A campus must overflow with hope if it is to be vital, while at the same time the hopeful must abrade self-satisfactions that endanger vitality.

Why is this framework – connection, coherence, agency, generativity, and hope as Leading Causes of Life – fundamental both to any discussion of ecologies of learning, and the importance of social abrasion? The word "academic" is frequently used pejoratively in our society. In some dictionaries the first two meanings listed are: (a) belonging to a school or place of higher learning; and (b) having no practical purpose or use. If we are to reclaim education as more than service to the market, we must do so by making our academic centers vital and "contagious" of hope. The Leading Causes of Life framework gives us language to summon forth that effort. Such an undertaking will be fraught with challenge as we confront the beliefs and habits that have prompted the pejorative views.

If learning is an emergent phenomenon from the self-organizing system that should be education, appreciation of complexity is required and essential to any institutional approach. We live in systems that we constantly co-create and constantly endure. The abrasions in everyday adaptation keep us engaged with others in the several contexts of our lives. Within the five Leading Causes of Life, abrasion is a necessary contribution to the ways the ensemble works to cultivate our lives. If, for instance, we become scattered by our multi-tasking, incessant connection, both our need to act (Agency) and our longing for purpose (Coherence) finally will abrade our excess and pull us back into balance. If we compartmentalize all of our various commitments and live attending only to the immediate tasks of living, we will stumble when faced with invitations to Generativity. Past and future intrude upon, and constructively abrade, our barriers.

When we use this framework to look at our educational goals, we immediately see beyond the constraints of artificial measurements and become clear about the impact schooling has on participants. If our faculty is not vital, alive to possibility and learning, they will not convey their passion to students. Repeatedly, undergraduates say that the best teachers are those who show passion, those who venture beyond their own particular interest, and who care to share that passion. Sadly, those same undergraduates admit that they fear to engage in debate until they can judge whether the teacher is fair, and since they perceive this as rare, most of the time they do not risk engagement.

The adventures of scholarship must be contagious, as are the Leading Causes of Life. As Christakis and Fowler remind us, the networks we create are constantly changing and we will be changed with them and by them. If we wish our graduates to love learning, or to act as contributing citizens, or to appreciate their own responsibilities in association, then we must, as teachers, both model what we seek to teach, and contribute to the vitality of the educational community.

Yet, we know that college experience is not unitary or generic. The strongest statement regarding the impact of college made by researchers stresses that impact is not due to pedagogy, or intentional transfers of knowledge, but to relationships:

> There is also replicated evidence to suggest that student critical thinking, analytical competencies, and general intellectual development are enhanced by an institutional environment that stresses close relationships and frequent interaction between faculty and students and faculty concern about student growth and development during college. This environmental emphasis appeared to have an influence on general cognitive growth that operated independently of an institution's scholarly environment.
>
> (Pascarella and Terenzini 2005: 205)

The efforts made to assess the impact of teaching around various methodological differences, perhaps would better inform us were they directed to the culture and traditions of the educational environment. I would argue we also explore for tolerances of abrasion within that culture and tradition. The abrasions of choice begin with the decision to enroll at a particular school, and continue with the choices of courses, residence, and academic alternatives. Within each of these contexts, the modifications wrought by relationship provide further abrasion. Gradually, over time, each student comes to accept or to resist such abrasions.

Part of the teacher's task is to support the vulnerability and rawness, which may result in a process that is developmentally desirable. We must acknowledge that abrasion is part of the culture of learning. We have encountered students who admit to being "lost" when what is familiar has vanished, and what is potential has neither been realized nor chosen. Engaging such a student in the adventures of exploration, and associations with others, will help to build the resilience necessary to deal with loss of coherence, and loss of a sense of agency. To deny that there is abrasion, or reassure a student that a particular college is permanently safe and stable, is dangerous.

Two of my own most vivid memories in my freshman year are of two students who did not want to be there; one attempted suicide and left school, the other struggled until she graduated, at which point she went off to cooking school, which is what she had always hoped to do. Teachers, advisors, and peers, all of whom were well-intentioned, repeatedly told both these students that their discontent would vanish because the college experience was so special and valuable. The young woman who became a chef repeatedly said that she did not question that it was special and valuable for others, but it was not her own choice. She stayed for the sake of her parents but it was clear that she was not being heard. Her story illustrates an important caution that may be forgotten due to the pressures for persistence and loyalty. We must be careful not to disregard the integrity of the student as a person illustrated in these examples. Just as when we are ill we do not wish to be treated merely as a diagnosis, or for our temporary role as patient, we are all persons before we become students on a particular campus and should be treated as such.

Now when mass enrollment in college has become the norm, we must ask, how many student voices are not being heard? While we may want our institutions to retain enrollment levels, we must nonetheless beware that there are some students who will find the experience destructive and deeply damaging. A scholarship student at McGill, who, like me, came from a small town, said to the dean that she needed to go home after freshman year and enroll in her local college. She wrote she needed to abandon the "famous" environment saying, "I have to fight against my roots and myself in order to be what the college wants me to be. I don't want to do that, and I don't believe the college cares who I am already." Abrasion at this university and for that time and place in her life was too great and too dangerous. This does not mean that she could not become a contributing and disciplined citizen in her own context.

We must be vigilant that our enrollees are willing participants in our chosen community, and that to cultivate the Leading Causes of Life we must respect the existing vitality of our students.

Over time, as our perspectives and preferences change, our associations will change. The club that seemed attractive to us as freshmen may have no appeal by senior year. We may abandon the intellectual pursuits that we found exhilarating in high school when we become aware of other choices in college. Faculty can assist by helping students to trust their own ability to balance change, and to learn from any given context. Even as we label the college experience unique and valuable, we must not diminish students' belief in their ability to learn anywhere and at any time. We must build upon formal and informal contributive associative experiences. We teach both content and character. We must be open to the challenge to abrade our own comfort in the context in which we find ourselves.

Among the neglected aspects of assessments of higher education is the emotional learning that takes place over the college years. Emotional maturity and the ability to apply reflective skills may in fact be the most valuable learning that takes place. This is yet another reason why the framework of the Leading Causes of Life is so important. Faculty can offer students a kaleidoscope for emotional development. As growing adults acquire the skills of independence and responsibility, they must also develop skills of emotional literacy. This is perhaps the most important contribution that abrasion can make. Now we have the opportunity to learn more vividly than when we were children that feelings are transitory, that alliances break, and that feelings shape how we learn just as much as our intellectual capacities. The disappointments and painful dilemmas of our college years are every bit as important to our future vitality as our successes, even though most of us are uncomfortable admitting the contributions made by our humbling embarrassments, failures, and growing awareness of limitation.

Some of this emotional awareness can come in our formal classes, as our intellectual curiosity leads us to explore the dark and shadowed areas of history and human lives. Some of the awareness will be nurtured, and then abraded, as our social efforts fail, or our desire for social justice misfires and we learn that good intentions can have regrettable results. It is in this arena that the culture of the college and the expectations of the faculty can be most important and most educative – in the real sense of *educo* – "to lead out of." If the college cultivates faculty who embrace their roles as catalysts in development of their students' emotional learning, it will be a natural and integrated aspect of their mentoring. If the college stresses that faculty must serve primarily as content providers and as researchers, the emotional aspect of education may be seen as less important, and less valuable.

The Association of American Colleges and Universities (AAC&U 2013) answers the question "What is a twenty-first-century liberal education?" by saying, "Liberal education is an approach to learning that empowers individuals and prepares them to deal with complexity, diversity and change."

In another time and place, perhaps the definition might include phrases such as "the pursuit of wisdom" or "the foundation of democratic liberties." No matter how it is defined education takes place in association with others, with ideas, with cultural norms and traditions, and also with every experience.

As we have evolved our curricula from grammar, logic, and rhetoric to the panoply offered today, we cannot forget that our purposes have to do with persons, each of whom seeks to glean both direction and identity. Andrew O. Fort (2011), writing for the AAC&U, comments on his own experience in "Learning about Learning Outcomes." "Incrementally and cumulatively, I have begun truly to see the point of focusing on student learning, and that doing so has improved my teaching and my students' learning." If our focus can shift to student learning, and if our understanding is that we are indeed helping students to become autodidacts, we can hopefully see that the outcomes of our teaching will be experienced as the Leading Causes of Life – vital connections, rigorous coherence, responsible agency, reflective generativity, and informed hope. All of these depend upon generosity and love, which are the foundations of true teaching.

Our pretentions and pride will be abraded throughout our lives. We can help our students understand the necessity of this constant friction that simultaneously polishes our potential and enables our gifts to be shared with others. In our universities we try to hire those with competence who know what to do and how to do it, those with courage who have the willingness to apply their skills to the unknown, and those with confidence, who have faith in the vision, using the tools available, and sharing their understanding. But above all, we must hire those with compassion who can engage students to care profoundly about what they can learn, what can be done, what can be dreamed and what can be given to those who come after us.

Notes

1 Notable exceptions include the Wabash Study of Liberal Arts Education, The National Survey of Student Engagement, and The College Results Instrument developed by the Institute for Research on Higher Education for the National Center for Postsecondary Improvement.
2 College staff and even administrators, for example, can be a critical part of this social learning, especially as they contribute to the ecology of the particular college. A financial aid counselor, a dormitory housekeeper, or a coach may have more interaction with the student over the entire length of enrollment, and possibly more sustained impact, than do specific faculty members.
3 Various studies have examined the role of active learning in undergraduate education, assessing its significance in the social integration and persistence of the student in college (Braxton *et al.* 2008). Most active learning is also social learning. Classroom culture that reinforces disconnection from others, specialization, or competition diminishes and degrades the value attributed to social learning (Palmer and Zajonec 2010: 91).

References

1919 Report, "Voluntary organizations and Adult Education," Chapter VII, http://infed.org/archives/e-texts/1919report.htm (accessed 27 June 2014).

Association of American Colleges and Universities (AAC&U) (2013) "What is a 21st century liberal education?" *LEAP*, Washington, DC: AAC&U.

Bennett, D. C. (2001) "Assessing quality in higher education," *Liberal Education*, 87 (2): 1–3.

Berry, W. (1987) "Real work," *Collected Poems*, San Francisco: North Pointe Press.

Bishop's University, "Vision, mission and values," www.ubishops.ca. (accessed 27 June 2014).

Braxton, J. M., Jones, W. A., Hirschy, A. S., and Harley, H. V. (2008) "The role of active learning in college student persistence," *New Directions for Teaching and Learning*, 115 (Fall) Hoboken, NJ: Wiley, pp. 71–83.

Brooks, D. (2011) *The Social Animal*, New York: Random House.

Bushnell, N. (2011) LAUNCH: Education and kids, keynote address, http://bliptv/learning-without-frontiers/game-based-learning-2009-nolan-bushnell-1915943 (accessed 27 June 2014).

Christakis, N. A., and Fowler, J. H. (2009) *Connected*, New York: Little, Brown.

Dewey, J. ([1938] 1997) *Experience and Education*, New York: Touchstone.

Follett, M. P. (1998) *The New State*, University Park: Pennsylvania State University Press.

Fort, A. (2011) "Learning about learning outcomes: A liberal arts professor assesses," *Liberal Education*, 97(1): 56–60.

Gunderson, G. and Pray, L. (2009) *Leading Causes of Life*, Nashville, TN: Abingdon Press.

Holt, J. (1972) *Freedom and Beyond*, New York: E.P. Dutton.

Ministry of Reconstruction, Adult Education Committee (1919) *Final Report* (Chaired by Arthur L. Smith and commonly known as "The 1919 Report") Cmnd 321, London: HMSO.

Palmer, P. J. and Zajonec, A. (2010) *The Heart of Higher Education*, San Francisco, CA: Wiley.

Para, E. A. (2008) "The role of social support in identity formation: A literature review," *Graduate Journal of Counseling Psychology*, 1(1): 97–105.

Parry, M., Field, K., and Sugiano, B. (2013) "The Gates effect," *The Chronicle of Higher Education*, Special Reports, 29 October.

Pascarella, E. T. and Terenzini, P. T. (2005) *How College Affects Students*, San Francisco, CA: Jossey-Bass.

Penn State, Office of Student Activities Learning Outcomes, http://studentaffairs.psu.edu/hub/studentactivities/outcomes.shtml. (accessed 27 June 2014).

Pomona College Mission Statement, www.pomona.edu. (accessed 27 June 2014).

Quinn, C. (2012) "College admissions: Five reasons to choose a liberal arts college," 4 June, www.golocalprov.com/lifestyle/college-admissions. (accessed 27 June 2014).

Rosenblum, N. L. (1998) *Membership and Morals*, Princeton, NJ: Princeton University Press.

Smith, M.K. (2012) "Association, la vie associative, and lifelong learning," *Encyclopedia of Informal Education*, Aurora, WI: George Williams College, http://infed.org/mobi/association-la-vie-associative-and-lifelong-learning/ (accessed 27 June 2014).

Turkle, S. (2012) "Alone together," www.TED.com (accessed 27 June 2014), and *Alone Together*, New York: Basic Books.

Warren, M. E. (2001) *Democracy and Association*, Princeton, NJ: Princeton University Press.

7 Communities of liberal learning as social spaces

Laura Grube and Virgil Henry Storr

Liberal arts colleges are special places. These communities of liberal learning ensure that their students are exposed to a diversity of ideas within and outside of the classroom. The best of these institutions also ensure that their students learn and live in communities characterized by diverse student populations. Liberal arts colleges provide a unique environment where (mostly) young adults can grow, and experiment, and challenge, and even reinvent themselves. They also provide students the opportunity to build meaningful, sometimes lifelong, and often close, social bonds with their fellow students and, occasionally, even college faculty and staff. Communities of liberal learning are, thus, social spaces where students can and do develop intimate and lasting social connections.[1]

That communities of liberal learning are also social spaces is not merely a side benefit of the college experience – not merely happy memories alongside the serious work of intellectual growth and developing into citizens ready and able to play their part in a self-governing society. The point deserves a more thorough analysis than we can offer here, so for now we will simply assert it. The intellectual growth that liberal arts colleges promise and their commitment to readying students to live impactful lives as local and global citizens is inextricably tied to the social space that such institutions create. We note that social space is an assumed, though not explicitly addressed, element in many of the contributions to this volume. Consider, for example, that the core lessons of the Chesapeake semester Chamlee-Wright, Goodheart, and Seidel describe are tied to the social space created among the students and between the students and members of the various communities with whom they engage. Though he does not reference "social space" explicitly, Garnett's description of a "polycentric classroom," in which students and faculty learn synergistically from one another, is one that at least resembles, and at best creates a healthy social space as it creates a healthy intellectual community. Wood Ion's "social abrasion" that grinds away the rough edges of students' reactions to the world can only happen if there are social spaces that allow it to happen. And, as Horwitz describes, the best pedagogical and programmatic innovations come from faculty talking to one another over lunch, in workshops, and in the conversations that co-teaching inspires. Or, to put the point more generally, if we are to cultivate the art of self-governance, we must also cultivate what Alexis de Tocqueville describes in *Democracy in America* as the art of association. And such arts cannot be developed without healthy social spaces.

There are several reasons why liberal arts colleges become social spaces that tend to foster the development of deep social relationships. Like all institutions of higher education, they contain a large concentration of 18–22-year-olds. There is, similarly, a mix of activities including classroom learning, studying, common interest clubs, fraternities, and athletics. But, unlike large universities, small, liberal arts colleges generally have student populations below 3,500 students and can, in some instances, have only a few hundred students. Moreover, classes are generally small, typically fewer than twenty students, and students are required to take classes outside their majors and sometimes take a majority of the classes that they need to complete their degrees in areas other than their concentrations. As such, it is not uncommon for students to build connections with fellow students that they met in class even if they do not share a major. Additionally, student to faculty ratios may be 12:1 or smaller, making it possible for students and teachers to build relationships.

Another important distinguishing feature is that liberal arts college students typically live on campus for all four years of their undergraduate education. Students learn together, eat together, live together, and play together. This constant interaction is one reason that we refer to small, residential liberal arts colleges as *communities* of liberal learning. This constant interaction is also why these communities tend to be social spaces that foster the development of deep social relationships.

We argue that by considering small, residential liberal arts colleges as social spaces, we can better understand what happens on these campuses and better understand the products, or outcomes of these types of institutions. The particular evidence that we present will focus on one institution in particular, Beloit College. Both authors are alumni of Beloit College (Storr '96 and Grube '08), a small residential liberal arts college in Beloit, Wisconsin. Grube is currently a visiting instructor of economics at the college. During the 2013–2014 academic year, Beloit College had 1,296 students. The student body represented 49 states and 40 countries; 18 percent from Wisconsin, 25 percent from Illinois, 17 percent from other Midwestern states, 12 percent from the Northeast/Mid-Atlantic, 12 percent from the West, and 6 percent from the South. Ten percent of students are citizens of foreign countries. The average class size is 15 students and the college's student to faculty ratio is 12:1. Outside the classroom, students participate in 17 varsity sports and over 75 student organizations.

As we will discuss, liberal arts colleges are environments where students can and do develop intimate and lasting social bonds with other students as well as faculty and staff at the college.[2] As such, liberal arts colleges can be thought of as training grounds where students not only become liberally educated but also learn valuable lessons about how to discover commonalities and identify shared interests in others who have potentially very different backgrounds. Specifically, we argue that the range of experiences that students have at Beloit College, their frequent interactions with one another as well as the faculty and staff, and the close proximity in which they live and learn, create multiple opportunities for Beloiters to meet and develop close friendships that can and do survive their time at Beloit.

The remainder of the chapter is organized as follows. In the next section, we explore how and why communities of liberal learning should be viewed as social spaces. Specifically, we focus on how students interact with one another as well as college faculty and staff to produce an environment where meaningful social relations can and do occur. We then offer some details about Beloit College and describe how it facilitates and fosters the development of social bonds between individuals with diverse backgrounds. We conclude by briefly commenting on the importance of this social aspect of liberal arts college life in fulfilling the liberal arts college's critical role in cultivating the art of self-governance amongst its students.

Communities of liberal learning as social spaces

The concept of social space was developed in the field of urban geography. Henri Lefebvre is one of the most influential figures on this subject. In *The Production of Space* (1991), a seminal work in the field, Lefebvre outlines his theory of space. For Lefebvre, space is simultaneously the result of spatial practice (i.e. it is produced and reproduced by social activity) and it is where social life takes place (i.e. it is where individuals interact).

Like spontaneous or emergent orders, social spaces are created by human action and interaction but are not deliberately constructed. As Lefebvre (ibid.: 26) writes, "(social) space is a (social) product." Similarly, as he explains, "social space ... remains the space of society, of social life ... all 'subjects' are situated in a space in which they must either recognize themselves or lose themselves, a space which they may both enjoy and modify" (ibid.: 35). And, as he writes:

> [social] space is not a thing among other things, nor a product among other products: rather, it subsumes things produced, and encompasses their interrelationships in their coexistence and simultaneity ... It is the outcome of a sequence and set of operations, and thus cannot be reduced to the rank of a simple object.
>
> (ibid.: 73)

Neighborhoods, for instance, are not naturally occurring phenomena but are, instead, man-made. They are produced by developers, and contractors, and construction workers and are constantly reproduced by residents and visitors as they enter, leave, interact, and fail to interact with each other. Cities, towns, streets, parks, offices, churches, stores, and homes are, similarly, social spaces that are produced by social activity and are the site of social action. As Lefebvre (ibid.: 73) notes: "itself the outcome of past actions, social space is what permits fresh actions to occur."

Different social spaces, according to Lefebvre, promote different social practices, come to be imbued with different social meanings and facilitate the development of different kinds of social bonds. As Lefebvre (ibid.: 35) writes, for instance, "all holy or cursed places, places characterized by the presence or absence of gods, associated with the death of gods, or with hidden powers and their exorcism – all such places qualify as special preserves." Similarly, a (peasant) dwelling, he (ibid.: 83) writes, "embodies and implies particular social relations; it shelters a family … and it is a component part of a particular site and a particular countryside." We worship in temples, churches, and synagogues, we work in offices, we shop in stores, and we play in parks. Additionally, we view our religious spaces as holy spaces, our workspaces as serious spaces, and our retail and recreational spaces as spaces of leisure. Moreover, the relationships between pastors and parishioners, between supervisors and employees, between retailers and shoppers, and between park goers differ in important respects.

Elsewhere, Storr (2008) has argued that the market is a particular social space created by particular social practices (namely, producing, buying, and selling) that facilitates the formation of particular social relationships including the potential of commercial relationships to develop into meaningful social friendships. As Storr (2008: 137) argues, the market can be understood as a social space where meaningful conversations take place, "conversations that are not just bartering and negotiations; conversations between socially bonded market participants concerned with more than simply making a deal."

Liberal arts colleges, we contend, are also particular social spaces. Communities of liberal learning present a social space with unique characteristics. Breneman (1994: 3–11) points to several key characteristics that distinguish liberal arts colleges. As he explains, liberal arts colleges (1) are not vocational schools but rather offer a broad range of courses, including courses in the social sciences and humanities;[3] (2) have a single purpose, which is to educate undergraduates; (3) have relatively small student bodies and class sizes; (4) allow for one-on-one interactions between students and faculty; and (5) have student bodies that live on (or near) campus.

The very features that make liberal arts colleges adept at providing their students with the opportunity to receive a liberal education (i.e. their emphasis on student growth and development, their smallness, and their residential nature) also combine to make them social spaces where students can and do develop intimate and lasting social relationships with others connected to the college.

Although the first liberal arts colleges appeared in the U.S. in the eighteenth century, liberal arts education can be traced back to ancient Greece. There were seven "liberal arts," divided into the verbal arts, or the trivium, which included grammar, rhetoric, and logic, and the mathematical arts, or the quadrivium, which included arithmetic, music, geometry, and astronomy (Wagner 1983). Today, the liberal arts retain elements of the ancient Greek tradition. Liberal arts colleges encourage students to study a breadth of subjects and offer courses in the natural sciences, the social sciences, and the humanities. The Association of American Colleges and Universities describes liberal education (and liberal arts colleges) as "an approach to learning that empowers individuals and prepares them to deal with complexity, diversity, and change. It provides students with broad knowledge of the wider world (e.g. science, culture, and society) as well as in-depth study in a specific area of interest."[4]

Not surprisingly, words like "nurture," "cultivate," and "develop" tend to find themselves into the mission statements of liberal arts colleges. The Williams College "Mission and Purpose,"[5] for instance, expresses a commitment to "nurturing in students the academic and civic virtues, and their related traits of character." Similarly, "the Mission of Vassar College is to make accessible 'the means of a thorough, well-proportioned and liberal education' ... [that] nurtures intellectual curiosity, creativity, respectful debate and engaged citizenship."[6] Additionally, "Carleton," according to the college's mission statement, "develops qualities of mind and character that prepare its graduates to become citizens and leaders, capable of finding inventive solutions to local, national, and global challenges."[7] Expressions of a commitment to student growth and development also appear in the mission statements of St. Lawrence University,[8] Hamilton College,[9] and Smith College.[10]

Moreover, liberal arts colleges' "statements of mission and purpose" tend to stress their commitment to promoting student growth and development both inside and outside of the classroom. Williams College's mission, for instance, emphasizes:

> learning that takes place in the creation of a functioning community: life in the residence halls, expression through the arts, debates on political issues, leadership in campus governance, exploration of personal identity, pursuit of spiritual and religious impulses, the challenge of athletics, and direct engagement with human needs, nearby and far away.[11]

Similarly, Bowdoin College's "Purpose" explains that a "liberal education rests fundamentally on the free exchange of ideas – on conversation and questioning – that thrives in classrooms, lecture halls, laboratories, studios, dining halls, playing fields, and dormitory rooms." Likewise, Knox College's "Statement of Mission" expresses the college's commitment that their:

> residential campus culture [encourages] the personal, cultural and intellectual growth of our students in a reflective, tolerant and engaged campus community through supportive residential opportunities, numerous student organizations, a wide array of creative activities and cultural programming, and opportunities for intercollegiate and recreational sports.[12]

The same is true of the mission statements of Skidmore College,[13] Middlebury College,[14] and many (likely most) other liberal arts colleges.

To the extent that these colleges are successful in achieving their missions, then, their students will experience significant personal transformations while living and learning in these communities of liberal learning. Because they offer a shared and significant growth experience, liberal arts colleges foster the development of a special connection between college students as well as between college students and their respective colleges.

Additionally, the smallness of liberal arts colleges means that students will tend to be at least acquainted with their fellow students and will frequently be quite familiar with a large percentage of the students in their cohorts. As noted above, liberal arts colleges will generally have small student populations. In 2013, for instance, Colgate College had a student population of over 2,800, Amherst College an enrollment of just over 1,800 students and Haverford College an enrollment of just over 1,200 students. Some liberal arts colleges, like Thomas Aquinas College and Principia College, have student populations of less than 500. Compare these to the student populations at major state universities, like Arizona State University, the University of Minnesota and Ohio State University, which can have populations of more than 50,000 students.

The smallness of liberal arts colleges also means that students will have opportunities to get to know their professors. Student to teacher ratios will tend to be quite small. For instance, Hope College and Knox College have a 12:1 student to faculty ratio. Similarly, Bates College, Colby College, and Colorado College have 10:1 student to faculty ratios. Again, compare these to the student to faculty ratios at major state universities – Oregon State University (21:1)[15] and Louisiana State University, Baton Rouge (23:1)[16] – which can have student to teacher ratios as high as 32:1.[17] As a result of these small student-to-faculty ratios, class sizes can be quite small; more often than not classes have fewer than 20 students. Departments can also be small, which means that, depending on their major, students can end up taking multiple classes from the same faculty members in order to complete their degrees. The small classes and departments alongside the open door policies that many liberal arts faculty adopt means that students can become quite close with their professors.

Likewise, the residential nature of liberal arts colleges means that students not only learn together but also live together. While it is not uncommon for many universities and colleges to require students to live on campus for at least a year and even two years, many liberal arts colleges require that students (who do not qualify for special exemptions) live on campus for at least three and sometimes even four years. As such, these residential liberal arts colleges are able to foster a rich campus life where students are also floor and dorm mates who study, and watch television, eat together, and party together, where late night study sessions or social gatherings turn into all night discussions and debates about silly matters and serious issues, where formal educational and social programming can extend into the evening and weekends.

The smallness and residential nature of liberal arts colleges also mean that students are given multiple opportunities to develop a facility in the art of self-governance outside the classroom. They are, for instance, given multiple chances to participate in student government and club governance where they learn to solve problems, work cooperatively, and manage conflicts. Similarly, dorms can become mini-polities where student-residents are sometimes given surprisingly large scope (though not unlimited) to decide the rules under which they will live, like whether the bathrooms will be coed or not and whether and when they will institute study hours, as well as what the rules will be around visitors or the use of common spaces. The importance of these experiences and the lessons they learn about building consensus, dealing with diverse perspectives, developing creative solutions when there are impasses and ensuring that their floor- and room-mates feel enfranchised throughout the process cannot be overstated.

Brann (2000) describes the importance of smallness and campus living to the liberal arts college experience. As she (168) writes:

> liberal education needs classrooms, quads, coffee shops, all the appurtenances of a community of learning. It needs residences where students ... may learn the ways of close conversational friendship ... It needs smallness, so that people may run into each other often for spontaneous conversation.

And, as she (ibid.) continues, "one mark of a liberal [arts] school is that its members carry the life of the intellect into casual encounters without the least shame."

Admittedly, that meaningful social bonds would be forged and that a genuine (close-knit) community would emerge in a context where a small number of people both live and work within very close proximity of one another for multiple years is not terribly surprising. That said, the importance of the lessons regarding civility and sociality that students in residential liberal arts colleges learn as they are creating these genuine communities is, arguably, underappreciated.[18] The importance of the close bonds that sometimes form between students in shaping their experiences while in college as well as after they graduate is also, we contend, underappreciated. If liberal arts colleges are fulfilling their core function, namely to offer their students a liberal education, this social outcome (i.e. the development of significant social relationships between students and the emergence of a genuine community) is not only an important complement but a likely side effect of these colleges successfully working toward their missions.

There is reason to believe that liberal arts colleges are, in fact, successfully working toward their missions. Scholars have identified a variety of products (or outcomes) associated with communities of liberal learning. Seifert *et al.* (2008), for instance, have analyzed the results of the Wabash National Study of Liberal Arts Education (WNS) and have found that liberal arts students exhibit (1) intercultural effectiveness, (2) an inclination to inquire and lifelong learning, (3) well-being, and (4) leadership. In another year, the study found that in addition to the four outcomes identified previously, students also illustrate (5) effective reasoning and problem solving and (6) an ability to transition to post-college life (Seifert *et al.* 2010). Likewise, Astin (1999) shows that liberal arts college students have (1) improved writing skills and (2) a cultural awareness. And, as Astin (1999: 83) finds:

> students attending private liberal arts colleges, compared to students attending other types of institutions, are more satisfied with the faculty, the quality of teaching, and are more likely to view the institution as student oriented ... [and] as being focused on social change.

Studies also find that liberal arts college students are capable of understanding various cultures and navigating cultural differences. Indeed, a growing number of studies have focused on liberal arts education and the ability to deal with people from different cultural backgrounds. Umbach and Kuh (2006), for example, find that students "understand diverse people," meaning here people with different races and ethnicities. And Aleman and Salkever (2003) report that, in addition to having a breadth of knowledge and an ability to communicate, liberal arts college students appreciate diversity.

Table 7.1 outlines the results of several studies of liberal arts colleges. With the exception of Heath (1976), the studies all use data collected from current students. There are, however, at least two surveys that provide this data based on alumni responses, the Higher Education Data Sharing (HEDS) Alumni survey and the Annapolis Group.[19] The 2011 Annapolis Group survey, for instance, found that 77 percent of liberal arts college graduates rated their undergraduate experience as "excellent;" 79 percent reported that they benefited very much from high-quality faculty; and 88 percent said that there was a sense of community among students at their college.

Although the Annapolis Group survey asks different questions, the reported results are not contradictory to the results from surveys of current students. The recognition of having benefited from high-quality faculty may be closely tied to an "inclination to inquire and lifelong learning" and students having developed "effective reasoning and problem-solving" skills. Presumably by high-quality faculty respondents are referring to those who illustrate the passion for lifelong learning and are good at teaching. Similarly, the "sense of community" that alumni reported is consistent with appreciation for diversity.

As we will discuss below, Beloit College is a community of liberal learning that successfully cultivates within its students the values, skills, and habits associated with a liberal arts education and is a social space where students can and do develop meaningful connections between students as well as between students and faculty and staff at the college. Moreover, Beloit College students are given opportunities to develop a facility with the art and science of self-governance both in and out of the classroom. In the next section, we offer some details about the College, describe the data that we utilize throughout the rest of the chapter and discuss how Beloit facilitates and fosters the development of social bonds between individuals with diverse backgrounds.

Table 7.1 Summary of findings on liberal arts outcomes

Authors	Liberal arts outcomes
Seifert *et al.* (2008)	(1) Intercultural effectiveness, (2) inclination to inquire and lifelong learning, (3) well-being, and (4) leadership
Pascarella *et al.* (2005)	(1) Leadership development, (2) responsible citizenship, and (3) prepared for first job
Astin (1999)	(1) Improved writing skills, (2) cultural awareness, (3) majoring in physical or social sciences, and (4) improved scores on the Medical College Admission Test (MCAT)
Seifert *et al.* (2010)	(1) Effective reasoning and problem solving, (2) intercultural effectiveness, (3) inclination to inquire and lifelong learning, (4) well-being, (5) leadership, and (6) ability to transition to post-college life
Umbach and Kuh (2006)	Understand "diverse people" (focus of the study was diversity)
Aleman and Salkever (2003)	(1) Appreciating diversity, (2) breadth of experiences, and (3) ability to communicate
Heath (1976)	(1) Stabilization of values, (2) intellectual curiosity, (3) independence, and (4) application of knowledge

Friendship and community in Beloit College

Beloit College is a small, residential liberal arts college that was founded in 1846 in Beloit, Wisconsin.[20] Beloit (population approximately 36,000), lies just north of the Illinois border, about 100 miles from Chicago and 75 miles from Milwaukee. The town of Beloit does not boast the social scene of a major metropolitan area, however, and as such, the Beloit College campus is the hub of both academic and non-academic student activities.[21] The forty-acre campus is roughly divided between a residential side (with residence halls, fraternities and sororities, a cafeteria, a student bar, and athletic facilities) and an academic side (with classrooms, faculty offices, administrative offices, a library and a student union). This divide between the academic and residential sides of campus, however, is a porous one. Students will attend performances and lectures, play capture-the-flag and frisbee-golf, and hang out in the student union and on the lawns on the academic side in the evenings and well into the night. Likewise, students will frequently study for exams and work on assignments, often attend club meetings, and occasionally share meals with faculty in the cafeteria.

Beloit College sees its mission as engaging "the intelligence, imagination, and curiosity of its students, empowering them to lead fulfilling lives marked by high achievement, personal responsibility, and public contribution in a diverse society."[22] As such, students are required to take 50–65 percent of their courses in a range of disciplines outside their major field. It is also not uncommon for Beloit students to double major.

The College has a student body of just fewer than 1,300. Most of these students (over 95 percent) live on campus in one of the residence halls or student townhouses. Most of these students also have a meal plan and regularly eat their lunches and dinners in The Commons Dining Room or in DK's café. The just over 100 full-time faculty members are spread among 30 departments. As such, most departments have around five faculty members including tenured, tenure-track, visiting, adjunct, and emeritus faculty members. This is the case in Computer Science, Education and Youth Studies, History, International Relations, and Sociology. Some departments like Classics and Geology have as few as three faculty members. For comparison, the University of Wisconsin–Madison's History Department has over forty faculty members. With Beloit requiring that students take at least ten courses within their major field of study, students will end up taking multiple classes from several professors within their major department.

Beloit College thus promotes the kind of spatial practices that would lead its students, faculty, and staff to produce a social space where Beloiters can and do build meaningful social connections with each other which can survive long after their time at Beloit. The data presented in this chapter bears out this claim.

We surveyed alumni of the Economics Department at Beloit College. The authors distributed the survey as an embedded link within an email explaining the goals of the project. Alumni were selected rather than current students for several reasons. First, we wanted respondents to comment on how their liberal arts degree and experience at Beloit College has affected their post-college life. Arguably, while students are in the midst of their education, it is sometimes more difficult to evaluate the experience. Second, we selected alumni because there are a greater number of alumni compared to current students. Alumni of the Economics Department were specifically selected for three reasons: the department is one of the most diverse on campus (diversity being defined as total number of domestic minorities and international students); it is one of the largest departments at the college; and email contact information was readily available for this population.

The data collected in the survey is a mix of quantitative and qualitative data. For example, survey data results will indicate aggregate figures and in some cases, provide qualitative information in the form of short sentence responses. This qualitative data comes from questions where respondents were asked to elaborate on their answers. The more detailed answers were in reference to the type of activities respondents had pursued with fellow Beloit College alumni (e.g. fraternity cook outs, staying with the family of an alumnus/a for an extended period, etc.).

The survey consisted of six questions. With the exception of the first question (which asked about the number of Beloit alumni to whom the alumnus/a was still connected), participants were not forced to answer any questions and were given an opportunity to select all the provided answers that applied. Additionally, participants were given an opportunity to expound on the answers that they provided to all but the first question. The questions focused on the types of relationships that alumni had while at the college as well as the value of their liberal arts experience more generally. Participants were asked about the persistence and origins of the friendships that they formed at Beloit and the various ways that their Beloit friends contributed to their post-college experiences. They were also asked about the liberal arts education that they received at Beloit.

In total, 864 online surveys were sent. Of these 864, 170 were completed, for a response rate of approximately 20 percent. In addition to the 170 completed online, another 16 were completed in person (for a total of 186 surveys completed). The range of alumni graduation years was from 1946 (approximately 90 years old) to 2013 (approximately 23 years old). Although we do not pretend that the data from this survey ought to be considered statistically meaningful (e.g. the students who responded are likely a biased sample of the overall alumni population), we do believe that it is suggestive of the experiences of many Beloit students and alumni and evidence that the College was a social space for at least some of its students.

In addition to the alumni survey data, we have also utilized data from current Beloit College students. This data comes from the Capstone Senior Reflective Survey of 2014 conducted by professors Natalie Gummer and Catherine Orr. Students in this survey were asked about what they learned during their time at Beloit that they expected to have a lasting impact on them. A total of 38 responses were collected.

Several themes can be gleaned from this data. First, Beloit students are likely to be engaged in a variety of activities while in college that can be opportunities for the emergence of meaningful and long-lasting social connections. Second, Beloit students do form social bonds with their fellow students as well as attachments to Beloit that survive their time in college. Third, as a result of their experiences of living and learning alongside and forming social bonds with fellow college students from potentially very distinct backgrounds, Beloit students develop several liberal values and (as will be discussed in the final section) skills in the art of self-governance.

Being active is something Beloiters have in common

Beloiters are likely to participate in a range of activities including athletics, clubs, and Greek life, which are opportunities to establish and solidify social bonds. For instance, a large percentage of the student body participates in one or more varsity sports, perhaps as many as one in four, certainly more than 20 percent.[23] In 2013–2014, 61 students were on the track and field team, 58 students were on the football team, 47 students played baseball or softball, and 39 students played lacrosse.[24] Beloit College is affiliated with the Midwest Conference and sponsors 17 NCAA Division III intercollegiate athletic teams. Although all the colleges in the Midwest Conference are within Wisconsin, Illinois, and Iowa, team members can spend hours together traveling to in-conference away games, meets, and tournaments.

Beloit College also supports a wide range of intramural sports including indoor soccer, basketball, softball, kickball, and ultimate frisbee. The majority of the student body, as much as two thirds, participates in at least one intramural sport. Teams are generally coed and can be comprised of club members, groups of friends, residence hall floors, and even faculty and staff.

About 8 percent of the male students belong to one of the three fraternities and 6 percent of the female students belong to one of the three sororities at Beloit, each of which has a house where a portion of the members live.[25] Beloiters also participate in one or more of the 89 clubs on campus.[26] Some of these clubs are arranged around activities (e.g. boating, yoga, writing, and the annual production of the Rocky Horror Picture Show) and others have social or civic missions (e.g. Black Students United, the College Democrats and Republicans, and Voces Latinas). Several campus groups occupy special interest houses where group members live and which can serve as meeting spaces and bases of operation for the clubs.

These group experiences can be both an opportunity and a basis for the formation of meaningful social relationships.[27] In addition to these group experiences, however, Beloit College students have an opportunity to participate in several activities individually that are unique to Beloit (at least in the particular form they are offered), thus, making them shared experiences around which Beloiters can connect. Three activities are worth noting: study abroad (and off-campus study) experiences, the Beloit Plan (1964–1978) and Liberal Arts in Practice. Although not a requirement, about 50 percent of Beloit students participate in an off-campus program during their four years (usually during their junior year) and often these programs are overseas.[28] Similarly, the Beloit Plan, which was established in 1964 and discontinued in 1978, replaced the more traditional two-semester format with a year-long three-semester format. Students spent their first three and their last three semesters on campus. They were expected to spend one of the middle five terms in an approved activity like an internship. Likewise, the Liberal Arts in Practice component of the curriculum requires students to participate in "applied or original work extending beyond the traditional classroom" and to "connect their experiences beyond the traditional classroom with ... learning in the classroom."[29]

Beloit relationships persist

As noted above, both authors continue to count Beloit College friends amongst our closest friends and one of us is actually married to someone she met at Beloit. Beloit relationships can and do persist. Our experience is not atypical.[30] Participants in the alumni survey we conducted reported still being in touch with as few as zero of their former classmates and as many as over 50. Of course, one would predict that the answer would be related with graduation year. For example, the longer a graduate has been away from the College, the fewer Beloiters she may still count as friends. This might be because new friendships are forged but also because of the physical and social distance that can develop as alumni live their lives. For respondents who graduated in the 1940s–1960s, some also indicated that friends had passed away.

The relationships that Beloit students form with peers, however, do appear to be long lasting. From the pre-1990 graduates (minimum age 46 years old), 10 percent stay in touch with at least 16 fellow Beloiters. From the post-1990 graduates, the figure is 25 percent who stay in touch with at least 16 fellow Beloiters. Many of the Beloiters they remained connected to they knew from the classroom and/or from a living arrangement. As noted above, small class sizes are conducive to knowing classmates and living together in the dormitories appears to be an important basis for the establishment of friendships.

If we divide alumni into two categories, those who graduated before 1990 and those who graduated after 1990, we find the following (see Table 7.2).[31]

Of these continued relationships, respondents indicated that they had met the individuals in a variety of contexts: 62 percent reported that they knew the individuals from a living arrangement, 53 percent through the classroom, 44 percent through a club or organization, 32 percent through another friend, and 31 percent through sports teams. The fact that "from a living arrangement" received the greatest number of votes illustrates that residential life is not a trivial aspect of communities of liberal learning.

These friendships have contributed to after-Beloit experiences as well. While 85 percent of respondents said that they valued the continued friendship, 24 percent reported that the contacts continue to be a source of social activities, 24 percent said that they were a source of additional networking (including career advice), and 18 percent indicated that they had exchanged job information.

Table 7.2 Continuing college relationships for pre-1990 and post-1990 graduates

	Before 1990, n = 104		After 1990, n = 75	
0	13%	14	0%	0
1–5	44%	46	23%	17
6–10	23%	24	40%	30
11–15	10%	10	12%	9
16–20	7%	7	9%	7
21–50	3%	3	15%	11
>50	0%	0	1%	1

While one respondent commented that the physical distance among friends makes it difficult to stay in contact, several others indicated that they still saw Beloiters from other places. In response to questions about how they interacted with Beloit friends after graduation, alumni offered several telling replies:

> [One friend] came to visit me in Ethiopia during [my] Peace Corps service, [and] I helped another find an apartment in Tampa when she moved there (I was also living there at the time).
> I stayed with a friend's parents when I went to Ecuador after graduation. I stayed with the mother of an alumna when I first moved to Johannesburg, South Africa, and while I was in South Africa three Beloit friends came to visit.
> Continued friendship, a sense of belonging to a wider group, world-wide contacts, a place to stay (to sleep, or visit).

Others indicated that a group of fraternity brothers had continued to get together once a year for the past 24 years. Another mentioned that several Beloiters had been at his wedding. The authors know of intramural teams (water polo and ultimate frisbee) with Beloit alumni in New York City and Seattle, Washington. A group of Beloiters (typically 6–10) get together at Dewey Beach, Delaware every summer; another collection of Beloit former cross country runners have competed in ultra-marathons and other runs around the country.

Not only do social relationships developed during students' time at Beloit survive their having graduated, their attachment to the College also survives. Another statistic (although not part of the alumni survey) that may provide insight to the continued connection between Beloiters and the College is the alumni-giving rate. Although several of the studies on small, residential liberal arts colleges mention the importance of student–faculty interactions, few mention the types of relationships that exist among students. This is peculiar given that alumni of liberal arts colleges are more likely to express a sense of belonging to their alma mater. This continued connection to their college is reflected in alumni giving rates. If we consider the top 100 universities/colleges, there are differences between large universities and liberal arts colleges in giving rates (see Table 7.3). Of the ten top colleges in alumni giving rates, nine are liberal arts colleges.[32]

Table 7.3 Alumni giving rates

	Best national universities	Best national liberal arts colleges	Beloit College
Mean	19.4%	31.8%	Actual rate: 27%
Median	16.5%	29.5%	

Beloit College is somewhat below the averages for liberal arts colleges (at 27 percent), but still above the averages for national universities.

Students develop liberal values that are useful in forming social relationships after Beloit

As mentioned above, Beloit College is able to successfully cultivate a number of core liberal attitudes and values as a result of students' experiences of living and learning alongside and forming social bonds with other college students and faculty from often very distinct backgrounds. These values include (but are not limited to) an appreciation for diversity and a commitment to lifelong learning and are, undoubtedly, useful as Beloiters negotiate their careers and form social relationships after they graduate. Beloit then is a social space that cultivates the habits, skills, and orientations that Beloiters can utilize as they inhabit, seek to build social connections and participate in political life in an increasingly global world. As another senior remarked, at Beloit, "I learned how to build strong, productive relationships with others. I learned how to form and defend my opinions. I learned how to interact with people from diverse backgrounds and to find common ground."[33] And, as another senior remarked, "an incredibly important thing I learned in my time here is to be especially aware that everyone I interact with has something to teach me and it's up to me to be able to understand and learn from them."[34]

Appreciation for diversity is a likely outcome of a social space that includes diversity.[35] Beloit students live and learn within a college community that is quite diverse. Beloit students cannot avoid interacting with students that are not like them. Moreover, this appreciation for diversity is fostered in the content of the liberal arts education they receive at Beloit, which asks students to learn different languages, consider alternative political systems, and learn about other cultures through studies in history, anthropology, and the arts. And, because Beloit wishes to ensure that students have a breadth of knowledge, students are required to take a variety of courses outside their majors. Students are, thus, constantly interacting with students who are majoring in other disciplines.

The faculty members at Beloit model a commitment to lifelong learning for Beloit students. As Pope (2012: 163) describes, "it's not a prestige-driven place. Its free-spirited culture embraces learning as an adventure and a thrill, not a means to an end." Again, a low student to faculty ratio (12:1) makes it possible for faculty to frequently interact with students and to take on a mentoring role. As one senior remarked, "Professors ... are extremely accessible" (cited in Fiske *et al.* 2012: 55). Faculty that can communicate the joy of learning may encourage students to seek out further opportunities to learn. In addition, as residential campuses that are singly focused on undergraduate education, students are challenged to be actively learning inside and outside the classroom. As noted above, a number of campus-wide programs facilitate this.

When participants in our alumni survey were asked what they thought was special about their Beloit College experience they highlighted the experiences

that liberal arts colleges hope to give their students and the values that communities of liberal learning hope to cultivate in their students. Almost an
equal number of the alumni who responded to our survey reported that small
classes and relationships with faculty were what made a liberal arts degree
unique (84 percent and 83 percent respectively). Similarly, 56 percent said that
the types of relationships were what made the degree unique and 40 percent
responded that it was a function of the number of extracurricular activities.

Regarding what makes a liberal arts degree unique, 20 percent of respondents
provided an elaboration. Of the 38, 18 mentioned something about the content
of liberal arts education, using words like "critical thinking," "problem solving,"
and "breadth of disciplines." One respondent stated, "[a] recognition that lifetime
learning and awareness of [a] wide range of knowledge is needed for a full life."

When asked to explain how attending a liberal arts college impacted their
after-college life, 53 percent said that it influenced the type of job they pursued and 55 percent said that it encouraged graduate education. In addition,
27 percent of respondents expanded on their multiple-choice selections. Of
these 51, 33 again stated that the content of a liberal arts education had
impacted their after-college life. For example, respondents said:

> [the] application of critical thought and problem solving to my job; self-
> confidence; not [being] afraid to pursue any career opportunity; con-
> tinued interest in a broad range of topics.
>   Well-rounded thinking and problem solving skills and ability to
> approach the world with an open mind.
>   I have a broad perspective in all my pursuits.
>   I work in a field that is a cross between economics, engineering and
> sociology. This is a field that requires [a person to be] cross-disciplinary.
>   [the] ability to think broadly, tackle complex problems, work with
> diverse teams.

Still others noted that it had provided them with an international perspective
and focus in their life. Again, these liberal values and habits of mind prove
useful in alumni's post-Beloit lives.

Conclusion

Beloit College students, we argue, live in close proximity with one another,
enjoy small classes, and participate in a range of activities that creates multiple opportunities for them to develop meaningful social relationships that can
last for decades after their time at Beloit. Like other communities of liberal
learning, then, Beloit should be thought of as a social space where students
receive a liberal education in and out of the classroom and where students
interact with and learn how to build social connections with others from different interests, ethnicities, and countries, and with different socio-economic
backgrounds and career goals. Like the students of many other liberal arts

colleges, Beloit students develop an appreciation for diversity, a commitment to lifelong learning and, importantly, skill in the art of association.

Alexis de Tocqueville, in *Democracy in America*, has argued that democracy is able to thrive in the United States because citizens have a general taste for and a skill in the art of association. But, as Nobel laureate Elinor Ostrom (in Aligica and Boettke 2009: 159) explains, "self-governing, democratic systems are always fragile enterprises. Future citizens need to understand that they participate in the constitution and reconstitution of rule-governed politics. And they need to learn the 'art and science of association.'" To the extent that liberal arts colleges give students experience in association, they can play an important role in preparing students for self-governance. Again, requiring that students live in the dorms and take classes in a variety of areas means that students grow comfortable interacting with others with different backgrounds, experiences and perspectives. Offering opportunities for students to participate in athletics and clubs gives students multiple arenas to work with each other to accomplish shared goals and multiple bases around which to build relationships. These communities of liberal learning give students opportunities to develop the tools they need to work and live alongside and to cooperate with one another to achieve shared ends in the political, social and economic sphere with potentially quite diverse others. The lessons that liberal arts students learn and the values that they develop as a result of their experiences in the classroom are reinforced and even enhanced during their experiences living together in small communities.

The important role that liberal arts colleges can play in preparing students for political and civic life in a democracy has been recognized. The tendency, however, is to focus on how aspects of the curriculum give students the tools of self-governance. But, as we have discussed, the social spaces that are created in the context of residential liberal arts institutions facilitate the formation of long-lasting social bonds between students of diverse backgrounds, and, as such, is critical to students developing a facility with association and self-governance.

Acknowledgements

We would like to thank a few individuals at Beloit College who made data available. We would like to thank Michelle Ping for her efforts with the alumni survey data. Also, we would like to extend our gratitude to Ellenor O'Byrne and Ruth Vater for data support through the Offices of Institutional Research, Assessment and Planning at Beloit College. Thank you Natalie Gummer for making the senior capstone reflections available. Thank you Aaron Joiner of the Office of International Education. Thank you Terry Owens for data related to athletics.

Notes

1 This certainly characterizes our experience. Both of us continue to count college friends amongst our closest friends and Grube is married to a Beloiter.

2 References to "liberal arts colleges" should be considered as "small, residential liberal arts colleges."
3 Further, there is an appreciation of education "for education's sake" (Breneman 1994: 3). Rather than have a direct, instrumental goal for studying a particular field, a liberal arts degree encourages learning and continued learning as an end in itself.
4 AAC&U, available online at https://www.aacu.org/leap/what_is_liberal_educa tion.cfm (accessed 19 May 2014).
5 Available online at http://archives.williams.edu/mission-and-purposes-2007.php (accessed 19 May 2014).
6 Available online at http://info.vassar.edu/about/vassar/mission.html (accessed 19 May 2014).
7 Available online at https://apps.carleton.edu/about/mission (accessed 19 May 2014).
8 Available online at www.stlawu.edu/philosophy/mission-statement (accessed 19 May 2014).
9 Available online at www.hamilton.edu/facts/mission (accessed 19 May 2014).
10 Available online at https://www.smith.edu/about_mission.php (accessed 19 May 2014).
11 Available online at http://president.williams.edu/college-mission-and-purposes (accessed 19 May 2014).
12 Available online at www.knox.edu/offices/registrar/catalog/statement-of-mis sion.html (accessed 19 May 2014).
13 Available online at www.skidmore.edu/about/mission.php (accessed 19 May 2014).
14 Available online at www.middlebury.edu/about/handbook/general/mission_state ment (accessed 19 May 2014).
15 Available online at http://colleges.usnews.rankingsandreviews.com/best-colleges/ oregon-state-university-3210 (accessed 19 May 2014).
16 Available online at http://colleges.usnews.rankingsandreviews.com/best-colleges/ louisiana-state-university-baton-rouge-2010 (accessed 19 May 2014).
17 University of Central Florida has one of the highest student to faculty ratios. Available online at http://colleges.usnews.rankingsandreviews.com/best-colleges/ university-of-central-florida-3954 (accessed 19 May 2014).
18 By "community" we mean both the elevated sense of community (e.g. a collective student response to concerns about shrinking diversity, or rising sexual violence) and the less elevated and a more pedestrian sense of the word (e.g. negotiation over what to watch in the common room).
19 For HEDS, more information is available online at www.hedsconsortium.org/heds-surveys/ (accessed 19 May 2014). For the Annapolis Group, see article in the *Chronicle of Higher Education*, available online at http://chronicle.com/blogs/headc ount/alumni-of-liberal-arts-colleges-see-value-in-their-degrees/29329 (accessed 19 May 2014).
20 Fiske *et al.* (2012: 57) describe Beloit College as "a bundle of contradictions: a small liberal arts college in the heart of Big Ten state university country, where the academic program has an East Coast rigor but the laid-back classroom vibe reflects the free-and-easy spirit of the Midwest."
21 As Fiske *et al.* (2012: 56) note, "the Beloit social scene remains largely on campus, and includes movies, concerts, art shows, dance recitals, and parties at the frats. 'A lot of social life occurs on campus due to the small size of the school and greater Beloit,' says a junior."
22 The Beloit College Mission Statement can be located online, at www.beloit.edu/ about/mission/ (accessed 19 May 2014).
23 This information is available online. See for example, www.beloit.edu/bucs/quick facts, which claims as many as 30 percent.

24 These figures were made available by the Beloit College Athletic Department.
25 Available online at http://colleges.usnews.rankingsandreviews.com/best-colleges/ beloit-college-3835 (accessed 19 May 2014).
26 This information is available by request through the Beloit Student Congress.
27 Godley (2008) found that propinquity (measured by shared academic major and participation in joint extra-curricular activities) was the strongest factor affecting friendship choice over the four years students spend in college. Her study looked at students at a small, residential liberal arts college in the Northeastern United States.
28 Available online at http://colleges.usnews.rankingsandreviews.com/best-colleges/ beloit-college-3835 (accessed 19 May 2014).
29 Available online at www.beloit.edu/registrar/lap (accessed 19 May 2014).
30 As one Beloit student remarked, "This isn't just a school – it's a home, it's a community, it's a lifestyle."
31 Seven survey respondents did not respond to this particular question. Therefore, only 179 responses are recorded and not 186.
32 Article available online at www.usnews.com/education/best-colleges/the-short-list-college/articles/2013/09/26/10-colleges-where-most-alumni-give-back (accessed 19 May 2014).
33 Capstone Senior Reflective Survey of 2014.
34 Capstone Senior Reflective Survey of 2014.
35 See Smith *et al.* (1997), Milem and Hakuta (2000), Antonio (2001) and Fischer (2008) for discussions about how curricula that demonstrate an appreciation for cultural diversity and student bodies that evidence racial and ethnic diversity contribute to students being open to diversity. That "racial and socioeconomic diversity among students" is an issue for Beloit students (a political science major cited in Fiske *et al.* 2012: 56) reflects their appreciation for diversity.

References

Aleman, A. M. and Salkever, K. (2003) "Mission, multiculturalism, and the liberal arts college: A qualitative investigation," *Journal of Higher Education*, 74(5): 563–596.
Aligica, P. D. and Boettke, P. (2009) *Challenging Institutional Analysis and Development: The Bloomington School*, New York: Routledge.
Antonio, A. L. (2001) "Diversity and the influence of friendship groups in college," *Review of Higher Education*, 25(1): 63–89.
Astin, A. (1999) "How the liberal arts college affects students," in *Distinctively American: The residential liberal arts colleges, Daedalus*, 128(1): 77–100.
Brann, E. (2000) "The American college as the place for liberal learning," in S. Koblik and S. Richards Graubard (eds) *Distinctively American: Residential liberal arts colleges*, Somerset, NJ: Transaction Publishers, pp. 151–172.
Breneman, D. (1994) *Liberal Arts Colleges: Thriving, surviving, or endangered?* Washington, DC: Brookings Institution Press.
Fischer, M. J. (2008), "Does campus diversity promote friendship diversity? A look at interracial friendships in college," *Social Science Quarterly*, 89: 631–655.
Fiske, E. (2012) *Fiske Guide to Colleges*, Naperville, IL: Sourcebooks, Inc.
Godley, J. (2008) "Preference or propinquity? The relative contribution of selection and opportunity to friendship homophily in college," *Connections*, 28(1–2): 65–80.
Heath, D. (1976) "What the enduring effects of higher education tell us about a liberal education," *Journal of Higher Education*, 7(2): 173–190.
Lefebvre, H. (1991) *The Production of Space*, D. Nicholson-Smith (trans.) Malden, MA: Blackwell.

Milem, J. F. and Hakuta, K. (2000) "The benefits of racial and ethnic diversity in higher education," in D. Wilds (ed.), *Minorities in Higher Education: Seventeenth annual status report*, Washington, DC: American Council on Education, pp. 39–67.

Pascarella, E., Wolniak, G., Seifert, T., Cruce, T., and Blaich, C. (2005). "Liberal arts colleges and liberal arts education: New evidence on impacts," *ASHE Higher Education Report*, 31(3): 1–23.

Pope, L. (2012) *Colleges That Change Lives*, New York: Penguin.

Seifert, T., Goodman, K., Lindsay, N., Jorgensen, J., Wolniak, G., Pascarella, E., and Blaich, C. (2008) "The effects of liberal arts experiences on liberal arts outcomes," *Research in Higher Education*, 49(2): 107–125.

Seifert, T., Goodman, K., King, P., and Baxter Magolda, M. (2010) "Using mixed methods to study first-year college impact on liberal arts learning outcomes," *Journal of Mixed Methods Research*, 4(3): 248–267.

Smith, D. G., Gerbick, G. L., Figueroa, M. A., Watikins, G. H., Levitan, T., Moore, L. C., Merchant, P. A., Beliak, H. D., and Figueroa, B. (1997) *Diversity Works: The emerging picture of how students benefit*, Washington, DC: Association of American Colleges and Universities.

Storr, V. (2008) "The market as a social space: On the meaningful extraeconomic conversations that can occur in markets," *Review of Austrian Economics*, 21: 135–150.

Umbach, P. and Kuh, G. (2006) "Student experiences with diversity at liberal arts colleges: Another claim for distinctiveness," *Journal of Higher Education*, 77(1): 169–192.

Wagner, D. (1983) *The Seven Liberal Arts in the Middle Ages*, Bloomington: Indiana University Press.

Part IV

Self-governing norms and practices across the academy

8 Polycentricity and the principles of effective co-governance

What the Bloomington School can teach us

Paul Dragos Aligica and Emily Chamlee-Wright

Though American institutions of higher learning vary greatly in terms of their size, complexity, and histories, any college or university professor can utter the phrase "faculty culture" to any another college or university professor, and know that the phrase will be understood. The specifics may differ, but there exists an overarching set of norms – norms of faculty autonomy and solidarity, for example – that are recognizable across the spectrum of institutions. Among those norms is the expectation that faculty play a significant role in governing their institution. Sometimes called "faculty governance," sometimes "co-governance," the expectation is that faculty wield influence not only in their courses but in how institutional decisions are made.[1] In any particular institution the culture of co-governance may be thick, its rules robust and considered inviolate or it may be thin, its rules deemed flimsy and processes more "governance theater" than reality, but the cultural expectations are at work in either case. Though faculty will often poke fun at their own culture ("we seem to delight in endless meetings") and at times find the practices of co-governance to be a source of deep frustration, the processes are upheld by a principled belief that productive outcomes emerge through deliberation, real decision-making authority, and collaboration. And despite the rules of co-governance being a favorite target of ridicule, faculty will be the first to cry foul if those principles and practices are usurped.

In this essay we take the principles and practices of co-governance seriously as a form of self-governance that is worthy of our analytical attention. What connection, for example, does a system of co-governance have to the underlying function of an institution of higher learning? What makes a particular system of co-governance work well or less well? What can systems of co-governance as practiced in higher education teach us about self-governance within civil society more generally? To address these questions we turn to the work of Elinor and Vincent Ostrom and associated work within the "Bloomington School" of political economy they established.[2] We begin by examining the phenomena of co-production and team production in liberal education in order to shed light on the governance structures that have emerged around them. We then examine the polycentric nature of decision-making authority within higher education, identifying both opportunities for robust well-functioning processes of institutional governance and common pitfalls administrators and boards encounter when they fail to understand the overlapping spheres of authority that define and limit their ability to control every aspect of college governance.

Forms of production and structural rules

Bloomington School contributions to the study of governance are applicable to a wide range of cases, and illuminate a variety of institutional and organizational forms. Many of the core insights of the Bloomington School emerge from the complex interface between public and private arenas. This work has helped researchers understand better the complex domain that includes individual and collective, public and private, voluntary and non-voluntary actions. Most critically, this work has shed light on how the rules structure within a system of governance frames and shapes actions in such circumstances.

Bloomington School analysis of any given system of governance begins with the basic analytical building block of production. Of particular interest to the Bloomington School are production processes that require inputs and/ or generate outputs that are held in common (such as a common source of irrigation). Such circumstances present potential social dilemmas, such as the tragedy of the commons phenomenon in which individual members of the community have the incentive to overexploit the resource, spoiling the long-term productive capacity of the group. The challenge from the community's perspective is to adopt rules that enable them to overcome these dynamics. The particular circumstances of production, the Bloomington School finds, are often the driving force behind alternative structures of governance that grow up out of these circumstances. For example, Elinor Ostrom (1990) finds that farmers in communities from California to Sri Lanka have avoided overexploitation and depletion of water resources by developing rules that provide limited access to all members of the community, as well as rules that ensure oversight and monitoring, graduated sanctions in the case of rule violations, and opportunities for community members to adjust the rules when circumstances require.

Starting with the analysis of how goods and services are produced, and then analysis of how they are delivered and consumed, the Ostroms and their associates built step by step a theoretical apparatus of how rule structures emerge to shape individual action and social interaction with respect to that good or service. Each category of production calls forth a different set of institutional arrangements whereby the community can effectively manage the production process and/or govern the use of scarce inputs required for the production process. The Bloomington scholars were clear that a wide variety of institutional arrangements might emerge in order to deal with the diversity of cooperation and social dilemma problems associated any given situation. "Thus, instead of recommending any particular institutional regime as the panacea" for solving socially complex problems, the Bloomington School scholars tended to recommend "that all institutional reforms be viewed as experiments that can inform both participants and others about the array of consequences that may be produced by the adoption of any one institutional regime" (Davis and Ostrom 1991: 328–329).

Co-production situations generate challenges and social dilemmas that have substantial institutional and governance implications. In their work on metropolitan governance, the Bloomington scholars noted instances in which collaboration between suppliers of a particular good or service and consumers of that same good, was the key condition determining its production and delivery. Consider community well-being, for example, as a "good." In preventing and responding effectively to fires and other forms of disaster, in providing effective police protection and other public goods to its citizens, a community depends upon both the professional quality of the personnel and on the informed efforts of individual citizens. Without the latter, the chances for an effective and successful delivery of the service are much reduced (Ostrom *et al.* 1973a, 1973b; Ostrom and Whitaker 1973). In other words, the effort of citizens to prevent fires and reduce criminal activity, and so forth, is part and parcel of the quality and the supply of such services. There are thus situations in which users of services have a double function: users of the service or good and at the same time, producers or as the Bloomington scholars put it, co-producers. These are circumstances in which the input of the service users is decisive. Without it, "the service may deteriorate into an indifferent product with insignificant value." Production and consumption are intertwined because the consumer has to proactively participate in the production process: "The resources, motivations, and skills brought to bear by the client or consumer are much more intimately connected with the *level* of achieved output than in the case of [standard] goods production" (Ostrom and Ostrom 1977, in McGinnis 1999: 93).

It is the pattern of co-production that, in turn, drives the governance arrangements that emerge from the production process. Schools, hospitals, homeowners associations, churches, and other civic organizations cooperate in the dissemination of information on fire prevention, for example. Further, some communities are too small and fires too infrequent to financially support full-time fire fighters and thus depend upon volunteer "suppliers" from the community. Or in the case of crime prevention, community policing models take advantage of the local knowledge that members of the community can provide to law enforcement, but this only works if there are substantial norms of trust between the "cop on the beat" and the community and between police officers and police administration. In order to establish trust between community members, the police officer needs substantial discretion in determining when to strictly adhere to the formal rules and when to let a violation pass without incident. In order to exercise this discretion, the police administration needs to remain closely connected to the communities they serve (with, for example, civilian oversight boards) to be in a position to know that officers are using their discretion wisely. As Ostrom *et al.* (1973a, 1973b; Ostrom and Whitaker

1973) found, community policing efforts more often than not fail when the governance structure does not align with the co-production framework. The point here is that the circumstances of co-production drive the governance structure that emerges, in terms of both the informal norms and formal rules (Boettke *et al.*).

The category of team production is another distinct form of production that presents social dilemmas that can shape both the formal and informal rules by which an organization is governed. Anyone who has ever produced in a team setting knows well the problems that accompany such circumstances, including free riding behavior that reduces productivity of the entire team, asymmetric information in which team members know more than supervisors what is really going on at the most local level of production, and so on (Alchian and Demsetz 1972). Organization leaders may seek rules of oversight and monitoring that weed out shirkers, but strict top-down monitoring can be expensive, attenuating the advantages that team production offers in principle. Formal rules that incentivize the team as a whole, for example a bonus structure tied to production targets, can lead to informal norms that tap the more robust local knowledge that team members possess of their teammates' behavior. If a team perceives that shirkers rob the group of a larger financial reward, informal norms that ostracize shirkers and confer status to hard workers are likely to emerge. Note for example, the significant informal pressure private sector construction crews exert on team members to ensure that each member of the team is carrying his own weight. The more complex the organization, the more likely we are to see formal rules of recognition by which the administrative leadership rewards team accomplishments. The point here is that the informal and formal rules of governance that emerge reflect the circumstances of team production.

Co-production and team production in liberal education

Both co-production and team production are at the heart of the enterprise of liberal education. The student–faculty relationship is a quintessential example of co-production.[3] Its quality is "critically affected by the productive efforts of students as users of educational services" (Ostrom and Ostrom 1977, in McGinnis 1999: 93; Parks *et al.* 1981). Through attitude, interest, and degree of involvement, the student is an integral partner in the educational process. This is true even in the acquisition of the most basic knowledge and skills, yet the enterprise of liberal education is particularly co-productive. The development of critical thinking and complex judgment, for example, require the student not only to exert effort in acquiring skills and subject area content, but also a willingness to go "off script" into intellectual terrain in which she exercises and develops her own judgment.

Team production, too, is a defining feature of education. Particularly as we move from narrow forms of training to the enterprise of "educating the whole person" that is the aim of institutions of higher learning, the team productive nature of the educational process becomes apparent, with faculty, coaches, student life staff, and fellow students all becoming part of the production process. Further, the abilities to think critically and exercise complex judgment are developed in part by being exposed to the multiple perspectives and ways of knowing that disciplinary diversity affords.

The co-productive and team productive characteristics of liberal education have implications for what choices are available to individuals within their respective roles, how individuals engage with one another, and how institutions as a whole are governed. In particular, the co-productive and team productive nature of liberal education shapes the rules by which faculty and students engage in the classroom and by which the faculty, the student body, the administration, and trustees engage with one another. Such rules determine degrees of freedom in each role, who is responsible for what, and who has authority to negotiate changes in the rules.

The most fundamental way in which co-production shapes the delivery of liberal education is seen in classroom governance. Though few of us use the language of "co-production" when describing how we teach, most faculty implicitly acknowledge its presence in the pedagogical choices we make. The common practices of assigning readings prior to introducing a new concept, or of assigning follow-up problems after the concept has been introduced, for example, recognize that student effort is part of the "production process" of what students are to learn. Pedagogies that stress active learning, student production of new knowledge, and opportunities for peer-to-peer learning capitalize on the co-productive nature of liberal education, more so than expert-centered pedagogical styles that rely on a one-way transfer of information to relatively passive students.[4]

The co-productive nature of liberal learning generates both formal rules and informal norms and expectations that govern faculty–student interactions. Formal course participation grades, for example, are an attempt to recognize the efforts students are exerting in the production process. Informal norms are also common by which students who successfully signal that they are "pulling their weight" in the co-productive relationship will earn the favor of the faculty member. While favoritism in grading is generally seen as "out of bounds," no faculty member will fault the colleague who finds the extra time needed to help the student who clearly has exerted extra effort all semester long; nor will he fault the colleague who resists requests to repeat lecture material for the student who regularly failed to do the reading or attend class. The former student has carried his load in the co-productive effort; the latter student has not. The co-productive nature of liberal education is also seen in student-to-student interaction. Such an impact is acknowledged in class discussion, of course, but also within the dormitory and on the athletic field, which serve as sites for the establishment, monitoring, and informal enforcement of complex social norms.

Formal rules governing the academic program also link back to the co-productive nature of the educational enterprise. Though in most cases faculty collectively determine the categories of experience the student must fulfill (e.g., three courses in the sciences, three courses in the humanities, and so forth), most institutions of higher learning allow a good deal of choice in what courses students can take to complete their degree requirements. As students move toward a particular field of study, course requirements are increasingly prescribed, but students typically have their choice of which major, and therefore which set of requirements, they will pursue. All this choice tacitly acknowledges the realities of co-production. Greater scope of choice is likely to foster on the part of the student greater openness to learning, thereby enhancing the co-productive partnership.

The notion that students should have a say in how the academic experience is structured has led many institutions to confer to students a formal role in the institution's governance processes. At many institutions, particularly smaller liberal arts colleges, and particularly those that have a history of engaged student activism, students are among the academic senators who determine academic policy. Similarly, through formal participation in honor boards, students often serve a critical role in establishing expectations for student behavior, monitoring that behavior, and sanctioning those who violate the established rules.

The team productive nature of liberal education is also reflected in the governance of the academic program. Though individual members of the faculty have a great deal of autonomy over what content to include and how to teach their courses, and departments have a great deal of autonomy over what they require of students majoring in their discipline, there are limits to these spheres of autonomy. Consider, for example, the course requirements a department selects for majors within its discipline. Despite formal authority curriculum committees and faculty senates enjoy to approve or reject course requirements within a specific department, most faculty will consider it "department business" if, say, the chemistry department requires advanced organic chemistry as part of the major. Yet, the issue may become an all-faculty concern if the total number of courses required by the chemistry department is perceived as too high, threatening to crowd out opportunities for students to explore other disciplines and take full advantage of the curricular breadth a liberal education promises to offer. In such circumstances, "department business" may quickly become "all our business." Because the full educational experience is considered a team effort, other members of the team may be more inclined to assert their authority in such circumstances. Similarly, most faculty will consider pedagogical choices to be a matter of faculty discretion but will nonetheless be willing to sanction colleagues who do not adhere to common standards of instructional quality. In other words, structures we take for granted, such as faculty committees on tenure and promotion, have their root in the team productive nature of the educational enterprise.

Faculty involvement in virtually all aspects of college governance, well beyond the strictly academic sphere, may seem puzzling at first blush. If an economist unfamiliar with faculty culture, for example, were to predict how college governance might evolve, he or she might assume that specialization and division of labor would confine faculty involvement to the governance of the academic program only, and that governance related to finance, athletics, residential life, admissions, buildings and grounds, and executive hiring would be the sole province of experts hired to attend to these matters. But in fact we see faculty involvement well beyond matters most immediately tied to the curriculum and faculty instruction. Why is this?

Contrary to the standard economist's view, faculty immersed in the culture of liberal education instinctively resist the notion that a strict model of specialization would serve as a formula for good governance, at least in that context. Arguably it is the co-productive and team productive nature of liberal education that leads us to think of colleges and universities more as civic spaces than organizations dedicated to supplying a service. If pressed, we can certainly conceptualize our institutions as providers of educational services, and we as hired labor, but most of us behave and think about our colleges and universities quite differently; that they either are or should be more than this. The idea that governance might be "supplied" by a specialized class (e.g., administrators) and "consumed" by another specialized class (e.g., faculty) runs counter to our notions that institutions of higher learning are (or should be) democratic civic spaces. What our intuition may be telling us is that good governance, at least within contexts like ours, is itself a co-productive and team-based process.

Clearly, specialization and division of labor are at work in systems of governance. (At the end of the day we want the chief financial officer to be accountable for the institution's financial decisions and the vice president for enrollment to be accountable for successfully recruiting the incoming class, and so on.) But in civic spaces, the resources, motivations, and skills brought to bear by the user are intimately connected with the quality of governance, at least much more so than with the production of standard goods. Similarly, the production of good governance is team based in that the perspectives and local knowledge brought forward by different groups are essential. Though faculty may not hold primary responsibility for managing the institution's finances or student recruitment, for example, faculty have critical insight that may inform strategies pertaining to resource management and the admissions process. As such, faculty membership on the financial affairs committee and admissions committee makes a good deal of sense. The concepts of co-production and team production thus give us a unified perspective. The production of quality education and good governance seem to share some deep structural properties.

What we have described so far are the underlying structures of production within liberal education that have shaped the structures of governance we commonly find within the academy. What we have not yet addressed is the question of what marks the difference between a well-functioning governance system and one that is not. For this, we turn to the concept of the polycentric order that is at the heart of much of the Bloomington School's work on self-governing systems.

Co-governance as a polycentric order

If asked to describe the governance structure of a typical college, we might be tempted to sketch out an organizational chart like the one below (Figure 8.1), with the Board of Trustees at the top, the president reporting to the Board, the provost reporting to the president, departments reporting to the provost, individual faculty reporting to department chairs, and faculty (in a manner of speaking) overseeing students. Universities would be more complex, with layers of deans sandwiched between the provost and departments, but the basic idea is the same. The emphasis here is on a chain of command.

But is this what we mean by "governance"? In one sense it is. Members of the Board do "govern" the institution in the sense that many decisions ultimately rest with them, and in the sense that they bear legal and financial responsibility for the policies and practices of the institution. Yet in another way, this is not what we mean when we are trying to describe the governance structure of a college or university. What we have described here is a set of power relationships, but not the rules that govern behavior of individuals on the ground, nor the rules by which decisions are made. In other words, a reporting structure is not the same thing as a governance structure.

Particularly in their work on common pool resource (CPR) management, Elinor Ostrom and her Bloomington School colleagues have identified the characteristics commonly found within well-functioning governance structures. These principles of good governance allow researchers to diagnose why some communities fail and others succeed in maintaining an order that leads to the appropriate use of resources. In its empirical research, the Bloomington School's approach is to track the rule structure, or more precisely, to track the *rules in use* as opposed to the rules on paper, so as to gain a clearer understanding of the underlying governing system, how it works on the ground, and why it succeeds or fails to provide the order the community is seeking.

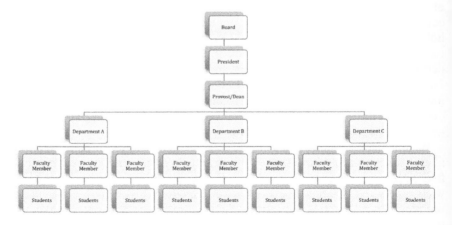

Figure 8.1 Hierarchical structure of governance

We can apply the same strategy to the context of higher education. If we follow the logic of the rules in use we will be able to reveal the deeper governance structure.

The cooperative and co-productive relationship between faculty and students form the first basic building blocks of co-governance. As students and faculty interact, their spheres of decision-making overlap, but they also preserve their autonomy.

Consider Figure 8.2.[5] Within the boundaries of graduation requirements, students have autonomy over their choice of classes, their choice of major programs, and so forth. Though there are consequences to their choices, they also determine the level of effort and engagement they put forth in any particular instance. In their relationship with students, individual faculty members likewise enjoy a sphere of autonomy and authority. Typically, for example, faculty members have primary authority over the content they cover, the choice of readings, assignments, and pedagogical practice. In other words, such choices would be inside the "Individual Faculty" circle. The intersection between these spheres represents the arena in which formal rules and informal norms of governance are required for the effective co-production of liberal education.

When it comes to matters of academic freedom, the autonomy an individual faculty member enjoys is sacrosanct. Such autonomy is often formally guaranteed, with institutional policies referencing AAUP's 1940 Statement of Principles on Academic Freedom and Tenure. Just as important, informal norms also protect this sphere as sacred. If there is anything akin to an academic creed, it is that faculty have a sphere of autonomy and authority – such as in the choice of texts, lecture topics, and teaching methods – that is inviolate. That said, colleges and universities are nonetheless *social* contexts, in which the multiple actors, each with their own spheres of autonomy and authority, interact within a complex system. Consider, for example, the interaction between individual faculty members and their respective academic departments (see Figure 8.3).

While assertions regarding academic freedom are part of a fiercely held moral code, we can also think of some exceptions, when the choice is not

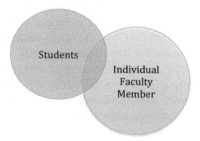

Figure 8.2 Overlapping spheres of autonomy and authority: faculty and students

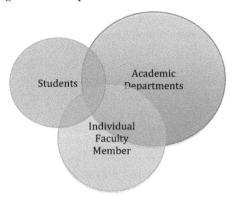

Figure 8.3 Polycentric governance: faculty, students, academic departments

completely up to the individual faculty member, but does not send us running to the AAUP website. Departments frequently have something to say about common course materials or pedagogical approaches. An economics department may agree, for example, to adopt a common text across all sections of an introductory course. A modern languages department may adopt a practice of immersive pedagogy, i.e., using the target language only, across all language instruction courses.

Viewed one way, departmental rules such as these may be seen as a violation of the individual faculty member's autonomy. Viewed another way, we have the beginnings of what the Bloomington School regarded as a polycentric order. While we as individual members of the faculty enjoy a sphere of autonomy and authority, so do academic departments. And as the previous examples suggest, on some matters these spheres overlap (again, see Figure 8.3). Consider also the role that academic departments play in review processes. While an individual faculty member may enjoy autonomy in how he teaches and the texts he assigns in most (if not all) his courses, if a parade of students marches through the department chair's office complaining about his teaching, he will soon discover the limits of that autonomy. He will be asked (told) to change whatever is deemed to be the source of the problem. The influence that academic departments wield in shaping the practices of individual faculty is not a contradiction of the principle of faculty autonomy; it is a recognition that both individual faculty and academic departments have spheres of autonomy and authority that do intersect.

It is important to note that while the spheres intersect, one sphere need not fully envelop the other, and this is certainly the case in the relationship between individual faculty and academic departments. While departmental influence might be felt in many aspects of a faculty member's activities, the typical teacher-scholar tends to enjoy a great deal of freedom (particularly if the faculty member is deemed to be doing a good job overall). The classroom is a remarkably "free" space in that most of the time we are not monitored by our colleagues.[6] And to the extent that our scholarly work is subject to scrutiny, the rules of academic freedom still apply, and ideally it is the quality of our work, as judged by the standards of the discipline, that matters. In other words, for most of us, there is indeed a sphere of autonomy free of departmental control.

As we continue to add on spheres of autonomy and authority, we begin to see the features of the polycentric structure of governance take shape. Matters of departmental curriculum, for example, rest squarely within the "Department" sphere rather than the "Administrative" sphere; whereas other decisions, such as budget allocation, fall within the "Administration" sphere (see Figure 8.4). And of course here too there are areas of intersection. Departments, for example, may make a recommendation of their preferred candidate in a faculty search, but such recommendations are (typically) made to a dean or provost who renders the final decision and sets the terms of any negotiated agreement.

Overlaying each of these spheres are standing faculty committees (see Figure 8.5). Individual faculty enjoy a sphere of autonomy, but they are also accountable to their colleagues in the form of committees on tenure and promotion and curricular oversight. The administration enjoys a sphere of autonomy, but it too is constrained by the authority the faculty hold over curricular issues and policies pertaining to faculty review and faculty status.

As depicted in Figure 8.6, a board of trustees also enjoys its sphere of autonomy and authority, but that autonomy and authority is attenuated by the fact that its sphere overlaps with others. We have purposely drawn Figure 8.6 such that the Board's sphere of influence does not intersect with the individual faculty sphere. We do this is in part to keep the figure from becoming muddled, but it is also to recognize an unwrittten rule that operates at most

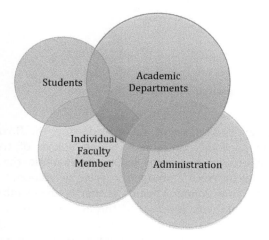

Figure 8.4 Polycentric governance, including administration

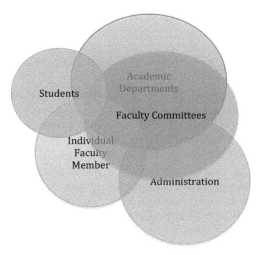

Figure 8.5 Polycentric governance, including faculty committees

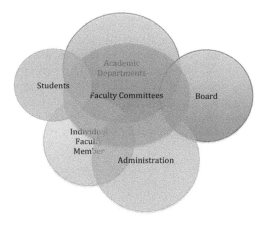

Figure 8.6 Polycentric governance, including the Board

institutions – except in the case of senior leadership, the Board does not get bogged down in personnel decisions. Though boards of trustees typically enjoy *de jure* authority over granting tenure, for example, the *de facto* reality is that they will not overturn a president's recommendation.

One way to view this common reality is that board members are shirking their formal responsibilities. But viewed through the lens of the polycentric order, a very different picture emerges. Boards adhering to the norm that they do not weigh in on matters pertaining to individual faculty, even though they could, is tacit recognition that to do so would undermine the process that is set up to render good decisions, grounded in local knowledge. The same could be said for any area of intersection. Though formally deans and provosts have the authority to override many decisions made at the departmental level, as we discuss below, doing so runs the risk of pursuing a course that is not informed by the local knowledge possessed by members of the department. Further, a dean who exercises formal authority that runs roughshod over informal norms of departmental autonomy undermines the integrity of the decision-making process pursued within departments. As the Bloomington School scholars describe, coordination within a polycentric system emerges as various constituencies simultaneously police, through formal and informal means, their respective boundaries that define their sphere of autonomy and authority.

The Bloomington School's emphasis on polycentricity emerged out of empirical work related to metropolitan reform.[7] Analysis of metropolitan governance structures revealed that underlying, seemingly fragmentary and chaotic, processes were patterns of order that were flexible enough to accommodate complex chains of production, provision, and consumption of public goods (Ostrom 1983a, 1983b). Contrasted with the ideal typical monocentric system, in which decision power is "vested in a single decision structure that has an ultimate monopoly over the legitimate exercise of coercive capabilities," in a polycentric system "many officials and decision structures are assigned limited and relatively autonomous prerogatives to determine, enforce and alter legal relationships" (V. Ostrom 1972, in McGinnis 1999: 55–56). That is to say, following Michael Polanyi's (1951) work, the Bloomington School identified two ideal typical methods of social organization. A deliberate or directed order having at its pinnacle an ultimate authority monitoring and controlling through a unified command chain; and a polycentric order where, "within a general system of rules ... individual decision makers are free to pursue their own interests subject to the constraints inherent in the enforcement of those decision rules" (V. Ostrom 1972, in McGinnis 1999: 55–56; Polanyi 1951). In practice, degrees of monocentricity and polycentricity can range within a given system, with one force always creating a tension of opposition with the other.

Relative to a standard command and control hierarchical structure, polycentric orders have features that make them more conducive to co-production and team production environments. Orders characterized by high degrees of polycentricism tend toward greater flexibility and adaptability that allow for experimentation and accommodation of a variety of co-productive and team productive arrangements. Experimentation, adaptive change, and pedagogical innovation in the classroom, for example, are far more likely if faculty enjoy a sphere of autonomy independent of the hierarchical chain of command.[8] That said, a polycentric structure of co-governance is no guarantee that it will work well (Ostrom 1990). This then raises the question of what the elements of a *functional* polycentric order are in the context of co-governance within an academic institution.

The principles of good governance: how we know we have them; what to do when we don't?

The most basic element of good governance within a polycentric system of co-governance is that every sphere – the individual faculty member, the department, the provost/dean, the president, the board, and we could add other spheres, such as governance structures within the student body and staff – has authority over issues for which it has the best access to local knowledge and the greatest incentive to "get the rules right." Administrations that receive votes of no confidence are often in this position because they have bypassed or overridden faculty authority in matters over which faculty have primary oversight. Administrative maneuvering of this kind should concern us not only because it undermines the principles of faculty governance over such matters, but also because it bypasses the local knowledge that faculty bring to the table when deliberating matters of which they have the greatest local knowledge, such as matters related to pedagogical practice or curricular design.

Second, in a well-functioning polycentric order, the boundaries of authority are clear such that everyone knows when it is their role to advise, to consult, to recommend, and/or to decide. Not understanding where the boundaries lie, and what role one plays in the deliberative process can lead to deep mis-understanding that may make it appear that the players are not adhering to the principles of good governance when in fact they may be. The president may *consult* with, say, the Faculty Affairs Committee to discuss the tradeoffs related to 2 percent or 3 percent salary increase, for example, but the advice she receives does not alleviate the need for the president to *decide* the matter. Faculty who do not understand that their role was to advise rather than decide may mistakenly claim that the president has not adhered to the principles of co-governance if she decides to go against the advice of the faculty committee. When it comes to curricular matters, on the other hand, it is the faculty's role, not the president's, to *decide*, for example, which courses are required for graduation. If the president misunderstands her role in this moment – if she offers advice as if it is a decree, or rejects the faculty vote on a curricular matter – she has stepped outside her formal sphere of authority.

Formal rules delineating decision-making authority, in the form of bylaws and policy handbooks, for example, are invaluable tools for gaining clarity on such matters. At the same time, any set of explicit formal rules will be accompanied by informal norms that may further define the *de facto* sphere of authority. The provost, for example, may have *de jure* authority over student suspension decisions, faculty requests for routine professional development funds, and so on, but the *de facto* decision-making authority may rest with the faculty committee charged with reviewing individual cases. The advantage of informal rules is that they allow for variation in practice necessary to adapt to local and changing circumstances. For example, the informal norm that it is the committee, rather than the dean that makes such decisions helps to avoid stifling bottlenecks in routine decision-making. At the same time, because informal norms will be different in every place, it is critical that newcomers take the time to "read" the local landscape such that they do not run roughshod over practices that have long-standing credibility in the community, despite the fact that they have no formal basis in policy.

Third, functional polycentric orders afford community members a great deal of influence over the rules that comprise the governance system. Faculty handbooks, Robert's Rules of Order, contentious and seemingly endless academic senate meetings are targets of ridicule, but they are artifacts of a process that takes rules, and processes that change the rules, seriously. When members of the community have a hand in establishing and significant control in changing the rules that govern interaction and define their scope of responsibilities within the organization, there is a greater chance that they will view those rules as having legitimacy.

Fourth, well-functioning polycentric orders charge community members with monitoring compliance with the rules. This feature of polycentrism is much more than compliance with formal rules (e.g., colleagues calling one another out for breaches in parliamentary procedures). A truly robust polycentric order recognizes through formal rules and informal norms, that community members are first and foremost accountable to one another. This aspect of polycentrism is at the heart of why faculty committees on tenure and promotion carry such weight in the evaluation process. And it is a mark of a highly functional polycentric order when a colleague can call out another for errant behavior, rather than waiting for the dean to notice and intervene.

Finally, and perhaps this last feature is summative of the points already made, in well-functioning polycentric orders, higher levels of authority do not encroach on the authority enjoyed at the lower levels. As has been discussed, sometimes our role is to recommend, and the person or group with the authority to decide may either accept or reject that recommendation. The point being made here is different. Polycentric orders flourish when actors with an appropriate scope of authority are able to put the local knowledge they possess to work for the benefit of the organization or community as a whole. A department chair, for example, has far greater access to the local knowledge needed to successfully manage the affairs of the department, be they interpersonal conflict between members of the department, deciding which adjuncts should be hired or dismissed, and so on, than any administrator holding a higher level of hierarchical authority. If a dean, president, or board member usurps the authority of the department chair, the lesson will quickly be learned that it is not worth the effort to manage departmental affairs locally. A dean who regularly intervenes in matters that are within the sphere of departmental authority, will in short order find himself in the role of "Super Chair" of all academic departments.

Given the principles articulated above, it is reasonable to ask how we know whether we have a well-functioning system of co-governance or not; how we know if we are close to or far from the ideal such principles imply. The glib response is that institutions that avoid votes of no confidence must be doing something right. The more serious response is that votes of no confidence and significant discord among faculty, administrators, boards, and so on, signal that *something* is wrong, but it is not necessarily clear *what* is wrong. The characteristics of well-functioning polycentric orders described above can provide a starting point for diagnosing the health of the co-governance structure and shed light on possible ways forward. A grander vision still is that in recognizing and making better use of the polycentric properties of our systems of co-governance, we model for our colleagues and our students the principles of effective self-governance that are key to robust civic life within and beyond the campus community.

The symptoms of a poorly functioning system of co-governance vary, but among the most common are deep-seated distrust between boards and the faculty, charges that the administration has not taken faculty governance seriously, and a widespread sense (among the faculty and the administration) that faculty committees have trouble getting anything accomplished. Again, the symptoms tell us that *something* is wrong, but diagnosing the problem is not necessarily obvious. Lack of trust between the faculty and the board, for example, may stem from unpopular decisions by the board, but it is important to ask whether those decisions fall into the "difficult but necessary" category. In such circumstances, better communication about what was decided and why, and the impact on various groups across campus, may be the best approach. On the other hand, if in making these decisions, the board overstepped the formal boundaries that define its scope of authority, such as imposing curricular change from on high, nothing short of a full reversal of the decision is likely to rebuild trust.

More difficult is if decisions are made that *formally* fall within the board's purview, but are *informally* seen as falling outside its sphere of decision-making authority. For example, a board that denies tenure to a faculty member after having received a favorable recommendation at every previous stage of the process, or a board that holds up approval of a curricular initiative that has passed through every layer of governance prior to reaching the board fails to uphold the principles of good governance even if they are acting within the letter of stated policy. In such cases it is the role of the president, the chief academic officer, and faculty leaders to counsel the board on both the formal layers of faculty governance and the nuances of local practice.

Concerns such as these are not likely to be remedied with a single conversation. The cultures of boards, often populated by people with a background in the for-profit business sector, can be resistant to faculty culture. In turn, faculty may unfairly attribute malevolent intent to board members precisely because they come out of a business environment and are not enculturated to the ways of the academy. This is where leadership, informed by the principles of good governance and armed with a great deal of patience, can make a difference, albeit over time.

Tension and lack of trust within administration–faculty relations are similar. It is important to sort out the difference between "difficult but necessary" decisions that are within the purview of presidents, provosts, and deans and those decisions in which an administrator has overstepped her formally or informally defined sphere of authority. Academic leaders will always be charged with having to make difficult decisions in which there are no winners. Particularly difficult are those circumstances when an academic leader knows she will be violating an informal norm, by for example overturning a tenure committee's recommendation, but concludes that the tenure committee has fundamentally failed to exercise good judgment in its review process. Slings and arrows are inevitable. One important lesson, however, is that the academic leader who has built a reputation for respecting the principles of good governance is more likely to withstand the firestorm of negative reaction when an unpopular decision has to be made. More generally, the academic leader well versed in the principles of good governance will override decisions at the lower level only when (a) she has the formal authority to do so and, (b) is certain that the decision rendered at the local level is the wrong one, and (c) the reversal is worth the damage she will do to the sense of authority and autonomy enjoyed at the lower level. It is worth stepping outside the local norms to avoid making a thirty-year mistake; it is not worth stepping outside those norms just to exercise managerial control.

It is commonly observed that co-governance is a time-consuming process. Yet there is an important difference between a deliberative process that moves forward slowly, ensuring that all points of view are considered and all decisions are weighed carefully, and a structure that is inherently averse to any change. The former will always be too slow for the taste of administrators and boards, but faculty insisting on such careful deliberation will ultimately offer up decisions that have legitimacy within the broader community and will therefore have greater likelihood of successful implementation. The latter situation – a structure inherently averse to change of any kind – however, runs precisely counter to the advantages a polycentric order affords, which is greater scope for flexibility, experimentation, and innovation. The sources of such rigidity are varied. The political economy of change is such that those who have adapted to the status quo may resist anything that deviates from the current path that minimizes risk and effort. Those proposing change may be deemed as advancing their personal interests, and therefore not to be trusted. Under such circumstances, faculty committees may be reluctant to propose anything new for fear of backlash from colleagues who prefer the status quo or may accuse them of driving a self-serving agenda. And in low-trust environments such as those we address above, any proposed change seen as coming from the administration may be deemed tainted by association.

Such postures – a self-interest so narrowly defined that it does not take the civic life of the intellectual community into account, a paralysis engendered by the fear of criticism, and an unwillingness to consider an idea because it wasn't one's own or offered by one's own kind – reflect the challenges we face in civil society more generally. Being cultural in nature, such problems may seem intractable. Arguably, however, intellectual communities are in a relatively strong position to shift cultural norms, as they are "in the business" of norm-shaping. Intellectual communities are in a perpetual effort to shape positive student culture, for example. The very virtues we impress upon our students as being critical to their education – responsibility to the intellectual commons that is a classroom, the importance of being engaged and taking intellectual risks, and an openness to consider even-handedly ideas different from one's own – are exactly those that are necessary to overcome anemic civic life within faculty culture. Perhaps the first step in improving civic life in our institutions is to admit the embarrassment that we have not always upheld these virtues in our dealings with our colleagues, even though we insist that our students uphold them with one another. Further, unlike many communities, academics are enculturated into a process of peer review in which ideas are proffered, vetted, and debated, which has obvious implications for the roles we can play in fostering open and engaged dialogue within the college community. Finally, because institutions of higher learning have formal structures of co-governance, there is some reasonable assurance that genuinely bad ideas have a fairly decent chance of being weeded out, so long as a diversity of faculty are fully engaged in the vetting process.

Conclusion

We have argued that the co-productive and team productive circumstances underlying liberal education and good governance require a particular rule structure that is best described as polycentric in nature. By viewing co-governance structures through the perspective of the Bloomington School, we come to recognize that co-production and team production in higher education are its functional principles that give rise to the polycentric framework that describes cultures of co-governance in institutions of higher learning. In practical terms, awareness of the co-productive and team productive nature of the collective enterprise by community members may provide intellectual support for structures that can often be perceived as frustratingly slow, cumbersome, time-consuming, and bogged down. A certain attitude is necessary in the deliberate effort to capture the benefits of the co-productive and team productive arrangements. This is certainly true in civic life generally. A good citizen understands that good governance cannot come without direct involvement, without the citizens' investment in building political competencies. In the same way, life in an intellectual community requires a specific attitude, the equivalent of citizenship and the civic attitude. A quality education requires a certain attitude, expression of the awareness of the co-productive and team spirit. The same holds true for robust co-governance within institutions of higher education.

By understanding better the polycentric nature of good governance, we are in a better position to recognize that colleges are (or could be) laboratories for civic life, in which the particular rules of governance and their accompanying implications for citizenship are tested, honed, and refined.

Notes

1 For convenience and because we discuss the intersecting spheres of authority between students, faculty, and administration, we use the phrase "co-governance." In using this phrase, we intend to include formal rules and informal norms of "faculty governance" as well.
2 The "Bloomington School" of political economic thought represents the work of Elinor and Vincent Ostrom and the interdisciplinary team of scholars working with the Workshop in Political Theory and Policy Analysis at Indiana University, Bloomington.
3 Historically, the university is the result of either students organizing as a collective unit of financing and consuming education/knowledge with a view toward attracting professors, or as a result of professors organizing as a collective unit of producing education with a view toward attracting the students-beneficiaries. In both cases the organizational arrangements grow around the basic co-productive nature implied in the acts of teaching and learning (Pounds 1968; Berman 1983).
4 See Garnett in this volume.
5 We have intentionally drawn the "Student" circle smaller than the "Faculty" circle to represent the fact that typically the faculty wield more influence in the institution's governance structure than students.
6 Peer review of teaching, in which faculty peers co-mentor one another by reviewing syllabi and visiting classes is becoming more widely practiced, but if such initiatives are voluntary, they need not diminish the degree of autonomy the faculty member enjoys in his or her classroom.
7 Bloomington scholars are clear that they are not the first to note the phenomenon. Alexis de Tocqueville made note of polycentric features of American democracy. Earlier, the framers of the American Constitution debated and fostered social arrangements that possessed polycentric features. Though the Federalists did not use the term polycentricity, their understanding of "the principles of federalism and separation of powers within a system of limited constitutions meets the defining conditions for polycentricity" (V. Ostrom 1972, in McGinnis 1999: 57; V. Ostrom 1990, 1973, 1971).
8 See Horwitz in this volume.

References

Alchian, A. A. and Demsetz, H. (1972) "Production, information costs, and economic organization," *The American Economic Review*, 62: 777–795.

Berman, H. J. (1983) *Law and Revolution: The formation of the Western legal tradition*, Cambridge, MA: Harvard University Press.

Boettke, P., Lemke, J., and Palagashvili, L. (unpublished working paper) "Re-evaluating community policing in a polycentric system."

Davis, G. and Ostrom, E. (1991) "A public economy approach to education: Choice and co-production," *International Political Science Review*, 12(4): 313–335.

McGinnis, M. D. (1999) *Polycentricity and Local Public Economies: Readings from the Workshop in Political Theory and Policy Analysis*, Ann Arbor: University of Michigan Press.

Ostrom, E. (1983a) "Analyzing institutions for the delivery of local collective goods," Prepared for the Annual Meeting of the American Society for Public Administration, 16–19 April.

Ostrom, E. (1983b) "A public choice approach to metropolitan institutions: Structure, incentives, and performance," *Social Science Journal*, 20(3): 79–96.

Ostrom, E. (1990) *Governing the Commons: The evolution of institutions for collective action*, Cambridge, MA: Cambridge University Press.

Ostrom, E. and Whitaker, G. (1973) "Does local community control of police make a difference? Some preliminary findings," *American Journal of Political Science*, 17(1): 48–76.

Ostrom, E., Baugh, W., Gaurasci, R., Parks, R., and Whitaker, G. (1973a) *Community Organization and the Provision of Police Services*, Beverly Hills, CA: Sage Publications.

Ostrom, E., Parks, R., and Whitaker, G. (1973b) "Do we really want to consolidate urban police forces? A reappraisal of some old assertions," *Public Administration Review*, 33(5): 423–432.

Ostrom, V. (1971) *The Political Theory of a Compound Republic: Designing the American experiment*, 2nd edn, Lincoln: University of Nebraska Press.

Ostrom, V. (1972) "Polycentricity," Workshop archives, Workshop in Political Theory and Policy Analysis, Bloomington: Indiana University. Presented at Annual Meeting of the American Political Science Association, 5–9 September, Washington, DC. Reprinted in McGinnis, M. D. (1999) *Polycentricity and Local Public Economies: Readings from the Workshop in Political Theory and Policy Analysis*, Ann Arbor: University of Michigan Press, pp. 55–56.

Ostrom, V. (1973) *The Intellectual Crisis in American Public Administration*, 2nd edn, Tuscaloosa: University of Alabama Press.

Ostrom, V. (1990) "American constitutionalism and self-governance," in M. Rozbicki (ed.) *European and American Constitutionalism in the Eighteenth Century*, Vienna: U.S. Regional Program Office, pp. 24–25.

Ostrom, V. and Ostrom, E. (1977) "Public goods and public choices," in E. S. Savas (ed.) *Alternatives for Delivering Public Services: Toward improved performance*, Boulder, CO: Westview Press, pp. 7–49. Reprinted in McGinnis, M. D. (1999) *Polycentricity and Local Public Economies: Readings from the Workshop in Political Theory and Policy Analysis*, Ann Arbor: University of Michigan Press, p. 93.

Parks, R. B., Baker, P. C., Kiser, C., and Oakerson, L. L. (1981) "Consumers as coproducers of public services: Some economic and institutional considerations," *Policy Studies Journal*, 9: 1001–1011.

Polanyi, M. (1951) *The Logic of Liberty*, London: Routledge and Kegan Paul.

Pounds, R. L. (1968) *The Development of Education in Western Culture*, New York: Appleton-Century-Crofts.

9 Meaningful change comes from the shop floor

Generating, growing, and governing in liberal education

Steven Horwitz

At any gathering of faculty who teach at institutions where commitments to teaching and liberal education remain central values, one is likely to hear a whole variety of complaints about the state of higher education today. The general tenor of those complaints is often about the combination of the rise of the professional administrator and the increasing demands for particular kinds of pedagogy and curricula that seem to be coming from "on high." The data on the growth of administrators/staff are unarguable, but it is important to disentangle the various factors involved, including everything from government mandates that have required new positions, to meeting the extra- and co-curricular demands of students that have led to a growth in Student Affairs positions, to what is the core concern of faculty, namely the growth in academic administrators in positions dealing with teaching and learning. Many of the latter positions are overseeing (or assessing) programs, often new ones, that have real implications for the work of faculty interested in liberal education. There is a sense that the faculty's control over the curriculum, and its ability to decide what sorts of pedagogies are appropriate to forward student learning, have been severely diminished by the rise of the professional administrator.

This loss of control to the hands of administrators who are perceived to be disconnected from the teaching and scholarship that faculty engage in provides the context for this chapter's exploration of curricular and pedagogical change and its relationship to self-governance. In the face of these concerns, faculty have to make the case that meaningful curricular and pedagogical change must come from the "shop floor." Faculty must create a culture of innovation among themselves out of which new programmatic initiatives and ideas about teaching and learning will emerge. Although programs imposed from the top down may well be successful at self-perpetuation, they are far less likely to be successful at achieving liberal learning goals than are those that emerge from the bottom up. One common example of failed "top-down" initiatives are pushes for more online learning. At institutions where faculty believe deeply in the value of face-to-face learning, and where they have built programs based on that belief, such initiatives are bound to fail. Even the use of technology in a face-to-face classroom can fail if it is driven by what IT staff or administrators think will work, or has worked elsewhere, rather than what faculty see as integrating best into their classroom practice. At some institutions, attempts to create writing requirements without sufficient faculty buy-in has led to the hiring of squadrons of adjuncts whose weaker connection to the institution suggests that such programs will not achieve their goals very well.

I will offer two related arguments from social science that bolster the case for thinking that decentralized, faculty-driven innovation is likely to be superior to that coming from the top down, and I will illustrate those arguments with examples from the role played by St. Lawrence University's First Year Program in generating innovation on our campus. Recognizing that innovation comes from the shop floor is only one of two steps necessary for faculty to reclaim their role in driving the curriculum and pedagogy. I will argue that taking responsibility for that innovation process by being willing to put in the time, energy, and resources to develop new ideas is one of the most important ways we engage in faculty self-governance. Too often, self-governance is conceived only in terms of committee work and voting on various proposals. Those are indeed part of the process, but they omit the most productive forms, which include things like faculty development workshops, peer-to-peer mentoring, team teaching, and a whole variety of other ways in which faculty can affect the culture and structures within which they work. If we define self-governance too narrowly, we end up buying into a conception of that work that sees it only in terms of its relationship to administrative edicts and the formal structures of bureaucracy, rather than as a way of shaping the culture and conditions of our work, including the curriculum and pedagogy. That said, in the modern university, administrative work cannot be avoided and new initiatives must be overseen. A second example of faculty reclaiming their role in the curriculum and pedagogy is a willingness to take on the administrative work of helping programs succeed. Faculty, as a whole, are resistant to taking on administrative work, though that might be different if more of the work that needed to be overseen were the product of their own work on the shop floor. To completely reclaim this work, faculty need to also create a culture in which they feel ownership of the curriculum and pedagogy to a degree that makes them willing to put in the work to ensure that it survives and thrives. Hoping that others will manage what we have created is a recipe for disaster. Genuine faculty self-governance in a project of liberal education requires that faculty be engaged in the entire structure of production of the curriculum and pedagogy of liberal education, from conception to maturity.

Structures of production and decentralized knowledge

My use of the phrase "structure of production" in the previous sentence was quite intentional. One of the ways that we can understand how faculty can engage in more meaningful forms of self-governance is to analyze the way in which new programs and pedagogies come into being and get adopted through the lens of the economic concept of the structure of production. Associated with the work of F. A. Hayek, the structure of production conceptualizes the way in which goods are produced as a series of stages that each passes through, starting from raw materials through to a finished consumer good.[1] The process moves through time starting from the "early" stages of production, which might include things like mining raw materials or research and development, through to the "intermediate" stages, which include partially finished goods (e.g., pressed and milled lumber that has not yet been transformed into a bookcase), to the "later" stages, which include finished products at a wholesaler or retailer.

As goods move from the early to the middle to the later stages of production, value is added to them until they become the final good on the shelf waiting for the consumer to purchase. If we imagine the structure of production for a bookcase, we can see this process at work. The earliest stages, or the ones farthest from the ultimate purchaser of the bookcase, would include cutting the wood (or even the purchasing of the machines that cut the wood) and shipping it to a mill. Note that a cut tree has more economic value than one still standing, and that a tree on a railway car headed to a mill has more economic value than one just lying in the forest. Because the source of economic value is the consumers' evaluation of how well a good satisfies their wants, each step that brings the raw material closer to the good that consumers want adds value. Milling the wood and turning it into the flat boards needed for a bookcase in the intermediate stages add value by moving the good even closer. The manufacturer who turns the boards into a finished bookcase adds value. The wholesaler who supplies the bookcases to retailers does the same, and then the retailer adds value in the final stages of production by bringing the product to a location where consumers can get it.

One feature of this model is that it assumes that the physical capital used at each stage, such as the various machines involved in all of these processes, has a certain degree of specificity to it. Any given machine is not capable of being used at more than a limited number of tasks and therefore can only be used at particular stages in the structure of production. For example, the machines used to cut down trees cannot be used to turn the trees into flat boards. The forklifts that move boxes of finished cases around a wholesaler's warehouse cannot be used to drill the screw holes in the wood. Each of these machines also requires human labor and that labor must have a set of skills (what economists call "human capital") that is complementary to the physical capital it works with. Labor's skills also have particular degrees of specificity, as workers who are very productive at one stage because of their complementarity to the physical capital there might be less so at other stages because their particular skills do not align as well with those machines. Oversimplified economic models often ignore these issues, preferring to treat capital as perfectly fungible with other capital, and the same with labor and other labor. Some even treat capital as perfectly substitutable with labor. In reality, capital goods and workers each have differing capabilities and the challenge for economic production is bringing them into alignment with each other to produce the most value.

More generally, the "economic problem" involves determining what it is that people want and how best to produce it. The structure of production gives us a way of seeing the complexity of how to answer those two questions. For example, how do we know whether people want bookcases or not, and how do we know whether to make them out of wood, steel, or plastic? Alternately, we have all this wood we might use, but what should we make out of it? Although economists disagree on much, there is a broad consensus that, in general, the best way to discover the answers to these questions is through the prices, profits, and losses of the market. Part of the argument for that position is that allowing individuals and the organizations they form to act on the basis of their own particular knowledge and judgments, supplemented by the feedback from prices, profits, and losses as to how correct they were, will do a better job than trying to impose answers from the top down. Just as we think that academics will do a better job in generating knowledge if we give them the academic freedom to explore the ideas each thinks is important, subject to the feedback of the process of peer review and the incentives of reputation, rather than dictating from the top what should or should not be researched, so do economists think that giving people the freedom to act on their specific knowledge of time and place will generate better results than orders from the top. The key to both is recognizing that no one knows everything and everyone knows different things. And both systems work because they have some kind of feedback process to inform people as to whether their actions have contributed to either creating value or enhancing knowledge.

Sorting out what to produce and how to produce it requires a delicate dance of coordination among all of the people throughout the structure of production. Those thinking about what consumer goods to produce have to not only think about what will create the most value for those whom they provide goods, they must also take into account which resources are available, how productive those resources are, and what they cost. Resource producers must also try to peer into the future and see what retailers might want (which is implicitly what consumers want) and therefore try to make available the resources they will need to produce those goods. The signals of prices, profits, and losses in the market help people sort out what others want and therefore help people to decide what they should be producing.

It is difficult to imagine trying to do this sorting out from the top down. The variety and quantity of knowledge that would be required to do so is beyond the ability of humans to collect and use effectively.[2] Attempting to tell manufacturers what goods to produce without knowing both what resources were available at what cost or without really knowing what it is that buyers want would lead to incredible waste and misallocation of resources, as has been the case in real-world economies that have gone this route. Societies that have attempted to dictate academic or scientific research from the top down have seen similar problematic results. In general, if the goal is to discover things that are currently unknown, processes that have freedom to experiment by decentralized agents and reliable feedback mechanisms to inform and incentivize their behavior will outperform those that attempt to consciously design outcomes. Such a decentralized feedback-driven process is also found in biological evolution by natural selection, and the same arguments against design there hold for similarly structured social processes.

The structure of production and self-governance in St. Lawrence's First Year Program

This conceptual framework enables us to think about how curricular and pedagogical change might take place in liberal education. The first point is to recognize that such changes, in order to be effective, have to go through a structure of production analogous to that of the market. One important implication of the structure of production view is that you cannot make goods without knowing what raw materials you have at your disposal. A second implication is that those who are at the front lines of dealing with the "customer" will be in the best position to know what goods should be produced. Creating new programs or demanding new pedagogies that do not align with the resources available, or what faculty know about their students, are unlikely to succeed.[3] In general, social institutions and practices that emerge from the actions of those who actually make use of them are far more likely to "stick" than those imposed from the top down. The educational practices that have the most impact are ones where faculty have developed them from the "raw materials" they know are available and have guided those practices through from the earliest stages of production to the final product that confronts students in the classroom. It is the faculty, with their local and contextual knowledge, who will be in the best position to know what needs to be done and how best to do it.

If the "final products" of this process are the curricula and pedagogies that constitute liberal education, what are the early and intermediate stages of this production process, at least ideally? How, in practice, do faculty take the relevant raw materials and start to turn them into programs and pedagogies that will be effective and stick? To answer those questions, I want to draw on examples from my own experience with the First Year Program (FYP) at St. Lawrence University (SLU).

The FYP began in the mid-1980s with a series of pilot initiatives that were designed to create living-learning communities as well as teach basic writing and research skills that it was perceived students often lacked. In 1988–1989, the program became mandatory for all entering students. In its first iteration, the program was structured as a year-long course, co-taught (normally) by three faculty members from different disciplines. The students in each course lived together in a residence hall, or a wing thereof, in what are referred to as "colleges." Early on, the program had a set of common texts with individual faculty teams adding their own additional readings and treatment of the common texts. The course replaced the standard freshman composition course and became the site for teaching writing and oral communication skills as well as research skills, which were emphasized in the spring. In addition to the common texts, faculty developed a set of common expectations with respect to the communication skills component of the course, providing additional programmatic integrity. Finally, the three instructional faculty also served as academic advisors for the students in their FYP college, each being assigned a third of the students.

The program has evolved in a number of ways over the intervening 25 years, with the two most important being abandoning the common texts and allowing faculty to develop their own course topics and texts (which happened in 1991) and separating the fall and spring semesters, with the latter being renamed the First Year Seminar (FYS) and not involving the team-teaching and living-learning components. The FYS courses more closely resemble a traditional first year seminar course, although the faculty teaching those courses are still held to common program-wide expectations around communication skills. One other change over the years was a move from three-person to two-person teaching teams as the most common option, as many faculty felt that made for easier intra-team coordination and more effective classroom size. Despite those changes, all of which were driven by the faculty in the program themselves rather than mandated from the outside, the FYP has continued its commitment to its four basic pillars: interdisciplinarity/liberal education, living-learning (at least in the fall semester), communication skills instruction, and high-quality academic advising.

The other important element of the program, as hinted at above, is that it was developed, piloted, structured, and administered by the faculty themselves. The faculty who first created the program did so because of problems they thought needed to be addressed in their work with students, ranging from having no space to introduce students to the idea of a liberal education, to weak academic advising, to a lack of alternatives to the Greek system as a model for living and learning, to no real follow-up on the writing instruction of freshman composition. Though the administration did mandate a 1991 review that led to some faculty-approved changes, almost all of the rest of the program's evolution has come directly from the shop floor. Many other schools have seen similar sorts of programs imposed from the top down, especially as a means to increase retention, but the FYP at St. Lawrence was a faculty initiative from the beginning.

The relevance of the program for my argument is not so much its own history, but rather the way in which the FYP became the catalyst for significant pedagogical, curricular, and cultural change on campus that has enhanced the faculty's ability to deliver a high-quality liberal education. I will look at three areas in which this change took place: communication skills instruction, interdisciplinarity, and general pedagogy.

Developing communication skills pedagogy

One ongoing challenge facing a program like the FYP was how to get faculty from outside of the English department to teach first-year students how to write, not to mention getting them to teach oral communication and research skills. Although we all write for a living, most faculty outside English departments have not had any formal training or experience in conveying that skill to students. We can all *assign* writing, but *teaching* it is another matter. An administrative mandate to expand writing across the curriculum does not make those skills appear. Having the faculty collectively commit to using the FYP as a site for writing instruction meant that the faculty were agreeing to figure out how to develop those skills to put that commitment into practice. Doing so required two distinct steps: figuring out what students needed (i.e., developing a set of learning goals) and providing faculty with the skills needed to deliver on those goals.

If the end product is to help students become better writers and speakers through more effective pedagogy, then the early stages of production are the focus on goals and skills enhancement. In developing a set of expectations (known in the program as its "Philosophy and Goals Statement"), faculty engaged in a series of conversations about the communication skills they wanted students to develop and then what sorts of pedagogies and how much writing and speaking would be necessary to achieve those goals. Although faculty with communication skills expertise were certainly leaders in those early discussions, faculty from across the disciplines brought their experiences with the sort of writing and speaking they expected of students after the first year and the places where they saw weaknesses in student preparation. By involving faculty from across campus in discussions of teaching first-year writing, the FYP was able to shape a set of goals and practices that did not just serve the particular needs of the program, but was in line with the program's sense of its obligation to the faculty as a whole to prepare students for writing beyond the first year. Notice the role of shop floor knowledge in these early stages of production: It was concerns of faculty working with students across the curriculum that fed into the development of programmatic goals.

One way that the commitment to those goals was overseen was another important form of self-governance exercised within the program. From the start, all of the syllabi for both the FYP and FYS were subject to a peer-review process by other faculty teaching in the program, and all were reviewed by the associate dean of the program, who was also a tenured member of the faculty and taught in the program. The particular form that review takes has varied over the years, but at the very least small groups of program faculty shared their syllabi and engaged in a group discussion of their strengths and weaknesses and whether or not they were meeting the program goals. This group feedback, along with that of the associate dean, frequently led to a round of syllabus revision before classes started. After the start of the semester, all of the syllabi were publicly available on the web for other faculty to see. This level of openness and mutual accountability was a particularly powerful form of self-governance and helped assure that the FYP philosophy and goals statement remained both a collective commitment and a living document.

Over the years, that philosophy and goals statement was revised periodically as faculty moved in and out of the FYP and as the perceived needs of students changed. At each of those moments of reflection, it continued to be the faculty teaching in the program who guided the revision process based upon their experiences, expertise, and perceptions. Subsequent versions of the philosophy and goals statement were approved by both a vote of the program faculty and then shared with the faculty as a whole, as were the major structural changes in the program, such as abandoning the common texts and separating the two semesters. The faculty in the program at any given moment recognized that "ownership" of the program rested in the faculty as a whole and saw the need to gain its formal approval as both an obligation of a university program and as a way to reinforce the program's legitimacy among the faculty and in the eyes of the administration. Although the program was sometimes accused of a certain degree of insularity by its faculty critics, it continued to recognize its obligations to the faculty as a whole over the evolution of the philosophy and goals statement.

Having developed a preliminary set of learning goals, the challenge was to create an environment in which they could be achieved. From the beginning, faculty with expertise in communication skills instruction found ways to share it with colleagues through a variety of methods. Faculty who taught in the program committed to participating in a number of faculty development workshops over the year, including an annual two-day retreat each summer. Those workshops were, for the most part, run by other faculty as a form of peer-to-peer instruction. Though the occasional outside expert was brought in, the program's thinking was that, again, the particular local knowledge of SLU faculty put them in the best position to do what was needed. As faculty in the program began to develop some expertise and experiment with new writing assignments and pedagogies, the faculty development process expanded to more comprehensive uses of peers, as faculty from a variety of disciplines shared their assignments with others, generating a social learning process by which better pedagogies began to stand out and spread across the program. When the program split off the spring semester and more tightly focused it on the pedagogy of research skills, it was FYS faculty from outside the English department who developed some effective pedagogical strategies that they then demonstrated in workshops for other faculty, who tried and adapted them for their own use. A decade later, the basics of that pedagogy still form the foundation of the way research skills are taught in a good number of FYS courses.

One of the hopes of engaging a broad subset of faculty in the work of communication skills pedagogy is that they would bring those pedagogies to their work in their home departments. That hope has largely been realized over the years as many faculty who have taught in the FYP and FYS have adapted the assignments and strategies they used there to enhance the writing, speaking, and research projects in their disciplinary courses. More generally, the focus on process that is central to the FYP has led more faculty to shift the balance of their courses away from being solely about disciplinary content to one that includes more explicit skills goals and instructions. By having responsibility for communication skills instruction spread out across campus from a more organic process based on pedagogies with demonstrated success, SLU has avoided the need for imposing a writing across the curriculum program top down, or having some sort of university-wide writing requirement. Instead, we have been able to embed those goals across campus by having a large percentage of the faculty with experience and knowledge of good communication skills pedagogy. Many of the same topics covered in FYP workshops have also been offered through our campus-wide Center for Teaching and Learning, offering non-FYP faculty a chance to learn as well. Rather than leaving the responsibility for communication skills instruction in the hands of specialists, SLU faculty have mostly taken on that responsibility themselves and, as a result, the faculty have become capable of doing that work, which is a much better assurance of an ongoing commitment to the communication skills goals of a liberal education.[4]

The evolution and development of the communication skills goals and pedagogy reflects a structure of production in which decentralized and local knowledge forms the foundation of the creation of value and in which that knowledge has to be coordinated across the various stages. In the case of the FYP, the coordination process was obviously not the prices, profits, and losses that we see in the market, but rather the process of faculty self-governance. The willingness of a sufficient number of faculty to take direct responsibility for first-year communication skills instruction, and the faculty ownership of the program in which that instruction took place, became ways in which faculty could guide the process from creating the necessary skills all the way through their implementation in the FYP and beyond. The ways in which this combination of shop floor commitment and willingness to self-govern led to good writing pedagogy spreading across campus reflects the degree to which these strategies "stick" in comparison to top-down ones.

Interdisciplinarity and a culture of teaching

Where faculty are willing to take on the task of self-governance and to guide curriculum and pedagogy through the necessary stages of production themselves, the results will be better and will be more sustainable through time. Two of the other key features of the FYP reflect this point. From the beginning, the interdisciplinarity of program courses, including the single instructor FYS after 2001, was a central means of achieving the program's learning goals around liberal education. Though it was not an explicit goal of the program, one of the results of the requirement of team teaching was to increase the degree of cross-disciplinary teaching and research that faculty engaged in beyond the boundaries of the FYP and FYS.

At many institutions, liberal learning goals include an emphasis on understanding important topics from multiple disciplinary perspectives. Normally this is conceived of as taking place over the course of the full four years as multiple classes across various disciplines are thought necessary to accomplish the task. It is fairly easy to put in curricular requirements that students take courses from various divisions of the college. However, the hard part is finding ways to connect those courses so that the disciplines are brought into direct contact with each other in ways that enable students to really grasp the different epistemological and theoretical perspectives that they bring to their subject matter. The interdisciplinarity that comes from two or three faculty from different disciplines occupying the same classroom space and bringing their perspectives, and a reflectiveness about them, into dialogue with respect to a particular topic is a much more powerful way of achieving that goal of liberal learning. Students can directly experience the ways in which disciplines are ways of constructing knowledge that ask certain kinds of questions and not others. The experience of seeing the world through a different set of disciplinary eyes, and the way in which it enables students to encounter their "home" discipline with the eyes of a stranger, is a much more transformative way to gain an interdisciplinary perspective than is checking off boxes on a list of distribution courses.

But for this to work, faculty need to be willing to take ownership of such courses and believe that it is possible to teach across disciplines in a meaningful way. In particular, they must get beyond the simple model of alternating presentations of discipline-based content to really engaging across disciplines and genuinely team teaching such courses. Being able, for example, to understand the other discipline well enough to teach it and to discuss its assumptions, strengths and weaknesses, and the scope of its explanatory power reflects a much deeper conception of interdisciplinarity, and one that is far superior to the distribution requirement approach, especially if it comes from the top down. When faculty engage the process of self-governance by creating and administering programs that build in such interdisciplinary teaching, and make use of peer mentoring and collective commitments to particular pedagogies and other similar strategies to help faculty improve their ability to do such work, they will more effectively guide the process that produces the desired liberal education goal. It will also build that interdisciplinarity into faculty's pedagogy and perhaps even their scholarship in ways that will stay with them and the institution down the road.[5]

One of the results of this work in the context of St. Lawrence is that the ethos of team teaching has become more embedded in the institution. It is not uncommon to see faculty team teaching outside of the FYP, and often doing so as an outgrowth of the work they did there. Faculty research has also tended in a more interdisciplinary direction, and faculty have worked across such lines in the arts and sciences in particular to create facilities and programs that provide students with a richer experience not bound by specific disciplines. Interdisciplinarity will be lasting and sustainable when it emerges from faculty using their power of self-governance to create and administer programs that make interdisciplinarity central, and also do the work of guiding its growth from that specific program through to the broader curriculum and into pedagogy.

An additional benefit of faculty-driven curricular innovation is that it is a more powerful method of campus cultural change. The kinds of early stage investments in faculty that are necessary to get them to produce the liberal learning that so many of us value will have a long-run payoff in the ways it shapes faculty culture. When new curricular initiatives are created, nurtured, and governed by faculty, they come with a legitimacy that is born of the ways in which faculty can more easily persuade other faculty of the benefits of such initiatives and develop effective ways to make them work. Doing what is necessary to get faculty to be able to meet the goals of such programs will often become the beginning of new practices of faculty governance and communication. For example, in a program such as the FYP where developing skills in teaching writing and speaking, or working across disciplinary boundaries, are so central, the program's culture of peer-led faculty development has opened a door to all kinds of conversations about pedagogy. As faculty figured out together how to make the program work and agreed to do things like share and peer-review syllabi, it created an atmosphere of trust around discussions of teaching that eventually ran deeper than the needs of the program itself.

For much of the program's first decade, it was by far the largest site on campus where comprehensive faculty development work was taking place, including all the sorts of topics mentioned earlier. The University Writing Program did some additional workshops, but the bulk of their work was in conjunction with the FYP. Faculty who wanted to improve their teaching by exposure to new, and often cutting-edge, pedagogies did so by participating in the program. As faculty took those new skills back to their departmental teaching, two things happened. First, they spread best practices to departmental colleagues who had not taught in the program through the general kinds of conversations that departments might have about teaching and curriculum. Second, students who were exposed to, for example, writing pedagogies that stressed multiple drafts and peer workshops, got used to that sort of work early in their college careers, which made them more receptive to such pedagogies in departmental courses. It also turned them into better writers, and faculty observing this success began to find more creative and discipline-specific ways to use the writing pedagogies they picked up in teaching in the FYP. Without any mandate from the top, the faculty culture around writing pedagogy had developed a very effective version of "writing across the curriculum" that had organic roots in a faculty initiative. The FYP had shifted the culture of pedagogy and curriculum from the shop floor.

A related development was the way in which team teaching de-privatized the classroom and opened up space for constructive peer engagement over teaching. One of the unfortunate aspects of teaching is that for most of us it is a solitary activity, at least with respect to our peers. We face a classroom of students, but our classrooms are private spaces with respect to our colleagues. Tenure and promotion evaluations at institutions where teaching is primary are an attempt to open that space up through classroom visitations and examinations of teaching materials. Classroom visits in the context of a formal job evaluation are difficult to turn into meaningful peer exchanges because the context of evaluation and the power dynamics that it produces are not especially conducive to open conversations based on trust. Even classroom visits as part of a mentoring program for new faculty have to overcome issues of their frequency and the sense that the relationship is not an exchange among near-equals, but a more one-sided flow of expertise. One of the hardest things to do is to create space for genuine and open discussion of a classroom experienced simultaneously by more than a solitary instructor.

Team-teaching opportunities provide an opening for this kind of work. Teaching for a full semester, or perhaps multiple semesters, with a partner exposes our normally private work to the eyes and ears of a colleague in ways that official mentoring and evaluation processes cannot. Where teaching teams have an ongoing and long-term partnership, they are able to build the trust and good faith necessary for very open and constructive conversations about what's happening in the classroom and how to get better. Faculty can learn from each other's strengths and gain from the perspective of colleagues from other disciplines by seeing them work in person. The conversations about teaching that happen within teams and then across teams as part of a program that requires team teaching are among the most powerful and effective forms of faculty development, and also demonstrate the power of the shop floor. When faculty can create the spaces to do their work and step up to the governance process to implement and manage them effectively, our best work in the classroom can become a kind of "open source pedagogy" to be shared and spread among colleagues.

The larger institutional change brought about by this work can be the creation of a culture of conversation around teaching that extends beyond teams and specific programs or departments. The faculty development work of the FYP led to the creation of a Center for Teaching and Learning on campus as well as various successful grant proposals that led to a variety of sites of faculty development and opportunities to talk meaningfully about pedagogy. The end result is a campus that has a great deal of talking about teaching in both formal and informal venues. The development of such a culture is an outcome that many administrators would love to see happen and believe requires top-down design. But the experience at SLU indicates that this sort of meaningful change really does come from the shop floor when faculty design, implement, and govern such programs themselves. This is also why faculty reluctance to step up to the administrative plate is so frustrating. The alternative is to dissociate existing programs from their faculty roots and to leave the creation of new programs to those without the grounding in the shop floor of the particular institutional culture. Producing high-quality liberal learning outcomes requires that faculty guide and coordinate the process from the earliest stages to the final product.

The argument for the superiority of shop floor approaches to innovation should not be read as dismissing the role of leadership in moving faculty ideas into implementation. That leadership can be of two sorts. First, faculty are notoriously not self-organizing. Leaders will have to emerge among the faculty to create the processes by which ideas will become concrete proposals and those with various forms of expertise will have to step forward to lead on particular pieces (e.g., the role played by English faculty in developing writing pedagogy and learning goals). In economic processes of production, raw materials do not move themselves through the stages of production. They require entrepreneurs with a vision of that final product to organize the inputs in ways that produce that output. Faculty leaders can be seen as curricular and pedagogical entrepreneurs who are organizing the process by which ideas become new programs. Second, even shop floor initiatives must eventually work their way through the administration. Deans and provosts who recognize the kinds of arguments I have raised here can exercise what one might call "facilitative leadership" by helping to create the conditions under which faculty can develop new programs from the shop floor. This might take the form of material resources, but it could also be things like connecting faculty with peers at other institutions who have done similar work, or simply offering public support for the work faculty are doing. Just as good economic institutions create the fertile ground in which effective entrepreneurship can take place, so can good academic leadership create the conditions under which faculty initiatives are more likely to thrive.

The problem of special interests

Any discussion of faculty-driven curricular and pedagogical change needs to address what might best be called "the problem of special interests." One of the criticisms made of the way in which curricula have evolved in the last few decades is that small groups of faculty with fairly particular interests have been able to capture financial and human resources in order to push through programs that align with those interests even though the faculty as a whole might not think the programs are sufficiently valuable. Over time, the result can be a curriculum that is a pastiche of these special interests rather than a more integrated whole reflecting the work of the entire community of faculty. For many faculty, especially those who think that a general education program as well as an entire curriculum should coherently reflect a set of underlying principles of liberal education, the unfolding of this process has been a source of much concern.

Political economy has had a long-standing analysis of special interest politics that can be applied here to understand this phenomenon.[6] The analysis begins by noting a key feature of the pleas of special interests: The benefits of creating the programs they want will be concentrated in the hands of a small number of people, while the costs will be dispersed among a large number of others. Moreover, the benefits tend to be very visible and appear in the short run, while the costs tend to be more subtle and hidden, and normally take more time to reveal themselves. So when a few politicians ask for a subsidy for an industry in their state, the firms in that industry benefit a great deal (as do the politicians indirectly), but the costs of that subsidy amount to mere pennies per person for the rest of the population. When Congress asks for testimony on the wisdom of this subsidy, the beneficiaries have very strong incentives to go to Washington and lobby hard for it, while the rest of us find it difficult to raise objections given that the costs of doing so will exceed the fractional cost each of us pays for the subsidy. Congress hears strong favorable arguments and few objections, and the result is that the program gets passed even though it might be the case that the majority of the community thought it was a bad idea.

Matters get more complicated when we understand the ways in which political actors will engage in the mutual favor-trading known as "log rolling." A further reason that politicians tend not to object to the special interest programs of other politicians is that they are assuming they will get the same free pass with their own. In fact, there is plenty of evidence that there is explicit trading of the "you vote for mine, I'll vote for yours" sort. This mutual backscratching is known in the literature as log rolling – as in the way that lumberjacks have to work in tandem to successfully roll logs down a river. The result, however, is that the incentives to ever object to special interest legislation are weakened as each politician knows that he or she can get the same forbearance in return and thereby get programs passed that will please their constituents and garner them the votes needed for re-election.

Academia does not work exactly this way, but many of the same features are present. Small groups of faculty who wish to create a new curricular program are often quite successful at "lobbying" administrators to support such programs by touting all of the benefits, many of which will be enjoyed by the faculty themselves, in terms of new colleagues or material resources or even required courses in their area. The costs of new programs have to be paid from somewhere. Even if funded by grant money, new programs rarely cover all of the costs, including the time of faculty or administrators that is being taken away from other activities. Programs that are not funded by grants, and especially those that claim to be able to run by using "existing resources," inevitably produce costs that will be dispersed across the entire faculty and staff as they cope with filling in the holes left by the resources used by the new program. As the political economy literature observes, the tricky part is that it is nearly impossible to identify these costs with any certainty before the programs are actually in place, whereas the benefits to such programs are easier to see. Opponents cannot point to specific costs in the way that supporters can point to specific benefits. Faculty are often subject to the same temptation to log-roll as are politicians. There are times that we may well choose not to object to our colleagues' proposals on the grounds that we might well be asking the same of them down the road.

This forbearance is often mixed with a commitment to a view of academic freedom that suggests we should not raise such objections. If we have allowed academic freedom to mean that we are unwilling to engage the critical discussion of what constitutes a good curriculum or good use of resources, we do not have much ground to stand on in criticizing the ways in which special interests have altered the curriculum.

One last feature of this process is that once programs have been established, it is notoriously difficult to get rid of them. Even something as relatively simple and low-cost as a new major can be hard to eliminate once established because its existence creates groups of beneficiaries who will fight vigorously to prevent it from being taken away, while those who are bearing the costs will have far less incentive to argue for the removal of that very small per-person burden. In the political arena, the logic of politics is such that special interest programs continue to grow in size and number, while serious reductions are very rare. In academia, similar patterns hold, although the Great Recession was a strong enough shock from outside the system to force the hands of many institutions in ways that were able to overcome the inertia in the process of program approval.

Getting it right: what it means for liberal educators to self-govern

If the special interest problem is real and if there is reason to believe that shop floor initiatives are far more likely to be successful than top-down mandates, how do we get more of the latter and less of the former? The answer is that faculty have to engage the process of self-governance in a meaningful way and take as much responsibility as we can for generating, growing, and governing the programs that define our curriculum and pedagogy. Often we have allowed ourselves to accept a far too narrow conception of faculty governance that ends up focusing almost explicitly on our role in the formal process of bureaucratic/institutional decision-making and far less on the ways we can construct and direct processes of pedagogical and curricular change from outside of those formal institutional structures. A community that self-governs is one that is willing and able to make collective decisions about how it will be organized and what it will do. To self-govern is to direct one's future, either as an individual or as a group.

Faculty have to accept this responsibility and realize that if we wish to make meaningful change, we have to find ways to work together and take charge of the process from the earliest stages to the latest. A key piece of self-governance in academia is the set of activities we engage in with each other where we talk about our work, both curriculum and pedagogy. Talking to each other about the shape of the liberal education we aim to provide and how best to provide it are the most powerful ways we direct our future. In particular, it does two things in light of this chapter's discussion.

First, talking to each other is the way we generate the ideas that will move through the structure of production to become the programs and pedagogies of which we will take full ownership. Creating the space to engage in dialogue across disciplines and departments allows us to find common ground in what we want to provide for students and how we think we can do so most effectively. As we begin to create new programs or talk about our teaching, we can also create a shared set of values around that common ground that can enable us to deal with the inevitable disagreements that change will involve. Too often, our governance processes are about how best to divide the limited spoils dispensed by others, or they get bound up in the tiny details of curricular requirements. Seeing these sorts of conversations as generative of both new programs and a set of values puts self-governance in the position of being the activities we engage in that generate and develop *most effectively* the ways in which we deliver on our promises of liberal education.

In addition, conversations about curriculum and pedagogy, through their potential to create that shared set of values, provide a possible way around the special interest problem. To the extent that faculty can find consensus about what we think is important and how best to do it, and particularly if we do that of our own accord in conversation with one another, that will enable us to resist either asking for programs that benefit only a few, or acquiescing when others do and we have principled objections. If those values are sufficiently shared, we can call each other to task if we feel that those values are not at the center of our work. Put differently: The formal, political structures of faculty governance will function best if informal processes of governance are in place that enable faculty to discuss their work and develop their values outside the formal process. If faculty have not had those conversations and clarified their work together, then it becomes much easier to take advantage of the formal governance processes in ways that put special interests before our common goals.

As noted at the outset, this also means that faculty have to be willing to engage the more formal elements of the governance process. The work of committee meetings cannot be just a necessary evil, but instead must be seen as part of the production process that helps turn our shop floor ideas into institutionalized programs and practices. Institutionalized programs and practices require administrators and faculty to step to the plate to take on those responsibilities. Finding willing administrators from within the faculty is more likely if the programs in question have originated on the shop floor through the more powerful informal forms of governance. If those early stages have created the "buy in" and the common set of values, faculty should be more willing to want to shepherd those ideas through the remaining stages of the production process and help guide them at maturity. This willingness to administer is key to helping such programs remain firmly in the province of the faculty rather than be taken over by professional administrators who lack the context and an overview of the entire process.

Many faculty preach the importance of workplace democracy. However, formal democratic processes are not the whole of what it means to self-govern. The hard work of true self-governance takes place not just in committee meetings and faculty votes, but in creating and guiding curricular and pedagogical initiatives that help us achieve our shared liberal education goals. And that means engaging in the conversations about what work we want to pursue with our colleagues to advance liberal learning, and using those opportunities to share our knowledge and expertise. Programs that emerge from this much richer notion of self-governance, like the St. Lawrence First Year Program, will have a greater likelihood of making it through the production process in a way that meets the curricular vision of faculty and needs of students. They will then only flourish if we recognize that part of our responsibility as faculty is to guide those programs as their administrators. If we forget any part of this process, we have little reason to complain that our "traditional purview" has been usurped by others. They will not have usurped our roles – we will have abandoned them.

Notes

1 This way of thinking about production can be found in Hayek ([1933] 1967) as well as later treatments by Lachmann ([1956] 1978) and Lewin (1999).
2 This point was at the center of the famous debate over the possibility of rational economic calculation under socialism in the 1930s. Again it was Hayek (1940, 1945), following Mises ([1920] 1935), who emphasized the role of markets in being better able to make use of knowledge than was socialist planning. An overview of that debate in the context of contemporary economics can be found in Lavoie (1985).
3 One of the limits of my analogy is my desire to avoid speaking of students as "consumers" without qualification. Our job as liberal educators is not to give them what they say they want, but to provide them with what we think they ought to have. It is not unlike market purchases of expertise, such as someone to fix your car, where you are trusting their judgment about what you lack and therefore what you should want. One way to think about this is that what one is really buying when one gets a liberal education is not a list of specific things that one "wants," but rather the faculty's judgment about what constitutes a good education. In other words, one is purchasing their judgment based on whatever evidence is available that one should trust that judgment.
4 See Horwitz and Oakes (2007) for more on how the FYP's strategy compares to what many institutions do with writing instruction.
5 My own experience in this regard might be illustrative. I was trained as a macroeconomist and monetary theorist, but after teaching a First Year Program course on the family with a colleague from psychology for a number of years, I became fascinated with the topic to the point of beginning to write on it professionally and teaching an economics of gender and the family course. All of that work took on a decided interdisciplinary edge. In 2014, that colleague and I co-taught a senior seminar comprised of both economics and psychology majors (including some double majors) that reflects an even deeper sense of interdisciplinarity than we had working with first-year students. The experience of team teaching across disciplines has fundamentally changed the way I think about economics and my own scholarship, and it has done so in ways that cannot be reversed.
6 There is a vast literature on the political economy of special interests. The place to start is Olson (1965). Many of the other ideas in this section emerge from Public Choice theory. An excellent overview is Simmons (2011).

References

Hayek, F. A. (1940) "The competitive solution," in *Individualism and Economic Order*, Chicago, IL: University of Chicago Press, pp. 181–208.

Hayek, F. A. (1945) "The use of knowledge in society," in *Individualism and Economic Order*, Chicago, IL: University of Chicago Press, pp. 77–91.

Hayek, F. A. ([1933] 1967) *Prices and Production*, 2nd revised edn, New York: Augustus M. Kelley.

Horwitz, S. and Oakes, H. (2007) "A writing program that works: St. Lawrence's faculty-driven first-year program," *The John William Pope Center for Higher Education Policy*, www.popecenter.org/commentaries/article.html?id=1888 (accessed 4 July 2014).

Lachmann, L. M. ([1956] 1978) *Capital and Its Structure*, Kansas City, MO: Sheed Andrews and McMeel.

Lavoie, D. (1985) *Rivalry and Central Planning*, Cambridge: Cambridge University Press.

Lewin, P. (1999) *Capital in Disequilibrium*, New York: Routledge.

Mises, L. ([1920] 1935) "Economic calculation in the socialist commonwealth," in *Collectivist Economic Planning*, F. A. Hayek (ed.), Clifton, NJ: Augustus M. Kelley, pp. 87–130.

Olson, M. (1965) *The Logic of Collective Action: Public goods and the theory of groups*, Cambridge, MA: Harvard University Press.

Simmons, R. (2011) *Beyond Politics: The roots of government failure*, Oakland, CA: The Independent Institute.

10 Academic freedom as a basis for self-governance

Jonathan B. Imber

In 1996, I published an introduction to the Transaction edition of Arthur O. Lovejoy's *The Revolt Against Dualism*, first published in 1930 and in a second edition in 1960, two years before his death. The title of that introduction was "The Vocation of Academic Freedom" (Imber 1996). My interest in the history of academic freedom was inspired by events on my own campus during those years, which have been chronicled by my colleague Mary Lefkowitz in *History Lesson: A Race Odyssey* (Lefkowitz 2008). I rely here generously on my own published introduction to Lovejoy's work in the recounting of that history while bringing up to date the fate of academic freedom in an era of global challenges to self-governance.

Arthur Lovejoy's contributions to the cause of academic freedom were instrumental in the development of formal principles of due process in the long struggle to define and protect the rights and promote the duties of the academic vocation, now entirely taken for granted by those who directly benefit from the legacy he and others created. He led in the formation in 1915 of the American Association of University Professors (AAUP), whose first president would be John Dewey and first secretary, Arthur Lovejoy (Hofstadter and Metzger 1955: 475). I begin with Lovejoy's encounters with the early challenges to academic freedom because they reflect the various dilemmas that the academic profession has confronted about its self-governance in the predictably never-ending struggle between faculty activities and administrative oversight. Lovejoy was a student of William James at Harvard during the time that James formulated his ideas reflected in "The Ph.D. Octopus," a repudiation of formal requirements for that degree. When he enrolled for graduate work in philosophy in 1895, Lovejoy became one of James's test cases for his objection to such requirements that diverted "the attention of aspiring youth from direct dealing with truth to the passing of examinations" (Wilson 1980: 26).[1] Lovejoy completed an M.A. but never completed the Ph.D.

Upon his first appointment as an instructor at Stanford University in 1898, Lovejoy is said to have remarked to then president David Starr Jordan that "I am personally very indifferent about it [the Ph.D. degree] and regard it as unwise for a man to go at all out of the way of his own philosophical interests in order to conform to the requirements of this exercise" (Wilson 1980: 26).

After only two years at Stanford, in 1901, Lovejoy resigned in protest to the firing of Edward Alsworth Ross (1866–1951) by the university. Ross, who would later become one of the most well-known sociologists of his time, was dismissed toward the end of 1900 by Jane Lathrop Stanford, the widow of Leland Stanford, a former governor of California and U.S. senator (Mohr 1970). Under terms establishing the founding of the university, both Stanfords had assumed complete authority over its operation, and when Leland Stanford died, the same authority passed to his wife. Mrs. Stanford had expressed disapproval of Ross over a number of years. David Starr Jordan had mediated on Ross's behalf in an earlier episode, but Mrs. Stanford could no longer be appeased when, in the spring of 1900, Ross spoke disparagingly of those who had profited from the construction of railroads with the use of cheap ("coolie") labor. The Stanford family fortune had been made in railroads.

An imposing man with, in the words of Mary O. Furner (1975: 230–231), "well over six feet of brawn," Ross had regularly expressed his opinions on many controversial subjects, and so he was not entirely surprised by his firing. He was also not an innocent player in the entire affair. By setting out consciously to make his dismissal a public event, Ross staged an early version of a drama that is now regularly played out in the academy. The public and press came thundering to his defense when his dismissal was reported across the nation. He hired news clipping services to keep track of the public's opinion, which was overwhelmingly in his favor. Mrs. Stanford was characterized as standing in the way of scientific progress, though Stanford students and alumni were largely supportive of her actions, perhaps fearing the consequences to Stanford's reputation in the early phase of its development.

Although the Ross case is now part of the hagiography of early efforts to define and defend academic freedom, both his actions and the reasons for his dismissal are not entirely pure or impure. Mostly lost in the historical mists is an account of the events following Ross's termination, which led Arthur Lovejoy to resign from the Stanford faculty. Not long after Ross was fired, one of the original members of the faculty, a historian named George E. Howard, who was 20 years older than Ross, is reported to have interrupted himself as he was about to lecture on the French Revolution to say that new forms of repression and bigotry were asserting themselves and that he deplored the firing of Ross and his denial of academic freedom. For his remarks in class as well as a similar statement to the press, Howard was also fired.[2]

As Richard Hofstadter and Howard Metzger describe (Hofstadter and Metzger 1955: 436–445), the dismissal of Howard, which President Jordan unsuccessfully sought to avert, produced a chain reaction. Lovejoy's only account in writing about what happened at Stanford (in distinction to what principles of academic freedom were at stake, about which he did write) is contained in the utterly flamboyant book *The Goose-Step: A study of American education,* by Upton Sinclair, published in 1923. I quote from a letter which Lovejoy sent to Sinclair and which Sinclair reprints almost in its entirety:

Late in the academic year, near the beginning of which Professor Ross was dismissed, a statement addressed to the public and designed for signature by members of the Stanford faculty was drawn – by whom I do not know – and an attempt was made to secure the signatures of all members (I believe) above the rank of instructor. Each teacher was invited to come separately to the office of one of the senior professors, a close personal friend of President Jordan; was there shown certain correspondence between Mrs. Stanford and President Jordan, which had not been made public; and was thereupon invited to sign the statement – which was to the effect that the signers, having seen certain unpublished documents, had arrived at the conclusion that President Jordan was justified in the dismissal of Professor Ross and that there was no question of academic freedom involved in the case. It was perfectly well understood by me, and I think by all who were shown the letters, that we were desired by the university authorities to sign the "round-robin"; and it was intimated that if any, after seeing the correspondence, should reach a conclusion contrary to that in the "round-robin," they were at least expected to keep silence.

Because of this last intimation I myself for some time refused to have the letters shown me; and consented finally to examine them only after stipulating that I should retain complete freedom to take such action afterwards as the circumstances might seem to me to require. When I read the letters they appeared to me to prove precisely the opposite to the two propositions contained in the statement to the public. They showed clearly (a) that President Jordan who under the existing constitution of the university was the official responsible in such matters – had been originally altogether unwilling to dismiss Ross, and had consented to do so only under pressure from Mrs. Stanford; (b) that the express grounds of Mrs. Stanford's objection to Ross were certain public utterances of his, and that, therefore the question of academic freedom was distinctly involved. I drew up a short statement to this effect, and after the "round-robin" was published, communicated it to the newspapers, at the same time declining the reappointment of which I had previously been notified. I was thereupon directed to discontinue my courses immediately. About the same time another man – one of the best scholars and the most effective teachers in his department – who had refused to sign, and was known to disapprove strongly of the administration's conduct, but who had given no public expression of his opinion was notified that he would not be reappointed; and it was currently reported in the faculty that the vice-president, then acting president, of the university, Dr. Branner, had announced a policy of (in his own phrase) "shaking off the loose plaster".

(Sinclair 1923: 156–157)

Sinclair further quotes Lovejoy as remembering that "one of the signers of the collective statement to the public told me that he had signed with great reluctance and with a sense of humiliation, but, since he had a family of young children, he had not felt that he could afford to risk the loss of his position." Lovejoy, who never married, acknowledged that "practically all the men who resigned were either unmarried or were married men without children" (Sinclair 1923: 157).

No conformity goes completely unrewarded, including the opportunity to retain a livelihood. The Ross case may now be remembered in the purer cause of academic freedom, but, in the mess that life is, several other insights about the assertion of personal principles are worth noting. First, Lovejoy's reactions were the unintended consequence of Ross's desire for public notice. Mrs. Stanford argued, however ineffectually, that she was defending an institution by purging it of someone seen to be hostile to it. By their actions, both Ross and Mrs. Stanford forced others to stand up and be counted or to remain silent. Loyalty, in contrast to dissent, is not one of the highly cultivated virtues among the professoriate. Personal principle and self-interest are obviously not mutually exclusive categories. We mistake one for the other, in ourselves and in others, regularly. The less that is known about E. A. Ross's ambitions, the less self-interest appears to have guided his actions; the more known about them, the more it does.

Second, everything that Lovejoy has to say about the circumstances of his own decisions speaks to a defense not simply of Ross's academic freedom but of the freedom of other faculty members to determine without threat to their livelihoods what their relationship would be to Ross's actions. I believe that Lovejoy objected most of all to the persecution of those who were in no way responsible for what Ross had done but who were nevertheless implicated in his disloyalty by simply defending his right to speak out. The worm in the wood was too obvious to ignore.

And third, with a sympathy that was characteristic of his feeling intellect, Lovejoy further recognized that anyone intimidated into signing for fear of losing his job was not to be singled out and humiliated as some condemnable species of coward.[3] On the contrary, Ross's own egocentricity amounted to a form of cowardice insofar as he used public intimidation to further his case. Today, anyone aggrieved in any way hires a lawyer who serves as a publicist in a war waged for a public opinion that is ever more fragmented and fickle. This desire to be heard above all others is one of the most peculiar disorders of intellectual egocentricity. Its remedy is first achieved in the silent struggle of writing at length rather than speaking in sound bites. Even Lovejoy's explanation to Upton Sinclair seems peculiarly out of place in a book that is otherwise strident in its depiction of higher education in America, however entertaining that depiction may be.[4]

Lovejoy was not a polemicist in his public role as an academic man. On the contrary, he would later in his life make a fateful choice about the meaning of membership in the academy, during the 1940s and 1950s, when higher education was rocked once again by accusations of subversion and conformity, a motif that stands for much of American intellectual life over the past two centuries.

The quest for academic freedom

Lovejoy's voluntary departure from Stanford University in 1901 shaped his commitment to the ideal of academic freedom. He accepted positions at Washington University and the University of Missouri, and in 1910 moved to Johns Hopkins University where he remained until his retirement in 1938. Instances of violations of academic freedom, in the form of dismissals, continued to occur in the first decade of the twentieth century, most of them reflecting the tensions between overbearing administrators and outspoken professors. Richard Hofstadter and Walter P. Metzger rightly argue that no consistent typology can be applied to all the cases of dismissal; nor is each one unique. To understand the complexity of Lovejoy's own commitment, it is useful to distinguish between the precipitating factors that may or may not have motivated him to personal action and the principles that inspired him to press for a greater formalization of due process in the many different types of cases. The absence of this due process is a perennial problem, as is evidenced in recent years in the fumbling of cases involving accusations of sexual harassment.

In 1910, Lovejoy helped to protest, without success, the withdrawal of support by the Carnegie Foundation for service pensions for college teachers. He maintained a consistent approach to speaking for the collective interests of faculty members in all ranks of colleges and universities. This approach, free of hyperbole and rigorously argued, was to be the aim of an association to oversee the special interests and concerns of faculty. Lovejoy's capacity to assess carefully such matters led him to preside over a case that is regarded as a principal reason for the formation in 1915 of the American Association of University Professors (AAUP).

Three years after joining Johns Hopkins, in 1913 Lovejoy chaired an investigation of the forced resignation of John Moffatt Mecklin (1871–1956), professor of philosophy and psychology, from Lafayette College. Because no national association of professors existed to evaluate the circumstances of Mecklin's departure, a Committee of Inquiry was formed by the American Philosophical Association and the American Psychological Association. Lovejoy was joined by six others, including William Ernest Hocking of Yale and George Herbert Mead of the University of Chicago. Together, they issued a report, "The Case of Professor Mecklin," published in *The Journal of Philosophy, Psychology, and Scientific Methods* in 1914 (Committee of Inquiry 1914).

John Mecklin had been called to the Lafayette faculty in late 1904. Like others of his generation, he studied in Germany and wrote his inaugural dissertation in 1899 on early church history. He was an ordained minister of the Presbyterian Church. His thorough knowledge of Christianity, combined with strong progressive convictions, resulted in a fascinating range of publications, including *Democracy and Race Friction: A study of social ethics* (1914); *The Ku Klux Klan: A study of the American mind* (1924); *The Survival Value of Christianity* (1926); *The Story of American Dissent* (1934); and *The Passing of the Saint: A study of a cultural type* (1941), all published after his departure from Lafayette.[5]

The subject of "social ethics" (in the title of Mecklin's 1914 book) symbolized the growing influence of evolutionary ideas in disciplines beyond the natural sciences. Lafayette, during the time of Mecklin's tenure, has been described by Hofstadter and Metzger as:

> facing in two directions: toward its early nonsectarian idealism and toward the orthodox high Calvinism of Princeton Seminary and its autocratic president. The desire to have the best of both worlds created great confusion as to what could be taught at the college.
>
> (Hofstadter and Metzger 1955: 475n).

In this interpretation, Mecklin was seen to endorse, by way of evolutionary ideas, a relativistic view of morals. This probably summarizes accurately what was at stake in the college's argument with him about teaching the newer ethical writings by philosophers such as John Dewey.

Lovejoy's Committee of Inquiry examined as much circumstantial evidence as it could obtain and concluded that Mecklin had been denied his academic freedom. The ostensible reasons for Mecklin's forced departure were of the deepest concern to the committee, but it objected just as much to the unwillingness of E. D. Warfield, president of the college (and of Princeton Theological Seminary), to specify the "precise restrictions imposed upon freedom of inquiry and teaching in philosophy and psychology at Lafayette College" (Committee of Inquiry 1914: 71). Warfield made it plainly clear that he did not recognize the authority of either professional association to raise questions about how his institution administered to its faculty. He did report that Professor Mecklin in resigning was "granted a year's salary."

In a footnote to the Committee of Inquiry's report, Lovejoy seemed intent on demonstrating that Warfield was not only undermining his own position as chief executive officer by refusing to cooperate but was also being undermined by others around him, in particular, a member of the Lafayette Board of Trustees who informed Lovejoy that the Board had not asked for Mecklin's resignation. Much of the intrigue in this case seems to have occurred at the level of Lafayette's curriculum committee, which had assumed responsibility for reviewing the specific contents of Mecklin's courses. Considerably more intrigue and argument must have followed, for two weeks after the committee released its report, Warfield was dismissed by the Lafayette trustees.

In contrast to the E. A. Ross case at Stanford, which was as much about his rights under the First Amendment as it was about the more restricted idea of academic freedom, the Mecklin case was about what could and could not be taught in the classroom. Lovejoy must have understood this very well when the committee noted:

> American colleges and universities fall into two classes: those in which freedom of inquiry, of belief, and of teaching is, if not absolutely unrestricted, at least subject to limitations so few and so remote as to give

practically no occasion for differences of opinion; and those which are frankly instruments of denominational or political propaganda. The committee does not consider itself authorized to discuss the question whether the existence of both sorts of institution is desirable. If, therefore, the present case were one in which a teacher in a professedly denominational college had in his teaching expressly repudiated some clearly defined and generally accepted doctrine of that denomination, the committee would not feel justified in proceeding further with the matter.

This passage is remarkable for its extraordinary concession to the second class of institutions it describes. Lafayette College was in the process of classifying itself – that is precisely what the internal struggle over Mecklin's case represented. Mecklin lost the battle, but the doctrinal war was to be decisively settled against the Warfields of this world. As mediator of this battle, Lovejoy looked for a way at least to acknowledge the claims of those second-class types of institutions that did not afford clear protection of academic freedom. The concept of "church school," for example, is fraught with ambiguities over what kind of authority prevails. This explains, in part, why the lower down one goes in the status system of higher education, the more likely the pieties will seem regressive in evolutionary terms.[6]

Politics inside and outside the university

Lovejoy's defense of academic freedom grew from his strong belief in evolution and evolutionary ideas (Lovejoy 1911, 1936). The study of the history of ideas is built upon the proposition that language and ideas evolve over time into new contexts and new meanings, even as they retain a distinctive identity that enables the scholar to recognize in the past, elements of the present, and *vice versa*. The development of academic freedom in the United States incorporates the idea of evolution as a secular ideal that progresses toward an ever increasing openness about everything, though ideal and reality have been and remain often at serious odds with one another, as conveyed in controversies over multiculturalism, political correctness, and more recently, "trigger warnings."[7]

The conflict between competing theological doctrines as well as between theology and science, dominated intellectual debate during the nineteenth century, although in recent decades *how* that debate has been characterized has changed (White 1896; Shapin 1998; Noll 2010). Arthur Lovejoy's academic career began just as the vindication of evolution in higher education had been fully achieved in the natural sciences. No longer principally a dispute about the relationship between science and religion, academic freedom was now said to be threatened by the conflict between science and wealth, that is, between the vested interests of the wealthy on the one hand and the scientific, and thus progressive, inquiries of the professoriate on the other.[8] Indeed, Upton Sinclair's polemic against the powers in control of higher education asserted that university leaders were entirely beholden to wealthy donors. The necessity of academic freedom – at least in the less sectarian colleges and public universities – had also evolved, rendering religious disagreements less significant than political ones. Political commitment remains the reigning emblem of authenticity in the university. At the same time, the sectarian impulse so deeply ingrained in the American experience has not dissipated in the evolving controversies over academic freedom; it has simply found new forms of expression.

The central piety of criticism in higher education belongs to the tradition best exemplified in the life and writings of Thorstein Veblen (Ross 1984). Yet that piety has also evolved to the extent that the rhetorical celebration of science in Veblen's work has been largely abandoned in the postmodern critique of every social activity. Veblen gave vivid shape to the concern about the accumulating wealth of *all* institutions. Lovejoy's apparent indifference to this concern was due in part to the fact that he distinguished between the responsibilities of institutions and the obligations of individuals. Hofstadter and Metzger conclude that "Critics of the period [such as Veblen] looked to the *culture of capitalism* [my emphasis], rather than to the machinations of capitalists, as the source of academic evils" (Hofstadter and Metzger 1955: 452). The "culture of capitalism" was the deep well into which was poured many inconsistent criticisms of American life. Lovejoy was not captivated by the authenticity of one type of critique over another because his evolutionism and abiding attention to history compelled him to rise above the full spectrum of opinions in order to place them all in a context that reaffirmed the goals of higher learning. In one era, before the Gilded Age, heresy was religious. At the dawn and demise of the Progressive Era, heresy was political.

Arthur Lovejoy's strong national loyalty led him to support with a full and uninhibited voice American participation in two world wars. This deeply patriotic, yet remarkably thoughtful man who helped to make academic freedom a piety among academics, never lost sight of the larger purpose of his intellectual responsibilities as they related to his institutional commitments. That purpose is perhaps best conveyed in what appears to be an inconsistent stand he took against the employment of members of the Communist Party in universities after the Second World War.

The same man who gave up his job rather than submit to the demands of university authorities to tell him how to think about another colleague never wavered in his belief that the university was a precinct whose standards of judgment and action were set apart from those of the larger society. It is terribly misleading to see in Lovejoy's vocation as a scholar and academic man any argument that equates academic freedom with the freedom of association, even though the Cold War disputes about communism have long been represented in universities in terms of freedom of speech.

In 1941, Lovejoy wrote, "No teacher should be dismissed for holding and expressing publicly the opinion that Communism is an economic system preferable to the existing one."[9] He defended the right of the teacher to express that opinion "so long as he did not proselytize and gave a fair hearing to alternative views."[10] His objection was not to the articulation of the theory of communism but to those whose actions in relation to that theory would undermine the purposes and goals of teaching and scholarship. Membership in the Communist Party represented, in his view, an action injurious to the university. What is perhaps less known in regard to Lovejoy's position is that he applied the same principle to members of "the Nazi or Italian Fascist parties."[11]

Lovejoy concluded that faculty abrogated their academic freedom by submitting their thoughts and actions to the dictates of party authority. They were no longer independent scholars in pursuit of the truth wherever it might lead them. Perhaps willing to accept the inevitability of the Ph.D., he drew the line on the Communist Party. In so doing, he found himself arguing for limits to academic freedom – the same man who had once been president of the association devoted to furthering its cause.

Academic freedom was not an abstraction. Its defense and abuse had real, human consequences for universities, research, and students. The university had evolved, in Lovejoy's mind, well beyond the conflicts that John Mecklin's case at Lafayette had symbolized. Communist party members were considered agents who were charged with overthrowing the very principles that academic freedom was intended to uphold. In contrast to President Warfield, who believed that Professor Mecklin's "social ethics" undermined the institutional authority of his college to educate students in the faith tradition in which it was founded, the communist did not appeal to the past or to faith traditions but instead accepted the political principle that all knowledge, including knowledge of the physical world, is subject to political approval. President Warfield was no Stalinist before Stalinism. He also lost his job, but for resisting rather than affirming the separation of faith and education, a separation that until the end of the nineteenth century did not cross the minds of the vast majority of defenders of the separation of church and state.

What is most striking about Lovejoy's stand on communists, which he expressed and argued for in both philosophical and public journals, is the absence of any call for help from the outside, for example, from government. The American Association of University Professors, like the American Medical Association, was supposed to police its membership. Because the AAUP has been historically portrayed as the defender of academic freedom, just as the AMA is portrayed as the defender of professional autonomy, the expectation that either organization would ever be capable of policing deviant members is sociologically naive. On the contrary, the growing role of courts of law in matters of professional association points to the failure of professions to define and defend little more than the minimum standards for gaining entrance to them. Lovejoy must have realized at some point that the AAUP could only realistically defend individuals against their unprofessional institutions rather than institutions against unprofessional individuals.

When he died on 30 December 1962, Arthur O. Lovejoy had been in academic retirement for almost 25 years. His death came before the next significant chapter in the history of academic freedom: the student revolts of the 1960s. Others carried on in Lovejoy's spirit, such as Sidney Hook, with whom he had worked on the question of communism and academic freedom. Hook's approach to academic freedom deserves fuller consideration than can be given here. In 1953, the American Philosophical Association sponsored a symposium on "The Ethics of Academic Freedom," to which Hook and George Boas delivered papers. Boas was a longtime colleague of and collaborator with Lovejoy at Johns Hopkins. Hook's paper was largely a response to Boas's paper. Hook wrote:

> Sometimes our language about academic and other freedoms betrays us into an absolutism we do not intend and which suggests that a right is unconditionally valid, i.e., irrespective of its consequences upon the complex of other rights involved. I know of no such absolute right not even the right to search for and speak the truth in all circumstances. Some of the Nazi scientists sought to discover the truth about the survival thresholds of torture by immersion. One of them in a court proceeding defended himself on the ground that important truths were thereby attained. Yet all of us would regard such a quest for truth as a moral abomination even if the results obtained might someday be useful in saving lives – which in fact was part of the plea in extenuation. A scientist who practices upon human beings as if they were experimental animals is a stock example of insanity in popular literature. But suppose a community felt about vivisection of animals somewhat as we do about vivisection of human beings, would it be a violation of academic freedom to forbid such experiment? In a world of limited resources and opportunities would it be a limitation of academic freedom to prevent, to stretch our fancy, say publication of a discovery that would abolish death, until some provision was made for the limitation of births? On Mr. Lovejoy's definition, the answer would be clearly yes, but most of us would agree that the limitations were justifiable just as we would agree that limitations on freedom of worship if such worship involves child marriage or infanticide are justifiable. This indicates that moral questions are relevant not *in* knowledge but *to* knowledge.
>
> (White 1953: 36)[12]

Hook's assessment of Lovejoy's contextless defense of academic freedom is misleading, but interesting nonetheless, considering Lovejoy's own concerns about political associations and truth-seeking. Hook was not really addressing the ethical responsibilities of scholars per se but rather the constraints on truth-seeking itself. This latter concern is finally less about academic freedom and its protections than it is about resource allocation and support for any project under the auspices of the university. Governance in this respect involves a larger frame of reference than protection of academic freedom. The undertaking of what in Hook's terms might be interpreted as controversial research could be taken up entirely outside academia, thus avoiding a focus on academic freedom.[13]

Yet already in the 1960s, the belief that universities could be transformative agents in society at large was heralded from within them in the writings of such figures as Herbert Marcuse and from beyond them in the criminal activities of student liberationists of many different stripes. The disruptions to teaching and learning, in the cause of some publicly defined hope of social transformation, continue to the present moment in new forms, led by smaller cadres of dedicated ideologues whose strategic interests are more narrowly defined and conducted for maximum notice, as in cases of disruptions of trustee meetings (e.g., Swarthmore College), and shout-downs of prominent public figures (e.g., Brown University).[14] These student-led disruptions about climate change and police conduct suggest a kind of normalization of protest that no longer rises to the level of scrutiny as attempts to suppress academic freedom, and for good reason. The protests of the 1960s and early 1970s in some instances brought out the National Guard and literally shut down college campuses. Nearly two generations later, the qualities of dissent are as much theatrical as they are largely politically innocuous. In some respects it may be judged as a peculiar expression of academic freedom, combined with free speech.[15]

Part of this peculiarity is due to the fact that academic freedom was first and foremost intended to protect the work of those gainfully employed in academic life and its various institutions. Today, public speakers at universities are not only often well paid but have only tangential if any association with academic life. That students would protest such a speaker on campus is rude and inconsiderate, but hardly qualifies as a violation of academic freedom in the traditional sense, any more than outbursts and shouting do at a public event off-site from a university setting. There is some confusion now over what counts as civility, a different but not entirely unrelated aspect of academic freedom. In other words, where academic self-governance finds itself at a crossroads is less with rebellious students than with those who are paid to run the university. Students will always tend toward incivility, it is an aspect of youth that perturbs every parent generation, though, by my measure, the taming of student behavior with respect to public protest speaks to the strengths of meritocracy; even the leaders of opposition to climate change are building résumés (Imber 2012). They may be the children of 1960s protesters who were themselves red diaper babies, but their ambitions are plainly a part of the institutionalization and normalization of protest in such broad academic disciplines as, for example, environmental studies. It could be said that the development of whole academic fields exemplify what in the 1980s and 1990s was described as political correctness. Although the protests against political correctness were effective in highlighting some of the ways in which alternative voices were being challenged or silenced, a resolute push back against a one-sided perspective on economic and social life was taken up by foundations and institutes beyond the university, the effectiveness of which has not been insignificant despite the well ensconced activist disciplines that also have taken root in the university over the past several decades.

Another perplexing matter that has changed how academic freedom is appealed to in different cases is the blurring of the line between academic freedom and free speech. The question that arises is how the responsibilities of academic administrators, that is, presidents, provosts, and deans, correspond with the notice given to controversial scholarly work and public pronouncements by members of a university faculty. There is now a growing number of cases in which such work or pronouncements receive more criticism from people and organizations outside the university than inside. How administrators cope with a publicity-drenched society relates to how they defend their faculty generally. In Lovejoy's time, the kind of speech engaged by Edward Alsworth Ross was sufficient to cost him his employment. Today, the concern is not about the loss of employment but rather how strong administrative support is or should be in defense of unpopular opinions expressed by faculty.[16] The irony cannot go unremarked that with an expanded idea of academic freedom comes an increase in expectation about entitlement.

The expansion of the relevance of academic freedom beyond the university proper is also important to note, in particular as it has been raised over the university's obligations in the matter of academic boycotts. In recent years, some faculty members have called upon their colleagues not to engage fellow academics in countries whose domestic policies they oppose. The State of Israel has received a disproportionate amount of attention in this regard. Opposition to such boycotts has been registered by many university leaders and by the American Association of University Professors. At the same time, some have extended the idea that it is a violation of academic freedom for professional associations outside the university to take such stands in support of boycotts. Here the full consequences of political advocacy parading in academic dress show themselves, where the leadership of such organizations as the American Studies Association seeks the approval of its rank and file to engage a boycott of Israeli academics. It is to be sure a profound violation of academic freedom insofar as it inhibits collaboration among academics across disciplines and borders, and it was the sociologist Robert K. Merton who first addressed the problem three-quarters of a century ago.[17] That such tactics of protest appear to be applied to a society where academic freedom itself is more robust than in many other nations suggests more than political convictions are at stake.

The new challenge to self-governance: globalization

Academic freedom is, on a world-wide basis, a fragile commodity, one which stabilizes with the relative distance between the pursuit of intellectual and scientific life and any form of government oversight. In democratic societies, the risk to such freedom appears to be undertaken by those whose commitment to political ideals outweighs any principled conviction that the aim of academic freedom is to protect rather than direct. Now that a number of elite universities and other colleges are forging alliances with nation states across the globe, the comparisons of the American achievement with those nations is growing unavoidable.

Distinguishing the role of self-governance in matters of academic freedom from state diplomacy reveals different stakes at work when considering how universities across the world can and should work with one another. Diplomacy requires governments' willingness to cooperate at the highest levels, despite what are often profound differences in their respective policies and procedures. The level of cooperation just below the diplomatic is economic, with an emerging global sensibility that the expansion of markets of production and consumption will enable all nations to flourish if government control is limited. These two forces, the diplomatic and the economic, have led to the process of globalization, and in certain respects, universities have begun to enter into new arrangements that have diplomatic and economic elements. The diplomatic arrangement comes in the form of special exchanges agreed upon by both parties, usually between specific schools. The economic arrangement is more about exchanging students, presumably paying ones. In whose interest the direction of exchange is more important or valuable should not be ignored.

Academic freedom has foundational qualities when raised and judged in relation to diplomatic and economic interests. At what point in any collaborative relationship should an American university hold a foreign university to the American standards of academic freedom? In certain areas of research, for example, in science, mathematics, music, and the arts, the potential cultural conflicts may be of less import than in social science. The purpose is not to go into specific situations here but rather to conclude with the observation that American diplomacy historically at its highest levels has represented moral and ethical ideals that will be met with challenges about how alliances between American and foreign universities should proceed particularly in matters of academic freedom. The implications for self-governance by American universities should not be underestimated moving forward.

Notes

1 Also see James (1987). The essay first appeared in 1903, four years after Lovejoy left Harvard. It might be viewed as the culminating expression of convictions that James must have routinely articulated to students under his influence and direction.
2 Burton J. Bledstein writes: "The competitiveness of professional historians revealed itself when within a week of the Howard vacancy, the president at Stanford hired a young Ph.D. from Harvard, who accepted the position on the recommendation of Harvard's senior historians" (Bledstein 1976: 305). He notes "The historical profession's inaction in Howard's defense has generally been ignored in the successful outcome of both Ross's own professional career and his case against Stanford" (Bledstein 1976: 305 n27).
3 Mary O. Furner characterizes Lovejoy's resignation much differently than I do, and she makes no reference to his letter quoted in Sinclair's book. Furner writes,

"From the related field of philosophy, Arthur O. Lovejoy was so appalled by the docility of most of his colleagues that he felt compelled to express his disapproval by resigning too" (Furner 1975: 242). Given his own characterization of events, Lovejoy's personal motivation to resign was unlikely to have been the result of his contempt for those colleagues who signed Stanford's loyalty oath.

4 If any doubt exists about a long tradition of holding colleges and universities culpable for the failure to educate youth, Sinclair's long-forgotten work may help to put the current tirades into perspective. Of course, a much less flamboyant tradition of institutional self-criticism exists alongside the racier one. For an example that stands up much better against Sinclair as a responsible criticism of teaching and that was published nine years later, see Waller (1932). For later examples of similarly responsible criticism that stand behind and above much of the more recent exposes, see Nisbet (1971), Minogue (1973), and Rieff ([1973] 1985).

5 Mecklin's autobiography was published under the title *My Quest for Freedom* (1945). From 1920, he spent the remainder of his academic career at Dartmouth College in the Department of Sociology.

6 Catholic institutions of higher education have been subject to precisely the criticisms that Lovejoy would likely have not considered legitimate, given his willingness to acknowledge doctrinal authority in private institutions as superior to any countervailing definition of academic freedom in public and self-declared non-sectarian schools. Lafayette's struggle with itself in 1913 was about how to become post-Protestant without abandoning Protestantism entirely. For discussions of the Catholic case on academic freedom, see Manier and Houck (1967), Gleason (1992), and Worgul, Jr. (1992).

7 The classroom remains an important site in the nature and challenges of academic freedom and university and curricular governance. An emerging tendency, in particular among students and some faculty in elite universities, to question not only the selection of what is taught but to demand warnings about how what is taught may be experienced by some students, advances the claims generally of therapeutic culture from the self-esteem movements in primary education to the potentially fragile emotions of late adolescence. In certain respects, this seems to have been entirely predictable. See Imber (2004).

8 By the end of the twentieth century, the view of professional powers (including academics) had become less a critique of the influence of wealth on freedom generally and on academic freedom in particular and more a sustained attempt to indict those professional powers as interest groups. See Derber *et al.* (1990) and Brint (1994).

9 Quoted in Wilson (1980: 201). These are Lovejoy's words.

10 Wilson (1980: 201). These are Wilson's words.

11 Wilson (1980: 231, n28). The words are Lovejoy's.

12 See also Hook (1969, 1971, 1987) and Glazer (1970).

13 The question of the scope of academic freedom in its relationship to research has implications for assessing the nature of consensus in science and the indeterminacy of where the line is to be drawn at any given moment between what can be known and what knowledge should be sought. See Imber (2014).

14 At Swarthmore College, see http://daily.swarthmore.edu/2013/05/06/student-protestors-take-over-open-board-meeting-state-wide-array-of-concerns/ (accessed 4 July 2014). At Brown University, see www.huffingtonpost.com/2013/10/30/ray-kelly-brown-university_n_4176985.html (accessed 4 July 2014).

15 This, of course, does not include wanton intimidation of and violence against academic researchers, who, for example, use animals in their experiments. The attack on academic freedom in this regard is no longer confined to the university alone.

16 A recent illustration of a century's worth of change in valence arose at Virginia Tech over the controversial remarks made by an English professor about patriotism.

See http://chronicle.com/article/Virginia-Tech-Professors-Fault/143171/?cid=at&ut
m_source=at&utm_medium=en (accessed 4 July 2014).
17 Originally published in 1942 as "Science and Technology in a Democratic Order,"
and later as "Science and Democratic Social Structure," see "The Normative
Structure of Science," in Merton (1973: 267–278).

References

Bledstein, B. J. (1976) *The Culture of Professionalism: The middle class and the devel-
opment of higher education in America*, New York: Norton.
Brint, S. (1994) *In an Age of Experts: The changing role of professionals in politics and
public life*, Princeton, NJ: Princeton University Press.
Committee of Inquiry of the American Philosophical Association and the American
Sociological Association (1914) "The case of Professor Mecklin: Report of the
Committee of Inquiry of the American Philosophical Association and the American
Psychological Association," *The Journal of Philosophy, Psychology, and Scientific
Methods*, 11: 67–81.
Derber, C., Schwartz, W. A., and Magrass, Y. (1990) *Power in the Highest Degree:
Professionals and the rise of a new mandarin order*, New York: Oxford University
Press.
Furner, M. O. (1975) *Advocacy and Objectivity: A crisis in the professionalization of
American social science, 1865–1905*, Lexington, KY: University of Kentucky Press.
Glazer, N. (1970) *Remembering the Answers: Essays on the American student revolt*,
New York: Basic Books.
Gleason, P. (1992) "American Catholic higher education, 1940–1990: The ideological
context," in G. M. Marsden and B. J. Longfield (eds) *The Secularization of the
Academy*, New York: Oxford University Press, pp. 34–58.
Hofstadter, R. and Metzger, W. P. (1955) *The Development of Academic Freedom in the
United States*, New York: Columbia University Press.
Hook, S. (1969) *Academic Freedom and Academic Anarchy*, New York: Cowles Book Co.
Hook, S. (1971) *In Defense of Academic Freedom*, New York: Pegasus.
Hook, S. (1987) *Out of Step: An unquiet life in the 20th century*, New York: Harper &
Row.
Imber, J. B. (1996) "The vocation of academic freedom," Introduction to the Trans-
action edition of *The Revolt Against Dualism* by A. O. Lovejoy, New Brunswick,
NJ: Transaction Publishers, pp. xi–xxxvii.
Imber, J. B. (ed.) (2004) *Therapeutic Culture: Triumph and defeat*, New Brunswick, NJ:
Transaction Publishers.
Imber, J. B. (2012) "The far side of meritocracy," *The American Interest*, 8(2): 91–96.
Imber, J. B. (2014) "Introduction" to N. L. Farberow (ed.) *Taboo Topics*, New
Brunswick, NJ: Transaction Publishers, pp. vii–xxi.
James, W. (1987) "The Ph.D. Octopus," in F. Burkhardt and F. Bowers (eds) *The
Works of William James*, Cambridge, MA: Harvard University Press, pp. 67–74.
Lefkowitz, M. (2008) *History Lesson: A race odyssey*, New Haven, CT: Yale Uni-
versity Press.
Lovejoy, A. O. (1911) "Schopenhauer as an evolutionist," *The Monist*, 21: 195–222.
Lovejoy, A. O. (1936) *The Great Chain of Being: A study of the history of an idea*,
Cambridge, MA: Harvard University Press.

Manier, E. and Houck, J. (eds) (1967) *Academic Freedom and the Catholic University*, Notre Dame, IN: University of Notre Dame Press.

Mecklin, J. M. (1914) *Democracy and Race Friction: A study of social ethics*, New York: Macmillan.

Mecklin, J. M. (1924) *The Ku Klux Klan: A study of the American mind*, New York: Harcourt, Brace.

Mecklin, J. M. (1926) *The Survival Value of Christianity*, New York: Harcourt, Brace.

Mecklin, J. M. (1934) *The Story of American Dissent*, New York: Harcourt, Brace.

Mecklin, J. M. (1941) *The Passing of the Saint: A study of a cultural type*, Chicago, IL: University of Chicago Press.

Mecklin, John M. (1945) *My Quest for Freedom*, New York: Charles Scribner.

Merton, R. K. (1973) *The Sociology of Science: Theoretical and empirical investigations*, Chicago, IL: University of Chicago Press.

Minogue, K. R. (1973) *The Concept of a University*, Berkeley: University of California Press.

Mohr, J. C. (1970) "Academic turmoil and public opinion: The Ross case at Stanford," *Pacific Historical Review*, 39(1): 39–61.

Nisbet, R. (1971) *The Degradation of the Academic Dogma: The university in America, 1945–1970*, New York: Basic Books.

Noll, M. (2010) "A. D. White's 'Warfare Between Science and Theology,'" http://biologos.org/blog/a-d-whites-warfare-between-science-and-theology-pt-1 (accessed 4 July 2014).

Rieff, P. ([1973] 1985) *Fellow Teachers: Of culture and its second death*, 2nd edn, Chicago, IL: University of Chicago Press.

Ross, D. (1984) "American social science and the idea of progress," in T. L. Haskell (ed.) *The Authority of Experts: Studies in history and theory*, Bloomington: Indiana University Press, pp. 157–175.

Shapin, S. (1998) *The Scientific Revolution*, Chicago, IL: University of Chicago Press.

Sinclair, U. (1923) *The Goose-Step: A study of American education*, Pasadena, CA: The Author.

Waller, W. (1932) *The Sociology of Teaching*, New York: John Wiley.

White, A. D. (1896) *A History of the Warfare of Science with Theology in Christendom*, New York: D. Appleton.

White, M. (ed.) (1953) *Academic Freedom, Logic, and Religion*, Philadelphia: University of Pennsylvania Press.

Wilson, D. J. (1980) *Arthur O. Lovejoy and the Quest for Intelligibility*, Chapel Hill, NC: University of North Carolina Press.

Worgul, Jr., G. S. (ed.) (1992) *Issues in Academic Freedom*, Pittsburgh, PA: Duquesne University Press.

Index

For Product Safety Concerns and Information please contact our EU
representative GPSR@taylorandfrancis.com
Taylor & Francis Verlag GmbH, Kaufingerstraße 24, 80331 München, Germany